LESSONS FROM THE CYBERSPACE CLASSROOM

The Realities of Online Teaching

Rena M. Palloff, Keith Pratt

JOSSEY-BASS
A Wiley Company
San Francisco

Jossey-Bass books and products are available through most bookstores. To contact Jossey-Bass directly, call (888) 378-2537, fax to (800) 605-2665, or visit our website at www.josseybass.com.

Substantial discounts on bulk quantities of Jossey-Bass books are available to corporations, professional associations, and other organizations. For details and discount information, contact the special sales department at Jossey-Bass.

Printed in the United States of America.

Library of Congress Cataloging-in-Publication Data

Palloff, Rena M., 1950–
    Lessons from the cyberspace classroom : the realities of online teaching / Rena M. Palloff, Keith Pratt.
      p. cm. — (The Jossey-Bass higher and adult education series)
    Includes bibliographical references (p.) and index.
    ISBN 0-7879-5519-1
    1. Teaching—computer network resources. 2. Computer-assisted instruction. 3. Distance education. I. Pratt, Keith, 1947– II. Title. III. Series.
    LB1044.87 .P34 2001
    371.3'58—dc21

00-011518

FIRST EDITION
PB Printing 10 9 8 7 6 5 4 3 2 1

THE JOSSEY-BASS HIGHER AND ADULT EDUCATION SERIES

For Gary, Dianne, Kevin, Dava, Nora Jo, Brian, Dynelle, Brittnie,
Alyssa, and Kaylee—for your love, support, and inspiration.

CONTENTS

FIGURES, TABLES, AND EXHIBITS

Figures

Tables

Exhibits

THE NATURE OF CHANGE IN ONLINE LEARNING

In the two years since we wrote our first book, *Building Learning Communities in Cyberspace: Effective Strategies for the Online Classroom,* we expected to see dramatic changes in the technology used for online courses. Although there has been slow, steady progress in this domain, this has not been where the most significant changes in online distance learning have taken place. Where we have seen the most change has been in the realm of course delivery. Corporate entities specializing in "total solutions" are offering complete course and distance learning program management tools to institutions. Textbook companies are putting books and lecture materials on websites that also include chat capability and gradebooks. In addition, organizations have emerged focused solely on the development of courses that are then licensed or sold to academic institutions and delivered by faculty members who were not a part of their development.

Online Distance Learning in the Year 2000

These developments are forming the complexion of online distance learning as we progress through the year 2000. They raise concerns that were not considered even two years ago, such as these:

Have and Have-Not Institutions

Increasingly, smaller colleges and universities are wanting to enter the distance learning market to increase their reach and resultant student base. However, the cost of acquiring both the hardware and software required to enter this arena can be prohibitive to a smaller institution with limited dollars. Consequently, we are beginning to see a rift developing between the institutions that have the money to enter the market and those that are struggling to do so.

Faculty Control Over the Academic Process

Faculty are also raising concerns about the process by which institutions are entering the online market. Decisions about course authoring software and course hosting arrangements are often being made without faculty involvement. Questions are being raised about the degree to which faculty should be involved in decisions that have serious implications for course delivery.

Course Ownership

Do faculty members own the courses they develop, or are these courses institutional property? This question is becoming an increasingly important one as institutions continue to move into online learning. Related questions are: Should faculty be paid to develop courses for academic institutions as "work for hire?" Should faculty who teach a course developed by someone else be permitted to alter that course to suit their teaching styles and both eliminate and include material that they deem either unnecessary or more important? In addition, the trend toward delivering course material to a company that posts courses and course material on a website that may or may not be owned by the institution is raising some concerns about course ownership. The result is that faculty are wanting to know who "owns" courses and course material. In the face-to-face classroom, as faculty develop and deliver their own courses, this has not been an issue. In the online classroom, however, it is.

Intellectual Property and Copyright

Related to the course ownership issue are the issues of intellectual property and copyright. Bates (2000) helps to distinguish between the two. Intellectual property can be defined as "the original ideas and thoughts of an academic or teacher" (p. 109), whereas copyright holds in cases where those ideas are given some physical or tangible form of embodiment. Thus, when faculty are hired to develop a course for an institution, ownership of the embodiment of their ideas regarding course material—or the online course—can become an issue of contention if there is not an express agreement between faculty and the institution. However, other copyright issues worthy of discussion arise in this area, such as the use of the digital material widely available on the Internet and the use of student material posted to a course site as we have done in this book, for example. An increasing awareness and sensitivity to potential issues of copyright and intellectual property are pushing institutions to reexamine their agreements and policies so that as many instances as possible are covered.

These are the questions that we are asked with increasing frequency as we meet with faculty and administrators across the country, and these are the questions that we will tackle in this book. Although we may not have definitive answers, we hope to provide enough information on these issues so that faculty and administrators can begin to answer the questions for themselves.

Continuing Training Needs

It is assumed by academic institutions that if online courses and programs are offered, teachers will know how to teach in that environment, and more importantly, students will know how to learn or engage with the material. Our experience both in teaching online courses and in consulting with faculty, faculty developers, and administrators across the United States is that the opposite is true. Faculty need training and assistance in making the transition to the online environment, but students also need to be taught how to learn online. Learning through the use of technology takes more than mastery of a software program or comfort with the hardware being used. It takes an awareness of the impact that this form of learning has on the learning process itself. As more institutions and their instructors enter the cyberspace classroom and encounter both successes and difficulties in the process, they are coming face-to-face with the realities of online teaching and asking more, not fewer, questions about how to make this transition successfully. Consequently, we will offer concrete suggestions for course development and delivery. We will also offer suggestions to faculty who are being asked to teach a class they did not create.

This book is a logical follow-up to our first book. In *Building Learning Communities in Cyberspace* (Palloff and Pratt, 1999), we discussed the importance of building a learning community as a part of the delivery of online instruction. We also provided a guidebook to the construction of an effective course for those entering the online arena for the first time. As we have lectured and consulted using the concepts from the first book and also continued to teach online, we have been learning more about the realities of online teaching today. This new book will help take instructors, faculty developers, and administrators further into the process as we explore the issues that they face on a regular basis. It is for these professionals that the book is primarily designed. It will also be helpful to those in the corporate sector who are being asked with increasing frequency to develop employee training programs that are delivered entirely online. Readers will gain greater understanding of the forces that are reshaping education in new and exciting ways. The book will also provide readers with new tips, tools, and insights to equip them to enter and participate with greater confidence in this new environment.

Organization of Contents

This book is divided into two parts. Part One creates a context by focusing on faculty needs and concerns, administrative issues, and the technological tools being used for course creation and delivery. Chapter One reviews in more detail the state of distance learning today. Included is a brief discussion not only of technological developments but also of the ways in which distance learning programs are now being delivered and the resultant issues for faculty. Research on the effectiveness of online learning is emerging, and we include the results of some of that research in order to assist readers in evaluating online learning for themselves. We also look at the newer trend in offering online education to high school students and other recent developments in the K–12 educational arena. Chapter Two is devoted to providing tips and suggestions for assisting faculty in making the transition from the face-to-face to the online classroom. This is becoming an increasingly important topic for instructional designers, faculty developers, instructional technologists, and faculty themselves. Chapter Three focuses on administrative concerns, such as compensation for course development and online teaching, program development, faculty support and training, governance issues, tenure issues, and concerns about intellectual property and copyright. In Chapter Four we revisit issues related to technology, including a discussion of new developments and courseware. We evaluate the elements that make for good courseware so that institutions can make informed decisions about which to choose. Finally, we discuss ways in which online courses and programs can be developed when financial resources are limited.

Part Two of the book focuses specifically on online teaching and learning. Chapter Five provides concrete suggestions for the development of a course and offers a course example as a model. Chapter Six looks at another increasingly important issue in online education as it is currently being delivered: how to teach a course that has been developed by someone else. Issues discussed include how to build community into the process as well as how to add or omit material that the instructor feels is important or unimportant. Finally, we offer suggestions for evaluating good course packages when looking to purchase or license material developed by another entity or individual.

Much of what has been written to date has focused on faculty needs in moving to the online environment, and an assumption has been made that students will intuitively know how to learn online. Our experience has shown us that this is not true. Consequently, we offer two chapters discussing the needs and issues of the online student. In Chapters Seven and Eight we discuss the characteristics of the successful online student and offer suggestions to faculty on how to maximize the potential for students to be successful online. We also offer suggestions for orienting students to online learning in Chapter Seven and discuss group dynamics in cyberspace in Chapter Eight. Included in Chapter Eight is a discussion of theories of group development and dynamics as well as how these theories apply when the group is virtual. The chapter also talks about working with difficult students in the online environment. Chapter Nine summarizes the lessons learned in the online classroom, provides suggestions for further course and program development, and takes a look at likely future developments.

Each chapter ends with summary tips to help readers quickly access the material contained therein. The tips should also serve as a guide to creating successful online courses and programs because they highlight the more important points to consider.

As with our previous book, we have included many cases and examples throughout in order to illustrate the points being discussed. Once again, we have included student posts to various types of course discussions, and as in *Building Learning Communities in Cyberspace*, because of the importance we ascribe to allowing student voices to emerge in whatever way they may, we have left these posts untouched except for length.

Changes in online distance learning are coming fast and furious. We could not possibly hope to capture all of the issues of concern to educators today. One of our esteemed mentors once likened doing research on a topic to approaching a fast-moving river. There is no way to study the entire river. Consequently, all one can do is take out a bucketful of water and examine its contents. This book represents another bucketful of water from the fast-moving river of online distance learning, a river that continues to provide many of us with much to study. We can only hope that we have done justice to those issues that faculty, students, and administrators deem to be most important at this point in time.

Acknowledgments

Just as it takes a village to raise a child, it takes a collaborative effort to write a book about interactive processes and community building in online courses. As a result, there are a number of people to whom we are grateful for their help and generosity in completing this work.

As in our previous book, we need to begin by acknowledging our students. We thank you for the spirit with which you have entered this online adventure with us and also for your willingness to share your experiences with people you do not know in order to ease their transition to online work. We would also like to thank Alpha Sarmian for his suggestions on Internet resources and his assistance in converting the graphics contained in this work.

Thanks to the following people and their organizations for their enthusiastic support of our endeavors to improve the quality of online distance learning: Julie Jantzi of Christian University Global Network; Gary Girard of the University of South Dakota; Rita-Marie Conrad of Florida State University; Don Hart of Thomas Edison State College; Jessica Somers and Brian Finnegan of the Georgia Board of Regents; Phil Chatterton of WebCT; Dan Burke of Convene; Bob Crook of the LeCroy Center at the Dallas County Community College District; Bridget Ahrend, Chris Rapp, and Sarah Allen of eCollege; Brenda Reiswerg and Parker Hudnut of University Access; Liz Osika and Denise Camin of Purdue University; and Gale Erlandson, David Brightman, and Melissa Kirk, our editors at Jossey-Bass. In addition, we would like to thank the staff at Datatel for allowing us to test out some of our ideas and helping us to develop our thinking in the area of planning. Finally, we acknowledge our families for their love and support— without them, we would be unable to do any of this work.

December 2000   Rena M. Palloff
                                                                                       Alameda, California
                                                                                            Keith Pratt
                                                                                       Norman, Oklahoma

ABOUT THE AUTHORS

Rena M. Palloff has worked extensively in health care, academic settings, and addiction treatment for over twenty years. She is a consultant to community groups interested in systems change and results-based accountability and to addiction treatment programs in the areas of program development, marketing, and the development of service delivery systems that are sensitive to the managed care environment.

Palloff is a member of the faculty of the Fielding Institute, teaching in its completely online Master's Degree Program in Organizational Management. She is also an assistant professor at John F. Kennedy University, teaching in the Holistic Health Department in the Graduate School for Holistic Studies, Liberal Studies, and Management. She is an adjunct associate professor in the Chemical Dependency Studies Department at California State University-Hayward, and an adjunct professor in Samuel Merritt College's Program in Health and Human Sciences. She also teaches classes in organizational behavior and management and leadership for the International Studies Program at Ottawa University in Ottawa, Kansas, at various sites throughout the Pacific Rim.

Palloff received her bachelor's degree in sociology from the University of Wisconsin-Madison and her master's degree in social work from the University of Wisconsin-Milwaukee. She holds a master's degree in organizational development and a Ph.D. in human and organizational systems from the Fielding Institute.

Keith Pratt began his government career as a computer systems technician with the U.S. Air Force in 1967. He served in various positions, including supervisor computer systems maintenance, chief of the Logistics Support Branch, chief of the Telecommunications Branch, and superintendent of the Secure Telecommunications Branch. After leaving the air force, Pratt held positions as registrar and faculty (Charter College), director (Chapman College), and trainer and consultant (The Growth Company).

Pratt was formerly an adjunct faculty member at Wayland Baptist University and the University of Alaska, teaching courses in communications, business, management, organizational theories, and computer technology. He was most recently an assistant professor in the International Studies Program and the chair of the Management Information Systems Program, main campus and overseas, at Ottawa University in Ottawa, Kansas. He is currently a project manager for Datatel, working with community colleges on the West Coast. Pratt is certified in the administration of the Meyers-Briggs Type Indicator.

Pratt graduated from Wayland Baptist University with a dual degree in business administration and computer systems technology. He has a master's of science in human resource management (with honors) from Chapman University. He holds a master's in organizational development and a Ph.D. in human and organizational systems from the Fielding Institute, and an honorary doctorate of science in economics from Moscow State University.

◆ ◆ ◆

Palloff and Pratt are the managing partners of Crossroads Consulting Group and the authors of the Frandson Award winning book *Building Learning Communities in Cyberspace: Effective Strategies for the Online Classroom.* Written for faculty, trainers, faculty developers, and administrators of distance learning programs, *Building Learning Communities in Cyberspace* is a comprehensive guide to the development of an online environment that helps promote successful learning outcomes while building and fostering a sense of community among learners. The book was based on their many years of teaching experience in the online environment and contains vignettes and case examples from a variety of successful online courses. Palloff and Pratt have been presenting this work across the United States and internationally since 1994 as well as consulting to academic institutions on the development of effective distance learning programs.

PART ONE

RETHINKING EDUCATION FOR AN ONLINE WORLD

CHAPTER ONE

ONLINE LEARNING
IN THE NEW MILLENNIUM

Because of the changing nature of today's students, economic pressures, and rapid implementation of distance learning courses and programs, definitions of what constitutes education and learning are changing, too. Whereas years ago instructors viewed their students as "blank slates" whose minds could be filled with the information they were imparting, current constructivist theory holds that students, through their interaction with one another, the instructor, and their environment, create knowledge and meaning. A more collaborative approach to learning, such as that promoted by constructivist thought, can yield deeper levels of knowledge creation (Brooks and Brooks, 1993). The use of distance learning technologies, and more specifically, online distance learning, have both grown out of and enhanced the changes now occurring in the delivery of education.

It is widely acknowledged that nontraditional students (that is, working adults returning to school or students who are unable to attend classes on campus for other reasons) make up a rapidly growing population in education today. Their educational needs and demands are different from those of traditional students and it is these students to whom online distance education is geared. We have also seen, however, an increase in the use of online classes for campus-based students, particularly with classes that combine face-to-face and online components.

The changes caused by the use of online distance education are being met with the support of educators but also with some discomfort. The American Association of University Professors devoted the September-October 1999 issue of its bulletin *Academe* to the topic of technology in higher education. The following is a sampling of the opinions expressed by faculty faced with the increasing use of distance education:

> Some students learn better in a course in which they can interact with the professor in person. Others, however, thrive in an online environment. Shy students, for example, tend to feel liberated online, as do many foreign students who are unsure of their spoken English [Maloney, p. 21].

> Being there is irreplaceable. . . . Education involves more than lectures and class discussions. Our students learn from us what scholars in our disciplines do. We show the discipline of the mind and evaluate whether our students are catching on. . . . When students feel themselves identifying with us and our disciplines, they come to appreciate the struggle for knowledge; some may even choose to become part of the intellectual adventure [Martin, p. 35].

> The reality is that technology is playing, and will continue to play, a critical role in teaching and learning. As a pedagogical tool, distance education probably leads to different educational outcomes from those achieved with traditional classroom-based instruction—some better, some worse. . . . The real debate needs to focus on identifying which approaches work best for teaching students, period [Merisotis, p. 51].

Regardless of the debate, distance education is a phenomenon that is here to stay. Ronald Phipps and Jamie Merisotis of the Institute for Higher Education Policy note in their 1999 report on distance education, "Technology is having, and will continue to have, a profound impact on colleges and universities in America and around the globe. Distance learning, which was once a poor and often unwelcome stepchild within the academic community, is becoming increasingly more visible as a part of the higher education family" (p. 29).

In 1997, the U.S. Department of Education noted that in the fall of 1995, 76 percent of higher education institutions with enrollments of ten thousand or more were offering distance education programs. It was projected that by the fall of 1998 that figure would grow to 90 percent (Carnavale, 2000a). An update to that study was released in December 1999, indicating that between the fall of 1995 and 1997–98 the percentage of all higher education institutions offering distance education courses increased by about one-third and that the number of course offerings and enrollments in distance education courses doubled (National Center for Education Statistics, 1999). Not all courses were conducted online. However, the institutions that offered distance education in 1997–98 or were planning to do so in the near future reported that they planned to increase their use of Internet-based delivery. The study concluded that "distance education appears to have become a common feature of many postsecondary education institutions and that, by their own accounts, it will become only more common in the future" (National Center for Education Statistics, 1999, p. vi).

Given these facts, what is the impact of this phenomenon on education? How does learning online affect learning in general? How should decisions be made about such elements as courseware, courses offered, faculty who will teach online, and course development? What are the ethical and legal implications of these decisions? How do we train faculty to understand and use distance learning and distance learning technologies effectively and about the new pedagogy required for the delivery of distance education? How do we teach faculty to build interactivity and community into what is otherwise a flat, text-based medium? We will explore these questions and more in this book as we discuss the lessons learned from the cyberspace classroom.

Online Learning Today

Most distance learning classes today are delivered either through interactive video or over the Internet. But not all online distance learning classes are created equal. A white paper posted on the website of Blackboard, a course authoring software package, defines online education as "an approach to teaching and learning that utilizes Internet technologies to communicate and collaborate in an educational context. This includes technology that supplements traditional classroom training with web-based components and learning environments where the educational process is experienced online" (Blackboard, p. 1). That definition, with which we agree, indicates that there is more than one way to deliver online classes. One is not necessarily preferable to the other. A good way for instructors to enter the online arena is by using technology to enhance an on-campus class. As they gain experience in teaching online, moving from an enhanced approach to one in which a class is wholly delivered online becomes easier.

Classes that use technology and the Internet as an enhancement to what is happening in the face-to-face classroom generally employ materials on CD-ROM, an electronic textbook including associated learning activities, "lecture" material or an asynchronous discussion board located on a course site online, or chat or synchronous discussions online; they may even simply use e-mail. All of this technology may be used in a class that is conducted completely or almost completely online, the difference being that there may be minimal or no scheduled face-to-face sessions associated with the class. Yet another form of online learning is the posting of course material on a static website, meaning that no means of interactivity is built into the course. In this type of class, the student interacts only with the machine and not with other students. His or her contact with the instructor is likely to be via e-mail.

Most institutions now offer classes that use technology in some form as an enhancement to face-to-face classes. Interactive classes offered using the Internet as a means of delivering course content are a growing phenomenon. The 1999 Department of Education study indicated that the percentage of institutions using asynchronous Internet-based technologies to deliver courses essentially tripled between 1995 and 1997–98 (National Center for Education Statistics, 1999). Asynchronous Internet-based technologies generally refer to electronic bulletin board or discussion board systems. Users can access the bulletin or discussion boards at any time, twenty-four hours a day, seven days a week, to add to the ongoing discussion. Users do not need to be online at the same time in order to participate.

The posting of course material on a static website is most common at this point in time, and it is the form of online education that many refer to when they raise concerns about online learning. It is this form of online education that is mistaken for online learning as a whole and has given it a "black eye" due to the lack of interactivity.

In a report published in *Internet Research* in December 1999, accounting professors who responded to a survey overwhelmingly disapproved of the use of the Internet to deliver courses in their subject area. Eighty-two percent agreed with a statement that student-to-student and student-to-instructor interaction is missing in Internet-based classes, making them less valuable to students (Saunders and Weible, 1999). The respondents also likened Internet-based classes to correspondence courses, which they clearly considered inferior in quality. When course delivery does not include any interactive component, we have to agree that quality will suffer. However, a well-constructed interactive online course or good use of technology to enhance a course can only serve to contribute positively to learning outcomes.

In order to do a good job of constructing online courses, faculty need training that few campuses currently offer. When they are simply presented with course authoring software and asked or told that a course needs to be developed and presented, the resulting course is likely to have minimal interaction and pay little attention to the development of a learning community, which promotes collaborative learning and helps to achieve learning outcomes. We will discuss faculty training needs and good course construction in greater depth in Chapters Two and Five.

New Technological Developments and New Modes of Delivery

Most courseware applications now allow instructors to customize their courses in many ways. Asynchronous discussions can be supplemented with the use of synchronous or "chat" sessions. Video and audio clips can be used. Instructors can post PowerPoint slides or other graphic illustrations of the material being studied. Support documents—such as handouts, articles, and lecture notes—can also be posted to a course site. Links to other sites of interest or to an electronic textbook can be established. Whiteboard sessions can be held, in which synchronous discussion can occur while graphics are annotated or brainstorming sessions are going on.

Examples of the use of electronic whiteboards can be seen in Exhibit 1.1. The exhibit shows how graphics or other material, such as the math formulas presented, can be uploaded to the whiteboard and then annotated by the instructor. At the same time, a synchronous discussion about the image can be held, allowing students to ask questions and explore the concepts being presented. A more detailed description of current course software can be found in Chapter Four.

Most courseware allows the instructor to assess learner progress. For example, the quiz building functions available in most courseware packages allow the instructor to create tests and quizzes or to poll students about their opinions on various issues. The results of the quiz or poll are encrypted and available to the instructor either via e-mail or on the course site. In addition, the test or quiz can be constructed to show the students their results immediately without allowing them to alter their responses. Many courseware packages now include gradebooks as well, so that both instructors and students can monitor progress as the course occurs. Frequently, quiz results can be linked to the gradebook so that they are automatically recorded.

Many of the technological developments may be helpful in accommodating various student learning styles. An auditory learner, for example, may feel more comfortable listening to a brief audio clip explaining a concept than reading about it. A visual learner tends to do well in an environment that presents mainly text or uses video clips. A learner who is more kinesthetic may appreciate assignments requiring visits to other websites on the Internet and the incorporation of online research. All of these techniques also help to keep things interesting for students who feel the need for more activity in a learning situation.

However, we present the new technological developments with a caution: not all students are capable of receiving a course that contains all of these technological "bells and whistles." Reduced prices on computer hardware have made

EXHIBIT 1.1. EXAMPLES OF ELECTRONIC WHITEBOARDS.

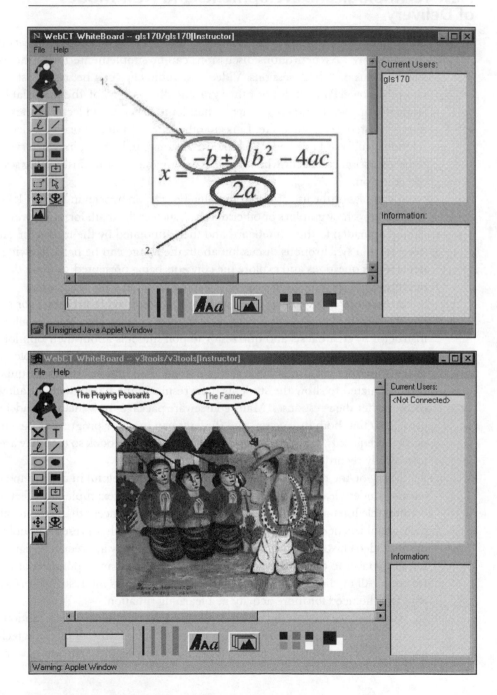

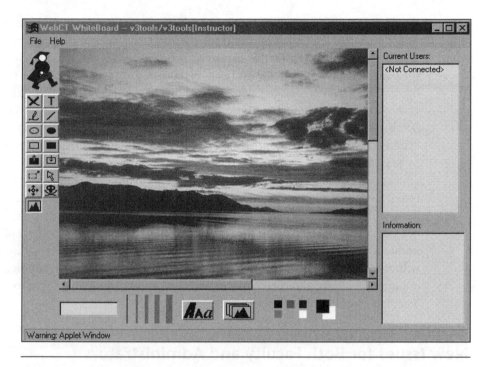

computers more available to a wider market. Even so, many students do not have access to a computer at home or are using older hardware and software to access their courses. Furthermore, it is difficult to compensate for a poor phone or Internet connection. For example, even though a computer might have a 56K modem, if the Internet connection available is only 28K, the user may have more difficulty working in a chat session or receiving a video clip.

Furthermore, although many institutions feel they need all of the technological advances in the courses they offer, rarely are those "bells and whistles" used in the delivery of a course. Brenda Reiswerg of University Access, an organization that develops business courses for institutions, likens the demand for all of the technological advances to the experience of buying a new car. She states, "When you go to buy a new car and the salesperson asks whether you want cruise control, of course you answer yes. But how often in a year's time do you really use it?" The staff at University Access have found that although their client institutions demand audio, video, and chat capability in their courses, rarely if ever are those elements used in the delivery of the course because many times faculty do not know how to use them effectively in an online course and students may not be able to access them.

In our experience, a well-constructed course is one that is logical in its design, easy to navigate, and inviting to the user. Further, we believe that asynchronous discussion is the most effective means of promoting online learning. Generally speaking, a simply constructed and easy-to-follow course site will be better received by students than one that relies too heavily on elements such as audio, video, and chat and is slow to download because of extensive graphics. Andrew Feenberg (1999), an early pioneer in online course delivery, supports this view when he states, "Could it be that our early experiments with online teaching, although constrained by primitive equipment, actually revealed the essence of electronically mediated education? We believe that to be true. Even after all these years, the most exciting online pedagogical experiences still rely on human interaction. And for the most part, these interactions continue to be text-based." Feenberg's statement echoes our own experience. When we ask students to evaluate the effectiveness of their online learning experience, it is the ability to engage in asynchronous discussion with their peers that they most value. Consequently, the choice of technology that enhances students' ability to connect with one another, enabling them to form a learning community, is critical.

New Issues for Both Faculty and Administrators

As development and acceptance of online distance learning continue to grow, new critical concerns for both faculty and administrators have begun to emerge, including such things as planning for a solid technological infrastructure, intellectual property rights, review and development of agreements with faculty that reflect good understanding of work for hire and copyright, and choice of software with which to conduct online courses. Many of these concerns relate to the degree to which faculty are being involved in the planning and decision making that surrounds the implementation of online distance learning courses and programs. Faculty argue that decisions should be made based on pedagogical need, but they feel that administrators are looking to the bottom line. However, the same issues that faculty face are also faced by administrators, albeit in a different way. For the purposes of this discussion, we provide Table 1.1, which compares faculty and administrative responses to commonly held concerns. A brief discussion of each of these issues follows.

Course Authoring Software Is Chosen Without Faculty Input

Andrew Feenberg (1999) states, "Professors aren't in the forefront of the movement to network education. Instead, politicians, university administrations, and computer and telecommunications companies have taken the lead, because they

TABLE 1.1. A COMPARISON OF FACULTY AND ADMINISTRATIVE RESPONSES TO COMMON CONCERNS.

Common Concerns	Faculty Response	Administrative Response
Course authoring software is being chosen by institutions without faculty involvement.	Want to be involved in choosing software that serves pedagogic needs.	Want software that will re-create the face-to-face classroom and will draw large numbers of students to online classes and programs.
Governance issues, including who decides which courses and programs will be delivered online, have emerged.	Want decisions to be made through faculty governance structures.	Frequently bypass consultation with faculty in attempts to launch programs quickly. Need to take the time to do adequate planning.
Intellectual property and course ownership issues have become paramount.	Want to retain ownership of courses or be compensated appropriately for development and "purchase" of courses.	See development of courses as "work for hire" or part of faculty role. Need to develop policies regulating these issues.
Just as faculty need training to negotiate the transition to online teaching successfully, so too do students.	Faculty training, both online and face-to-face, needs to occur to teach them not only the software but also the skills of electronic pedagogy. There is also a need for student orientations to online learning.	Need to support ongoing training for faculty and students. Administrators too should be informed and educated about the realities of online work.

see money in electronic ventures" (p. 26). Faculty's lack of involvement in decision-making processes that directly affect the way in which online courses will be
delivered is widening the rift between faculty and administrators. Feenberg further states, "In educational computing, the choice of infrastructure largely de-
termines how a program can be applied. If administrations consult corporations
instead of faculty about this choice, the outcome isn't likely to foster the kind of
educational community that faculty culture and traditions encourage" (p. 28). In
fact, involvement in the decision-making process required for the selection of
course authoring software can help elevate the level of faculty expertise required
to teach online just by their testing out various software packages before they begin.
This can give faculty a leg up in the course development process.

If faculty are being asked and even expected to teach online courses, and the
type of course authoring software that they are expected to use can significantly
affect the teaching and learning process, should they not be involved in its selection? Unfortunately, in our experience, rarely are they brought into the selection
process in any meaningful way. Feenberg states, "Salespeople often seem to have
the ear of administrators in a way that faculty do not, and they use their access to
sell not just devices but also the idea that the new tools can be used to reproduce
the live classroom experience or, better yet, to automate its elements and deliver
it as a package" (p. 30). Although administrators have the dollars and authority
with which to spend them, faculty are the end users of the software and should
have a say in its choice. Involvement of faculty will help them to "buy into" the
online teaching process and facilitate use of the software, thus allowing them to
focus more on pedagogical rather than technical issues.

Teaching online requires a new approach to pedagogy. The online re-creation
of the face-to-face classroom can be a dismal failure for both faculty and students.
A recent comment in an article in the *Chronicle of Higher Education* (Carnavale, 2000b)
indicated that students find nothing more boring than reading screen after screen
of text when an instructor is attempting to re-create a lecture online.

Administrators, along with faculty and students, need to be educated about
the realities of online teaching and the impact that good courseware can have
on this process. The concern should not be budgetary, but instead pedagogical.
"Administrators and businesspeople should forget the idea that distance education
systems based on videoconferencing or CD-ROMs and star professors will replace
face-to-face classroom education" (Feenberg, 1999, p. 31). As we have already discussed, technology can be an effective enhancement to the face-to-face classroom.
Well-constructed online courses can enhance and expand institutional offerings,
thus attracting students who prefer this mode of learning. Online learning is not
appropriate for all students, however, and is not likely to replace the face-to-face
classroom.

Governance Issues Have Emerged

As with the choice of courseware to be used for online courses, the selection and design of courses and programs to be taught online is also being made with little or no faculty input. In many institutions, department chairs are being asked which courses they will offer and programs are being designed by people involved in new departments devoted solely to distance learning or are being delegated to extension divisions or departments of continuing education. The new departments are hybrids, generally coordinating distance learning efforts that cut across numerous other departments in the university. Although some are organized in order to offer complete degree programs, most have been developed simply to coordinate multiple distance learning offerings. Often, faculty from many departments are asked to teach courses through the new distance learning departments. This is not inherently bad, as long as there has been good planning of the university's program as a whole. "When administrations in their hurry to launch potentially lucrative online programs forgo the usual channels of faculty consultation, quality suffers" (Maloney, 1999, p. 21). Faculty also object to the creation and spin-off of for-profit arms of universities devoted to the development and delivery of online courses, citing poor quality. Some entities are the result of collaborations between several colleges and universities, whereas others are partnerships between for-profit companies and universities (Grimes, 2000).

Accreditation raises yet another set of issues related to governance. As courses and programs are delivered online, those charged with judging academic quality are faced with the challenge of developing new standards. There is a belief that distance learning classes cannot be evaluated through the traditional model of academic accreditation. Some feel that new standards need to be developed because online courses are not a reproduction of those delivered face-to-face. There are additional fears that quality standards are being bypassed, thus degrading public perception of the value of a college degree (National Center for Education Statistics, 1999). However, others believe that new standards for the quality of online courses and programs should be determined through student feedback and institutional responsiveness, resulting in new sets of accreditation standards. Clearly, the jury is still out on this issue, and in the meantime the long-held accreditation standards normally applied to face-to-face classes prevail.

Nothing takes the place of good planning in the creation of any new academic endeavor. Some institutions have bypassed a planning process in the development of an online program, claiming faculty pressure to get courses online or the need to expand their market share quickly. However, as with the creation of a single course, planning with the end in mind can only serve to move the institution closer to a realistic use of technology to enhance teaching and learning.

What this means is that the institution should conduct an assessment of the learning and programmatic outcomes it hopes to achieve through online courses. The inclusion of faculty in this process should assist in creating a balanced approach focused on both pedagogic and budgetary goals.

"Administrators hope to use new technology to finesse the coming crisis in higher education spending, and to accommodate exploding enrollments of young people and returning students" (Feenberg, 1999, p. 28). Online distance learning will not save the academy by attracting large numbers of students while reducing infrastructure costs. However, through good planning and evaluation processes, institutions can avoid costly mistakes by developing realistic programs that address realistic student needs.

Intellectual Property and Course Ownership Issues Have Become Paramount

Numerous articles appearing in journals and on the Internet discuss who owns courses developed by faculty for online delivery. Interestingly, this is rarely a subject of discussion when it comes to the face-to-face classes that faculty members have taught for years. When members of the faculty leave for another institution, their courses generally go with them and another instructor is hired to develop and deliver the same course. Furthermore, it is usually not questioned that two instructors teaching the same course may choose to incorporate different concepts and material and be likely to approach the course very differently.

In the online arena, however, a growing trend is for the institution to claim ownership of courses. Because online courses are generally housed on a university server and can be archived or kept intact indefinitely, the question of ownership has become a bone of contention. Some institutions are calling the courses "work for hire" and claiming ownership, whereas others have few policies regulating how online courses are viewed. "Ownership is one of the most contentious issues in online education, because who owns a course bears directly on who profits from it" (Maloney, 1999, p. 23).

In addition, many institutions are hiring faculty from outside the institution—people who are considered to be content experts—to develop courses or are purchasing or licensing such courses, which the institution's own instructors are then expected to teach. "When professors have to use online materials prepared by others, their hands are tied. They can't draw on their own knowledge of content and the needs of their students in teaching" (Maloney, 1999, p. 22). The quality of development and degree to which these courses can be customized is an issue that we will discuss in more detail in Chapter Six.

Just Like Faculty, Students Need to Be Trained to Learn Online

Many of those we have spoken with around the country continue to believe that the key to faculty training lies in familiarizing them with the software they will be using to deliver courses. However, as we have conducted our faculty training seminars we have frequently encountered faculty who tell us that although they mastered the use of the software they still wondered how to deliver the course effectively. Why were students not participating? Why was it that most or all of the interaction occurring in the class was between students and instructor rather than between students? Why was it that students seemed unwilling or unable to take the initiative in making the course "happen"? Both the problems and the answers may be related to one issue: faculty training in more than just use of software. Faculty need instruction in the differences in online teaching and what is required to build a learning community online. We will return to this subject in Chapter Two.

However, faculty are not the only ones who need training. The same mistakes are made with students. Again, it is assumed that if students can navigate the courseware being used, they should successfully complete the class. In our experience, students also need training to learn what is expected of them in the online classroom. In Chapter Seven, we will discuss the issues involved in working with the virtual student.

Finally, administrators, politicians, and all those involved with decision making for distance education programs also need training. The financial realities and the ability of technology to resolve budgetary problems should be conveyed to the decision makers, along with the realities of online teaching and learning. Administrators and decision makers have been persuaded that online distance education could replace campuses and faculty. This is a myth that needs to be dispelled so that faculty and administrators can work together to create pedagogically sound, learner-centered online programs.

Recent Developments in K–12 Online Learning

Higher education professionals can begin their own learning process by taking note of the exciting developments occurring in the K–12 online learning arena. Although technology has been used as an adjunct to elementary and secondary teaching for a while, new virtual high schools and other virtual support services for school districts are emerging. Some of the new high school initiatives have been funded through grants available through the U.S. Department of Education. Some are collaborative partnerships between school districts and institutions of higher education. Others are Internet start-up companies hoping to provide services to the K–12 market, including offering school districts the ability to construct their own websites, which might include online classes, the posting of assignments, and discussion forums for teachers, parents, and students. Other features facilitate communication between parents and schools, enable parents to monitor their child's school progress better, or provide homework assistance for students, ongoing training for teachers, and community-building tools for use between schools and school districts to allow completion of collaborative projects and communication across the country and internationally for students and teachers. Resource C contains a list of contacts for readers who wish to explore some of the many developments in this arena.

One of the more innovative of these efforts has been the development of the Virtual High School, funded through the assistance of a Department of Education Technology Innovation Challenge Grant. The program, developed by the Concord Consortium of Concord, Massachusetts, allows students attending member high schools to take online classes with students from all over the country who are attending other member high schools and with an instructor who may or may not be at their own school. The project is also looking to create courses for middle school students and has created means by which elementary school students can collaborate on projects. Few of the programs being developed at the high school level allow students to complete a high school degree online. Instead, most, like the Virtual High School, provide advanced placement, honors, and college-preparatory courses. These efforts are being hailed as a means by which students who attend school in districts with limited funds to offer such classes can have access to them.

Just as with college-level online programs, however, accreditation concerns have emerged regarding online high school programs. Their quality is an issue that has been raised by accrediting bodies and faculty of four-year institutions. Although the schools of higher education have their own accreditation, there have been questions about the quality of the high school curricula they offer. And as with college-level programs, for-profit organizations are now offering high school level courses. Some companies offer their courses directly to students, which raises the highest level of concern. Others sell their materials to schools and colleges for high school student use. At present, it is difficult to monitor the quality of these courses. There is also some concern about whether the courses will be accepted by colleges and universities when students present them as part of their college applications.

Yet another concern about the online high school alternatives relates to access. Can the poorer districts to which the high school initiatives are directed support their students with equipment and Internet access? As virtual high school classes are developed, there also needs to be concern about the kind of computer equipment students may be using. Although computer prices have plummeted, a thousand dollars may still seem exorbitant to a district struggling to pay teacher salaries and purchase textbooks. Many districts are using older, donated equipment that may not be able to accommodate such elements as audio and video. Some two- and four-year institutions are opening the doors to their computer labs to allow younger students access. But greater efforts need to be made to provide computer equipment to the poorer school districts in order for students to have equal access.

We hope that high school and middle school alternatives will continue to develop but that they will not be seen as a replacement for the face-to-face high school. High school age students are in far greater need of socialization opportunities than are adults returning to school. Still, the courses, programs, and services can fill a definite need among students who might not otherwise have access, and thus provide a great service in narrowing the gap for the technological have's and have not's.

In any case, the growing trend toward virtual high school education is one that we in higher education cannot ignore. The students who participate in online high school classes are likely to seek out the same forms of education when they enter college. They will likely be skilled in navigating the online environment and in working collaboratively with their peers. The question then becomes, Is higher education ready for them?

The Effectiveness of Distance Delivery

A debate that is likely to continue for quite some time is whether online distance learning is as effective as the face-to-face classroom in achieving learning outcomes. Research on this topic continues to emerge as, for example, in a recent report released by the Institute for Higher Education Policy entitled *What's the Difference?* (Phipps and Merisotis, 1999). The essence of this report is a review of the research, which compares the outcomes of online and face-to-face instruction. Because it is almost impossible to engage faculty in a discussion of online learning without this topic emerging, we feel that it is important to review some of that literature here.

Phipps and Merisotis, the authors of the report, in summarizing their review of the literature on the effectiveness of distance learning, noted that the studies conducted tend to fall into three broad categories: student outcomes (including test scores, grades, and comparisons to on-campus students), student attitudes about learning through these means, and overall student satisfaction with distance learning. One such study, conducted by Schutte (1996), randomly assigned students in a course on social statistics to face-to-face or virtual classes. Lectures and exams were standardized between the groups. The study found that the students participating in the virtual class produced better results on tests. Schutte concluded that the performance differences could be attributed to the enhanced ability for students to collaborate in the online class. "In fact, the highest performing students (in both classes) reported the most peer interaction" (p. 4). However, Schutte noted that the element of collaboration is a key variable that would need to be controlled in future studies.

Phipps and Merisotis (1999) note, "With few exceptions, the bulk of these writings suggests that the learning outcomes of students using technology at a distance are similar to the learning outcomes of students who participate in conventional classroom instruction" (p. 2). Others who have also compiled the research on distance learning have come to the same tentative conclusion (Hanson and others, 1997; Russell, 1999). Phipps and Merisotis offer this conclusion with a caution, however, feeling that most of the research conducted on learning outcomes from distance learning classes is questionable. Many of the researchers, such as Schutte, have noted variables that cannot be controlled, and many studies are based on qualitative rather than quantitative measures. In addition, good research does not yet define what is meant by learning outcomes or conceptualize what knowledge looks like (Boettcher, 1999). Consequently, much of the research attempts to paint the picture of "an illusory 'typical learner,' which masks the enormous variability of the student population" (Phipps and Merisotis, 1999, p. 5) and does not account for differences in learning styles. Despite problems with the research being conducted on effectiveness, Phipps and Merisotis (p. 8) offer important implications that have come out of it. They state:

> Although the ostensible purpose of much of the research is to ascertain how technology affects student learning and student satisfaction, many of the results seem to indicate that technology is not nearly as important as other factors, such as learning tasks, learner characteristics, student motivation, and the instructor. The irony is that the bulk of the research on technology ends up addressing an activity that is fundamental to the academy, namely pedagogy—the art of teaching. . . . Any discussion about enhancing the teaching-learning process through technology also has the beneficial effect of improving how students are taught on campus. . . . The key question that needs to be asked is: What is the best way to teach students?

The debate over the effectiveness of online distance learning is far from over. We have found, however, that our involvement in teaching online has made a significant difference in the ways in which we approach our students on a face-to-face basis. No longer do we lecture about material that is contained in the textbook.

We now assume that our students will and do read. Our face-to-face teaching is far more collaborative and empowering.

Despite the criticim and skepticism, and with this hopeful outcome and implication of online learning as a backdrop, we now turn our attention to what it takes to assist faculty in developing high-quality courses. In so doing, we offer the following Principles of Good Practice in Undergraduate Education. They were first published by the American Association of Higher Education in 1987 and reproduced at the conclusion of the Phipps and Merisotis report (1999, p. 32) as a guide.

Encourage contact between students and faculty;

Develop reciprocity and cooperation among students;

Use active learning techniques;

Give prompt feedback;

Emphasize time-on-task;

Communicate high expectations; and

Respect diverse talents and ways of learning.

These principles form the backbone of a well-constructed online course because they encourage interactivity, active learning techniques, and the expectation that the instructor will be present and involved but not control the process. With the Principles of Good Practice in mind, we now turn our attention to the important topic of faculty training.

CHAPTER TWO

THE ART OF ONLINE TEACHING

Teaching in the cyberspace classroom requires that we move beyond traditional models of pedagogy into new practices that are more facilitative. Teaching in cyberspace involves much more than simply taking old, "tried and true" models of pedagogy and transferring them to a different medium. Unlike in the face-to-face classroom, in online distance education attention needs to be paid to developing a sense of community in the group of participants in order for the learning process to be successful.

We continue to find, as we work with academic institutions throughout the country, that faculty are ill-prepared to make the shift to the online academic arena. We hear stories about poor student and faculty participation in courses, difficulties with course construction, and poor course evaluations by students. A student in instructional design told us about the experience of a friend of his who, because of the convenience of taking a course in this way, enrolled in an online class in algebra. As the course progressed, she became increasingly frustrated and complained that she should have taken the class face-to-face. The instructor had set up the course simply by posting text-based lectures and lessons online. Students were expected to access the course site and read what was there in addition to reading material in the textbook. Homework assignments were e-mailed to the instructor, with whom there was no other contact. Exams were taken online. There was no ability to interact with other students or even to know who else was enrolled in the course. When this student e-mailed questions to the instructor, she received no response, and therefore felt that she was learning less and making less progress than if she had taken the class on campus. She did poorly on quizzes and exams and was confused by and frustrated with the whole experience. This may seem to be an extreme example. But stories like this are conveyed to us on a daily basis, and we have been asked why online courses continue to be developed in this way.

Such stories tend to discourage those who hear them from teaching online or suggesting that students take online courses. A new book advising working adults returning to college recommends that they avoid distance learning programs. The author's concern stems from the reports of students in distance learning programs, describing a sense of isolation and frustration as well as an inability to gain exposure to a wide range of subject areas. She also expresses concern about what she describes as the "money-making, opportunistic enterprise" that distance learning has become (Young, 1999b, p. 1). As we will continually stress throughout this book, online learning can be very powerful and effective if classes are constructed and conducted in a thoughtful manner, using the concepts and guidelines that we have developed and will provide in this chapter. The key to well-developed classes is training faculty not only in the use of technology but also in the art of online teaching.

Who Should Teach Online?

Not all faculty are suited for the online environment, and academic institutions are making some serious mistakes when deciding who should teach. Faculty who may be resistant to making the transition to the online classroom are being told that they have no choice and are being sent on to develop courses with little preparation or training in how to do so. In addition, choices about who should teach online are often based on faulty criteria: it is usually either someone who is considered a content expert or someone who is deemed entertaining in the face-to-face classroom who is chosen. Stephen Brookfield (1995) notes that often the most popular faculty who get the best course evaluations are the ones who are able to entertain. This popularity does not translate well online.

The problem with these decisions rests on the lack of attention to the personality type that tends to do best in the online arena. Research by one of us reveals that the introvert does particularly well online (Pratt, 1996). We believe that this finding generally applies to faculty as well as to students. With the removal of facial and body cues, introverts can easily establish a presence online, thus exhibiting aspects of themselves that might not otherwise be seen. Introverts generally appear far more extroverted online, frequently becoming quite verbal and interactive. Their ability to take time, reflect, and present themselves through text serves them well. Self-consciousness diminishes because the instructor is out from under the physical scrutiny of students. The extrovert, in contrast, who is used to being able to establish presence quickly through verbal and social connection, may have more difficulty in the flat, text-based online environment. Taking time to reflect is not the forte of the extrovert, who tends to process ideas out loud at the time they occur. Consequently, the asynchronous online environment with its absence of immediate feedback on ideas can be frustrating to these individuals. "People who are introverts are more adept at creating a virtual environment because they can process information internally and are less outgoing socially. It is more comfortable for an introvert to spend time thinking about information before responding to it. It is more difficult—but not impossible—for extroverts to interact this way, perhaps because they have less need to. Extroverts tend to feel more comfortable processing verbally and in the company of others" (Palloff and Pratt, 1999, p. 22).

We were told the story of an extremely extroverted professor, also considered an expert in his field, who was asked to develop a course that would be used online by other instructors. He became increasingly frustrated as he worked with instructional designers because they were unable to capture the essence of his personality in the online course. It was not so much conveying the subject matter that concerned him. Rather, it was the inability to convey who he was to prospective students—not an easy thing to do through text. Consequently, the instructor who may not present in a lively fashion in the classroom yet who has subject matter expertise, is flexible, and is willing and open to the development of a more collaborative way of teaching may be the better candidate to develop and deliver online courses (Brookfield, 1995; Denning, 1997; McGrath and Hollingshead, 1994; Palloff and Pratt, 1999; Palmer, 1998; Turkle, 1995).

Another important consideration is the instructor's willingness to give up some control in the teaching and learning process in order to empower the learners and build a learning community. An instructor who is open to giving up control of the learning process, using collaborative learning techniques and ideas, allowing for personal interaction, and bringing in real-life experiences and examples, and who builds reflective practice into teaching, is a good candidate for teaching online. Certainly, not all of these criteria need to be met, but a good measure of openness and flexibility is key to a successful transition to the online realm.

How do we find these instructors? At many institutions this is being done through a process of attraction rather than coercion. Those who are interested in giving online teaching a try—also known as *early adopters*—may develop or post a course or two. As they struggle but also succeed with the process, they will attract others to join them in this effort. The support that they need to make the transition successfully, however, rests in training and mentoring.

Training, Training, and More Training

Faculty cannot be expected to know intuitively how to design and deliver an effective online course. Although courses and programs about the use of technology in education are emerging in institutions of higher education and are available to teachers in training, more seasoned faculty have not been exposed to the techniques and methods needed to make online work successful. Current software applications make it easy for faculty simply to transfer material to a course site. The lure to do this is enhanced by the fact that institutions, seeing online distance learning as their lifesaver in times of declining enrollment on campus, are enrolling such large numbers in online classes that the burden on faculty is enormous. The result is the development of poorly constructed classes, like the algebra class we described earlier.

Providing training for faculty in order to help them get started and also to support their ongoing work in online teaching does help. In our experience, the pairing of faculty who are more experienced online with those who are just starting out helps to break down barriers and provide real, concrete examples of what works and what does not. The *Chronicle of Higher Education* reported on an effort by the University of Washington to attract faculty to online teaching by providing them with a lab situation and consultants—mainly undergraduate and graduate students at the university—to assist them with learning technology and teaching strategies (Young, 1999a). What better way to teach faculty to teach online than through the students who will be the recipients of that work?

With the assistance of a grant, the University of Central Florida established a comprehensive faculty development program that addresses four key areas of readiness: the institution, faculty, courses, and learners. Institutional readiness looks at the following elements, which can be used as a checklist: the course or program is a good fit with the institution's character and mission; it is a good fit with learner characteristics of the institution; it has a clearly articulated mission and strategic plan; there is demonstrated faculty interest; there is a robust campus infrastructure to support courses and programs; there is leadership for the initiative; and there are commitments to faculty support, course and program support, learner support, and assessment. Faculty readiness is determined by willingness to learn, willingness to surrender some control over class design and teaching style, ability to collaborate with peers, willingness to change their traditional role, ability to build a support system, patience with technology, and ability to learn from others. Course readiness depends on faculty understanding of the technology in use, the pedagogy required for online teaching, and the logistics of the course production process. Learner readiness is determined through informed self-selection, ability to take responsibility for their own learning, an access plan for taking the course, awareness of their own learning style, some technical skill, ability to build a support system, and ability to deal with the uncertainties of using technology to take courses (Truman-Davis, Futch, Thompson, and Yonekura, 2000).

We have found that even experienced faculty have something to learn about the creation of a learning community online. An instructor who was participating in one of our training sessions asked why he could not get students to talk to him or include him in their conversations. Instead of seeing this as a good thing and evidence of a developing learning community that was able to carry on without the input of an instructor, he felt excluded and anxious. Another instructor bemoaned the fact that in the courseware her institution was using there was no way to generate a transcript of the "chat" sessions (synchronous discussions) that were occurring during collaborative learning activities. The absence of a transcript and the fact that the instructor was not being asked to participate in the chat sessions left her feeling worried and uncomfortable. She was not in control of the learning process, which she felt was expected of her as an instructor. These examples illustrate that it is not easy to let go of traditional values and ideas in the academic arena. When instructors are given the opportunity to discuss their concerns and even fears emerging from their online experiences, it frees them to try new and better techniques to enhance learning.

Online training courses are another useful way to deliver training to faculty who will be teaching online. In an online training course, faculty can experience firsthand what it is like to be both an instructor and a student in the process. In our experience, the courseware to be used in the development and delivery of courses should be the software used in the training. Faculty, as a part of the training, should be encouraged to develop a course or even a lesson that other participants can critique. The facilitator of the training, who is likely to be a faculty developer or a faculty member who has been trained or is skillful in the delivery of online instruction, should model good techniques for building a learning community and empowering the participating faculty to explore both the medium and the material. We have found that it is best to include faculty who are about to embark on their first course in online training. Delivering such training to all faculty, whether they will be teaching online or not, tends to limit participation in the course. Faculty who are about to teach online are highly motivated to learn good techniques for doing so; faculty who are simply interested but will not immediately be using the material may not participate to the same degree. We have found that when the group is mixed, those who will not be teaching in the immediate future tend to drop away, frustrating those who are staying with the training and depending on the group in order to get something from it. But regardless of the form training takes, it is important to include techniques for course development, facilitating learning in the online environment, and building a learning community.

New Processes, New Relationships

In our previous book we described in detail a number of techniques and ideas for building and sustaining an online learning community, in addition to discussing the importance of developing community in order to enhance the learning process. The attention to community is not just "fluff," or something extra that an already overburdened faculty need to pay attention to. It is a means by which students become empowered as learners, thereby taking charge of their own learning, and in fact lessening the "teaching" burden on faculty. Instead of increasing the teaching load, good online teaching only serves to increase the faculty's responsibility as a learning facilitator. This is not a responsibility to be taken lightly, but rather than a burden it can in fact be a way to infuse teaching with new energy and passion. Working online certainly takes more time than teaching face-to-face. However, that time is well spent if students are taking responsibility for the learning process.

Online distance learning courses and programs can take many forms. For example, they may be *static courses*, in which material is placed on a website and left unchanged. Students can access the website at any time, but these courses include minimal interaction among the learners. A course also may involve the use of asynchronous discussion as the basis for teaching and learning, or it may use other technological advances, such as synchronous chat and streaming audio and video. Regardless of the technology in use, the more that instructors involve their students in the learning process online, the more likely they will be to achieve a successful learning outcome.

Our preference is for asynchronous learning environments in which students can read material and post to discussions on their own time schedules. The asynchronous environment allows students the luxury of time for thought and reflection on material, which we believe enhances the learning process. In asynchronous mode, students can read assigned material, search out new, additional sources to complement what is being studied, engage in lively discussion with one another—discussion that demonstrates good critical thinking skills, the ability to do some research on a topic—and reflect on the material presented in the text, by the instructor, and by peers. The result is a greater ability to make meaning out of the material under study and to engage with it. How that happens is the essence of what we call *electronic pedagogy*.

Electronic Pedagogy

The online classroom is a potentially powerful teaching and learning arena in which new practices and new relationships can make significant contributions to learning. In order to navigate the power of this medium in education successfully, faculty must be trained not only to use technology but also to shift the ways in which they organize and deliver material. Making this shift can increase the potential for learners to take charge of their own learning process and facilitate the development of a sense of community among the learners.

The shift to online learning poses enormous challenges to instructors and their institutions. As we noted earlier, many believe that the cyberspace classroom is no different from the face-to-face classroom and that approaches used face-to-face will surely work online. Many further believe that all they need to do to teach online successfully is to "convert" the course material by placing content on a website. We believe, however, that when the only connection we have to our students is through words on a screen, we must pay attention to many issues that we take for granted in the face-to-face classroom. It is our best practices that must follow us into the cyberspace classroom, and those practices are the basis for what we term electronic pedagogy, or the art of teaching online.

Keys to Success

The transition to the cyberspace classroom can be successfully made if attention is paid to several key areas: ensuring access to and familiarity with the technology in use; establishing guidelines and procedures that are relatively loose and free-flowing and generated with significant input from participants; striving to achieve maximum participation and "buy-in" from the participants; promoting collaborative learning; and creating a triple loop in the learning process to enable participants to reflect on their learning, themselves as learners, and the learning process. All of these practices significantly contribute to the development of an online learning community, a powerful tool for enhancing the learning experience. Each will now be reviewed in more detail.

Ensuring Access to and Familiarity with Technology

In a sense, it is a mistake to begin by talking about technology. Many institutions believe that all it takes to implement an online distance learning program is to install a fancy software package and train faculty to use it. Certainly, an instructor needs to be knowledgeable about the technology in use and comfortable enough with it to assist a student should difficulty be encountered. An instructor should also be able to construct a course site that is easy for students to access, use, and navigate. However, the instructor's responsibility must not end there. "Technology does not teach students; effective teachers do" (Whitesel, 1998, p. 1). The issue, then, is not the technology itself but rather how we use it in the design and delivery of online courses.

The most visually appealing course, complete with audio, video, and chat, is useless if a student is using old hardware or living in a remote area with limited Internet access. As students enter online degree programs and courses, they are generally told that in order to access a particular course they must have access to a certain level of technology. However, the most up-to-date computer technology will still not function well in an area with poor phone connections and slow Internet access. Consequently, the software used for course delivery should be:

- Functional, offering the functions necessary to design and deliver the course
- Simple to operate for both faculty and students
- User-friendly, visually appealing, and easy to navigate [Palloff and Pratt, 1999]

As we visit various academic institutions and talk with faculty and students, we have found it interesting that even when they are able to use chat or streaming audio or video, they do so infrequently. Students quickly become bored watching a "talking head" video lecture on their computer screen, particularly with the quality currently available. One of us participated in an online course involving fifteen-minute lectures in streaming audio and found that it was impossible to sit and listen for even that seemingly brief period of time without tuning out.

A recent issue of *Syllabus* reviewed the efficacy of using streaming audio and video in distance learning classes. While evaluating the pro's and con's of using video, Barry Hampe (1999) stated, "There has been an unfortunate tendency in recent years to create video programs which consist of nothing but people talking. . . . Taping someone talking is usually the least interesting thing one can do with video for a presentation" (p. 14). And yet, most current attempts at using streaming video in online classes generally involve taping a professor delivering a part of a lecture.

It has also been shown that few web users will read more than one screen of text. Long web pages that require readers to scroll large distances and remember what was previously on their screens tend to be disorienting (Lynch and Horton, 1999). Consequently, keeping it simple by using concise "chunks" of information is the best rule of thumb. Brief informational posts that stimulate thinking and discussion serve the learning process far better than attempting to post a lecture online or using audio or video.

Synchronous discussion does have its place in online courses in limited ways. Synchronous discussion—also known as "chat"—refers to online conversation that occurs in real time. All users are online at the same time and interacting in the same discussion space. It is best used to enhance collaborative learning experiences and enable teamwork. In order to make the best use of chat, groups should be kept very small and an agenda for the discussion should be created in advance in order to help keep participants on track. Otherwise, it is very easy for a chat session to wander off into areas unrelated to the course or the collaborative exercise. Small groups also create an environment in which all voices are likely to be heard. Because dominance in a chat session often goes to the fastest typist or the person with the fastest Internet connection, keeping a group small allows participants to keep up with the flow of conversation and enter when it feels appropriate.

Chat is also a good adjunct to a whiteboard session. As we illustrated in Exhibit 1.1, in "whiteboarding" an instructor or student might post an image or diagram that can be annotated as it is being presented. Chat can be used to discuss the image or to ask questions as the presentation is being made. Whiteboarding is also a good brainstorming technique. Consequently, chat might be used effectively to supplement that activity as well.

Chat is not well used to deliver lecture material, however, although many mistakenly believe that it is. If an instructor uses chat to lecture, once again what students will receive are lengthy pieces of text that are not likely to capture their interest or attention. Consequently, synchronous communication needs to be used judiciously in an online course.

Finally, the technology in use should be transparent to the students enrolled in the class. Instructors do not want to be faced with technological struggles throughout the course in addition to working to build a good learning community. The instructors also need to be familiar enough with the software to work around any difficult issues it might present. The technology, then, should serve only as a vehicle for delivering the course, allowing both instructor and students to pay attention to more important matters.

Establishing Guidelines and Procedures

We cannot stress enough that an important beginning to an online course is to present clear guidelines for participation in the class as well as information for students about course expectations and procedures. Guidelines are generally presented along with the syllabus and a course outline as a means of creating some structure around and in the course. If clear guidelines are not presented, students can become confused and disorganized and the learning process will suffer.

Once the course begins, the instructor should also make an assessment of the group he or she is working with in order to determine what modifications to the guidelines might be necessary. One of us learned this lesson the hard way with a group of graduate students who were having difficulty making the transition to the online learning environment. A course was posted that the instructor had taught previously, using the same set of guidelines that had worked well with previous groups. This group, however, needed far more structure. Believing that they were asking for help, two students "flamed" the instructor on the course site, causing participation in the course to dwindle. (*Flaming* is when one participant in an online discussion sends to another any kind of derogatory comment. A flame is frequently interpreted as an attack rather than a discussion of the participants' positions. It is, thus, a very heated exchange.) Once guidelines and course expectations were clarified and the angry feelings of the students were attended to, participation increased but never reached acceptable levels for the remainder of the term. One student responded to the clarification as follows:

I have felt like I poured my personal self out online, and receive little to no feedback, so your prompting will help a lot. I was beginning to feel that this would be a course where I got the most from self-reflection, not the dialogue, but I would welcome a change in this. Sometimes I think the early online tensions in the course created some rifts. I think we are on our way to recovering as a group. *Beth*

In evaluating their experience with this class, students made comments such as that they learned more from the reading than from each other—a clear indication that learning objectives were not met with this group and that a learning community never successfully formed.

The guidelines for an online class also should not be too rigid and should contain room for discussion and negotiation. "Imposed guidelines that are too rigid will constrain discussion, causing participants to worry about the nature of their posts rather than to simply post" (Palloff and Pratt, 1999, p. 18). Guidelines should not put students in the position of wondering, "Am I doing this right?" They should instead provide a safe space within which students feel free to express themselves and discuss material related to the course.

It is useful to use the guidelines as a first discussion item in a class. Doing this enables students to take responsibility for the way they will engage in the course and with one another, and it serves to promote collaboration in the learning process. We offer two caveats, however. The instructor should retain veto power—meaning that if a proposed change would substantially alter the course and send it in a direction that will not achieve learning outcomes, the instructor needs to step in and say no. The instructor also holds ultimate decision-making power in the area of assignments and grading. Frequently when we ask students for their input on guidelines, we state that assignments and grading are not open for negotiation. Deadlines, however, are. If we have established an assignment deadline that conflicts with other courses students may be taking, we will certainly entertain the notion of changing deadlines. The second caveat is that if one student offers a suggested change, the other students should be polled to see if the change rests well with them. We will not change the way in which a course is structured based only on one student's input. Because online learning should be collaborative, all voices should be heard when a change is proposed.

Achieving Maximum Participation

Participation guidelines in an online course are critical to its successful outcome. As online instructors, however, we cannot make the assumption that if we establish minimum participation guidelines of two posts per week, for example, students will understand what that means. We must also explain what it means to post to an online course discussion. "A post involves more than visiting the course site to check in and say hello. A post is considered to be a substantive contribution to the discussion wherein a student either comments on other posts or begins a new topic" (Palloff and Pratt, 1999, p. 100).

In addition to being clear about expectations for participation, the following are some suggestions that we have found will enhance participation in an online course (Palloff and Pratt, 1999):

• *Be clear about how much time the course will require of students and faculty in order to eliminate potential misunderstandings about course demands.* Students sometimes assume that taking an online course is the softer, easier way to earn credit. They learn quickly, however, that this is not the case. If the instructor forewarns them through accurate course information in an introduction to the course, it will help students make informed decisions about whether this is a course they can successfully complete. In addition, it helps to reduce or eliminate the possibility that they will drop out once the course begins. If some students are having significant difficulty managing their time as the course progresses and if their participation is dwindling as a result, the instructor may need to work with those students to assist them in establishing good practices to help them achieve their learning goals for the course.

• *Teach students about online learning.* Instructors and academic institutions assume that when students enter the online classroom, they will intuitively know what online teaching is about and how to learn in the online environment. What we have found, however, is that students need to be oriented to the online classroom and taught how to learn online.

• *As the instructor, be a model of good participation by logging on frequently and contributing to the discussion.* The workload in an online class not only is significantly higher for students but also is significantly higher for the instructor. Online instructors cannot post a course and then go on vacation for a week—unless they are willing to take a computer with them! An instructor is unlikely to keep up with student discussion by logging on once or twice a week. Furthermore, an instructor who does so is likely to see poor participation in the course. The instructor's role as a learning facilitator is to follow the discussion and gently guide and redirect it by asking clarifying and expansive questions. This practice keeps the discussion moving and also reassures students that the instructor is present and available.

However, the instructor needs to maintain a balance between too little and too much participation. Because the learning community is a critical feature of the online course, the instructor need not respond to every student post but instead should determine the appropriate time to jump in, make a comment, ask another question, or redirect the discussion. Too much participation by the instructor can have the effect of reducing the amount of interaction among the students and create an unnecessary degree of reliance on the teacher. Too much instructor participation is often evident in the form of questions or comments being directed to him or her rather than to other participants, or if the group waits for the instructor to post before they move on. Balance is the key to facilitating a good online discussion.

• *Be willing to step in and set limits if participation wanes or if the conversation is headed in the wrong direction.* Being a learning facilitator does not mean being uninvolved in the learning process. The instructor needs to act as a guide in order to ensure that learning objectives are met. Consequently, if students are headed down the wrong path, the instructor needs to let them know it so that they can get back on track. We had an experience with a group of undergraduate students who, when asked questions designed to help them critically analyze the material they were reading in the textbook, would respond by regurgitating material directly from the text. When one student would begin the week's discussion in that fashion, the others would follow suit. We needed to step in often to push them gently to reflect on the material they were reading and to move away from what was comfortable into territory that was new to them.

• *Remember that there are people attached to the words on the screen. Be willing to contact students who are not participating and invite them in.* When students drop away from the online discussion, the learning process of all participants is affected. Therefore, it is important to monitor the participation of each student and to make contact either when there has been a change (for example, someone has been a good participant but his or her participation wanes for a week or so) or when there has been minimal or no participation. Sometimes the reasons for nonparticipation have to do with technical problems and personal issues, with which the instructor may be helpful. At other times, the instructor may find that the online mode of instruction simply does not suit the student. When this is the case, students should be encouraged to find other means to take the course, such as returning to the face-to-face classroom.

Good participation is essential and should be stressed by the instructor. In the face-to-face classroom, the absence of one or more participants may not be noticed. But a student's absence from the online classroom significantly affects the quality of the online discussion and should be dealt with as soon as it is noticed.

- *Create a warm and inviting atmosphere that promotes the development of a sense of community among the participants.* During one of our presentations at a conference in Europe, an instructor from Holland expressed concern that he was unable to get his online students to respond to him as a person rather than as an instructor. He was hoping to develop a sense of community with his participants and was finding this a difficult task. We encouraged him to share a reasonable amount of personal information with his students as a way of inviting them to do the same. For example, in an introduction, instead of simply telling students about academic accomplishments that demonstrated why he was competent to teach the course, why not include information about a spouse or partner, children, pets, and interests outside of academic pursuits? Sharing this information with students presents the instructor as a real person who is interested in hearing about his students as real people as well.

It is always important to remember that in the online environment, we present ourselves in text. Because it is a flat medium, we need to make an extra effort to humanize the environment. In the face-to-face classroom, students have the opportunity to get to know one another as people—before or after class, during classroom discussions, and in other campus locations such as the student lounge. In the online environment, we need to create these opportunities more purposefully.

If you incorporate these suggestions into the development of an online course, they will promote the development of a learning community and can also assist in the promotion of collaborative learning. Both potentially contribute to stronger learning outcomes and more satisfactory learning experiences for all involved.

Promoting Collaboration

Collaborative learning processes help students to achieve deeper levels of knowledge generation through the creation of shared goals, shared exploration, and a shared process of meaning-making. Jonassen and others (1995) note that the outcome of collaborative learning processes includes personal meaning-making and the social construction of knowledge and meaning. Stephen Brookfield (1995) describes what he terms *new paradigm teachers,* who are willing to engage in and facilitate collaborative processes by promoting initiative on the part of the learners, creativity, critical thinking, and dialogue.

Given the separation by time and distance of the learners from one another and from the instructor, and given the discussion-based nature of these courses, the online learning environment is the type of learning arena that "(a) lets a group of students formulate a shared goal for their learning process, (b) allows the students to use personal motivating problems, (c) takes dialogue as the fundamental way of inquiry" (Christiansen and Dirckinck-Holmfeld, 1995, p. 1). Collaborative learning assists with deeper levels of knowledge generation and promotes initiative, creativity, and the development of critical thinking skills.

Engagement in a collaborative learning process forms the foundation of a learning community. When collaboration is not encouraged, participation in the online course is generally low and may take the form of queries to the instructor rather than dialogue and feedback.

Promoting Reflection

When students are learning collaboratively, reflection on the learning process is inherent. "The learning process, then, involves self-reflection on the knowledge acquired about the course, about how learning occurs electronically, about the technology itself, and about how the user has been transformed by their new-found relationships with the machine, the software, the learning process, and the other participants" (Palloff and Pratt, 1999, p. 62). In addition, when students are learning collaboratively online, reflections on the contribution of technology to the learning process are almost inevitable. They should be encouraged to reflect on their own learning process, how learning with the use of technology has affected that process either positively or negatively, and what they might have learned about the technology itself by using it to learn.

Constructing a course that allows these naturally occurring processes to unfold greatly enhances the learning outcome and the process of community building. It is more than reflection on the meaning and importance of course material. The reflection process transforms a participant in an online course from a student to a reflective practitioner, and ideally, sets in motion the potential for lifelong reflective learning. Purposeful facilitation of this process involves incorporating the following questions into a course (Palloff and Pratt, 1999, p. 140): "How were you as a learner before you came into this course? How have you changed? How do you anticipate this will affect your learning in the future?"

The following student post presents a good example of the reflective process. In her comments, Juliet reflects on the course content, some "aha's" about online interaction, and her own learning style:

A major realization was that the same leadership competencies such as vision, trust, building relationships, communicating, celebrating and rewarding, etc. are needed in the virtual and real world. These competencies are challenging to model in the real world and they take more effort and consciousness for leaders to model in the virtual environment. In virtual conditions leaders also need to be current and proficient in the many electronic tools available for leading.

There were two surprises for me. The first was that people online could have electronic personalities that may be different than how the person is experienced by others in a face to face situation. The readings on multiuser domains [or MUDs, virtual games that allow users to navigate, converse, build, and collaborate, which are considered a new form of community (see Turkle, 1995)] and multiple identities stretched my imagination and challenged me to remember how diverse we are as a human species. I now can understand how expressing a hidden or less used side of oneself in an online environment could provide an opportunity to work through emotional issues, not likely to be dealt with under more "real" conditions.

I was also surprised to realize that communicating online favors introverts. When I decided to have a distance learning experience I experienced a lot of resistance and fear around using the technology and being able to communicate effectively in writing. I am an extrovert and it is not a comfortable medium for me. It has been a learning experience, an opportunity to develop a less developed side of myself, and I have really improved my writing and analytical thinking skills. It makes a lot of sense that an introvert would feel safe, has the time they need to express themselves, and prefers this medium. *Juliet*

The reflective process embedded in online learning is one of its hallmarks and most exciting features. If an instructor is willing to give up control of the learning process and truly act as a facilitator, he or she may be amazed at the depth of engagement with learning and the material that can occur as a result.

The Final Transition: Evaluating Students and Ourselves

Harasim, Hiltz, Teles, and Turoff (1996) state, "In keeping with a learner-centered approach, evaluation and assessment should be part of the learning-teaching process, embedded in class activities and in the interactions between learners and between learners and teachers" (p. 167).

In the spirit of collaboration and reflection, evaluation of student progress and performance should not fall to the instructor alone. Students should be encouraged to comment on one another's work, and self-evaluation should be embedded in the final performance evaluation of each student. As the course progresses, we ask that students provide feedback to one another on assignments. In addition, at the end of a term we request that students send us a private e-mail with a descriptive evaluation of the performance of their student colleagues as well as their own performance. We use this feedback along with quality and quantity of participation and performance on assignments and in discussion as measures of overall student performance.

Based on our experience, we feel that examinations may not be the best measure of student performance in the online environment. Unless an exam is well-developed it will not necessarily measure critical thinking skills appropriately. Well-developed exams are comprehensive, contextual, relate to the material being studied, and promote reflection and critical thinking rather than regurgitation of material (Wiggins, 1998). A student's performance online should be a better indicator of whether learning objectives are being met. When exams become part of the process, concerns about cheating emerge. However, in a truly collaborative learning process, concerns about cheating become irrelevant because students learn from one another and together create higher levels of knowledge and meaning.

Evaluation should not just be focused on student performance, however. Ongoing course evaluation should also be embedded in the learning process. Instructors should make means available to students through which they can express their opinions about the course, the way it is proceeding, and how well it is meeting learning objectives based on the way it is configured. Course evaluation, then, should not be relegated to the end of the term and simply be a measure of instructor popularity. Instead, it should become part of the collaborative process of course delivery to meet learning expectations.

Supporting Instructors to Make the Transition

Making the transition to the online learning environment means developing new approaches to education and new skills in its delivery. It means engaging in self-reflection as we determine our own comfort level in turning over control of the learning process to our students. It means promoting a sense of community among our students to enhance their learning process. But, most of all, it means abdicating the tried-and-true techniques that may have served us well in the face-to-face classroom in favor of experimentation with new techniques and assumptions. In so doing, we will meet the challenges of preparing our students to navigate the demands of a knowledge society, and in the process, learn something new ourselves, thus supporting our own quest for lifelong learning.

How to make all of this happen is one of the most challenging issues facing online instructors. To make it happen, instructors need good training, technical support, and the ability to participate in the process in the company of others. Nothing substitutes for the support of other colleagues as they make the same journey. Encouraging faculty who are teaching online to join discussion groups, attend conferences about online distance learning, and attend training sessions on campus can greatly assist them in making the move to the online classroom.

We close this chapter with some tips for successful online courses that summarize the essence of electronic pedagogy.

Tips for a Successful Online Course

- Establish guidelines for the class and participation that provide enough structure for the learners but allow for flexibility and negotiation.
- Mandate participation and incorporate it into student evaluation and grading. A good idea is to mandate at least two posts per week. Another good idea is to equate posting with the number of credit hours for the course—for example, a standard three-credit course would require three posts per week.
- Promote collaborative learning through small group assignments, case studies, simulations, and group discussion of readings and assignments.
- Have students post their assignments and encourage feedback to one another on their work. Although some instructors and students feel comfortable having grades shared on the course site, we feel that grades should be shared privately. Whether grades are shared or kept private can be discussed along with the guidelines at the beginning of a course; this also may be regulated or controlled by university rules and requirements.
- Set up a well-organized course site that includes a place for students to socialize.
- Include an area where students can reflect on what it is like to learn online; we call these *Electronic Reflections*.
- Encourage students to bring real-life examples into the online classroom. The more relevant the material is to their lives, the more likely they are to integrate it.
- Don't lecture! An outline lecture becomes just another article that students are required to read.
- Stay present! Let your students know you are there by commenting on their posts and asking additional questions for them to consider. But also avoid being intrusive or overbearing. Balance is the key to successful participation.
- Become comfortable enough with the technology to be able to answer students' questions about its use and assist them when they run into difficulty.
- Act like a *learning facilitator* rather than a professor.
- Most of all, have fun and open yourself to learning as much from your students as they will learn from one another and from you!

~

CHAPTER THREE

ADMINISTRATIVE ISSUES
AND CONCERNS

W hy, in a book that has been written primarily for the team of professionals engaged in the design and delivery of courses—faculty, instructional
designers, faculty developers, and instructional technologists—would we devote
attention to administrative issues and concerns? Consider the following two scenarios as a means to begin answering this question:

A college has a number of faculty members dispersed across all departments
who are interested in using technology to support, enhance, and deliver their
classes. Many have put up web pages for their courses, some on the college's server
and some housed on the faculty member's private website. Some are using the
websites only to support their face-to-face teaching. However, a number of faculty primarily in two departments are offering courses delivered completely online. All of these ventures into technology are using differing forms of software
with differing support needs. Faculty are interested in continuing to teach using
technology but are concerned about their workloads as a result. Support staff are
also concerned about their burden given their limited resources. All are calling
for the development of policies and procedures relative to the delivery of online
courses for the institution.

Another college is engaged in discussion about the use of distance learning
technologies to deliver courses. A few faculty have put up web pages to support their
face-to-face classes, but no classes are being delivered entirely online. Meanwhile,
competing colleges and universities in the area are beginning to offer numerous

courses and even entire degree programs online. The president of the college has been approached by an organization devoted to the outsourcing of the design and delivery of distance learning courses. He has opted to go that route and has asked ten faculty members to work with the organization to get courses up online in time for the start of the next term.

As we have been discussing, colleges and universities today are undergoing a significant transition. There are economic pressures from mounting costs, demands by the business world for graduates who are able to function in a knowledge society, and greater diversity among students who choose to go on for higher education. In addition, today's graduates are expected to be able to demonstrate good critical thinking ability, good analytic skills, and the ability to work collaboratively in a team setting. What both of the preceding scenarios point out is the need for comprehensive planning involving a team of professionals, including administrative personnel, to deliver a coherent online distance learning program successfully. In developing a comprehensive plan for the institution, all participants in the delivery of the program must understand the needs and concerns of the other participants. In the next chapter, we will discuss administrative concerns about the choice of technology and the creation of a technological infrastructure for the institution. These are not, however, the only issues administrators are faced with as they seek to develop an online program or begin offering online courses.

Frequently as we present and consult we are asked about issues such as compensation for course development and online teaching, given the amount of time it takes to teach online courses. The issue of compensation is a controversial one, with no clear answers emerging to resolve it. In this chapter, we will review current thought on this issue as well as discuss other administrative issues and concerns, such as online program development, faculty support and training, governance issues, and tenure issues. An additional question in the area of governance that will be addressed is this: Should the administration of online courses and programs belong to departments or should a separate entity be developed in the institution? This question refers to issues of responsibility and control—in other words, who controls the development and delivery of online courses and, furthermore, who *should* be in control?

All of the issues embedded in the administrative arena are controversial and have been the cause of disagreement and even outright conflict between faculty and administrators. They are, however, important issues for all elements of the institution to consider. The policies—which, ideally, are the outcome of the discussion of these issues—should become the foundation of a technological infrastructure in an institution. Richard Katz (1999) describes the need for educational leaders to develop strategic frameworks to address the changing cultural, organizational, economic, and survival issues of the institution. All of the issues we have just outlined need to be included in such a framework. As Katz and others have noted, the demand for higher education is increasing, albeit with students who do not resemble the traditional students our institutions have served in the past. In order for our colleges and universities to rise to the challenge of delivering education with and through the use of technology, they must overcome what Katz refers to as the *natural conservatism* of their faculties and engage in the difficult discussions that will lead them to develop strategies to keep them fiscally sound while delivering high-quality educational programs. What this means is that administrators need to start working with and listening to their faculties. We will now examine each of the issues in the administrative arena and end with some tips for creating a sound technological infrastructure.

Faculty Time, Compensation, and Questions of Tenure

A 1999 survey of sixty faculty conducted at Arkansas State University yielded results that appear to be the norm of faculty experience for those who teach online: 90 percent indicated that they needed substantially more preparation time to develop a course, 75 percent had not participated in any additional training opportunities other than what they needed to understand the technology in use, and more than 88 percent indicated that they were given neither additional compensation nor a reduced workload for developing or teaching distance learning courses (Dickinson, Agnew, and Gorman, 1999). Considering these statistics, it is no wonder that some faculty resist the call to teach online.

However, another study (Rockwell, Schauer, Fritz, and Marx, 1999), designed to look at what faculty feel are incentives and obstacles to participation in online teaching, yielded interesting results. The primary incentives for faculty to teach at a distance were personal or intrinsic rewards, rather than monetary rewards. Included in the list of incentives was the opportunity to provide innovative instruction, use new teaching techniques, and receive recognition for their work. The main perceived obstacles, however, correspond to the issues outlined in the Arkansas study: the need for time, training, and support. Monetary rewards were seen as neither an incentive nor an obstacle to participating in online teaching.

That is not to say that the time differences required for course development and delivery along with increased workload should not be considered when developing a reward structure for faculty. Eric Boschmann (1998) asks an important question about the role of technology as he explores the ways in which institutions develop self-monitoring systems for rewards such as granting tenure, promotion, and merit increases. He asks, "Is technology simply a tool, or does it have real potential for scholarship and the promise of rewards?" In the face of the impact of technology on teaching and learning, others too are questioning the general use of the single criterion of research publication in consideration of tenure (Finnegan, 1997; Bates, 2000).

When the educational landscape is changing as rapidly as it currently is because of the impact of technology, administrators, faculty, and all others affected by the changes need to be talking and agreeing on new ways of negotiating that territory. Boschmann (1998) proposes a set of agreed-upon premises for technology: learning is not bound by place, time, speed, or style; learning takes place best when students are engaged; technology is the best tool to foster student engagement; and research in these areas is bona fide scholarship. He further proposes that rewards should be based on true scholarly activity as it relates to these premises. If, in other words, the outcomes and products of our engagement with online learning are shared, peer reviewed, published, funded, and presented at conferences, then these activities should be given the same consideration as the traditional criterion of research publication when rewards are made.

Faculty are afraid of feeling overwhelmed and overloaded when entering the online arena (Bates, 2000; Boschmann, 1998; Clark, 1993; Finnegan, 1997). Faculty do respond positively and express interest in becoming involved in online work when appropriate incentives are put in place, however (Boschmann, 1998). Incentives such as the provision of in-house grants for course development, significant blocks of time off to engage in course development and training activities, reduced teaching loads while teaching online courses, and adequate support to assist with course development and delivery can help to allay the fears of faculty members who are entering the online arena for the first time. Incentives can also support those who are considered the pioneers or early adopters in pursuing this work.

Program Planning and Development

As illustrated by the two scenarios presented at the beginning of this chapter, often the move to implementing online courses and the use of technology to support teaching is done without much planning. G. Phillip Cartwright (1996) describes the current state of technology planning this way: "Statewide and higher education planning activities are a continuing effort in some places, but are not as widespread as you might think" (p. 1). As we have previously discussed, planning should begin with instructional design and overall outcomes in mind. The technology tools that fit the needs of instructors, students, and the curriculum should then be chosen and integrated (Lytle, Lytle, Lenhart, and Skrotsky, 1999).

Cartwright (1996), with tongue in cheek, describes four ways in which technology planning seems to occur on campuses. They are:

- *The End-of-Year Scramble,* in which long-range planning is put aside in favor of honoring short-term budget requests before the end of the fiscal year
- *Neo-Passe Chaos,* where no planning process is evident but department heads are authorized with a budget to acquire hardware and software suited to individual needs; also termed the "Faculty Knows Best" approach to planning
- *Father Knows Best,* where decisions are made by the technology administrator or a small, handpicked group made up primarily of technology professionals
- *Pollyanna-Phillpanna Utopia,* where all institutional activities are put on hold for several weeks a year while all departments engage in a consensus-building approach; this can result in a long-term plan with annual updates, but may result in no action [pp. 2–3]

In summary, the mistakes that institutions make in the planning process revolve around lack of support or guidance from senior level administrators, lack of knowledge or contact with the marketplace (this is, the students and their needs), a lack of specific action steps with which to implement plans, and an inability to implement plans rapidly.

Interestingly, most of the comprehensive technology planning that is happening is occurring at the statewide level, primarily in the K–12 arena. Once again, higher education could benefit by reviewing the scope and intent of these plans in order to begin a comprehensive planning process on individual campuses. In the list of online resources compiled and presented in Resource C, we have included some sites where it is possible to review statewide technology plans.

In addition to focusing on teaching and learning outcomes, a comprehensive technology plan for distance education should clearly identify the students the institution intends to serve and realistically assess the access to technology of that target group (Bates, 2000). Often institutions intend to use distance learning to extend their reach without much thought about who those students really are or how they will access programs and courses.

We consulted with an institution that had this intent in mind. The thought was that offering distance learning to a nationwide audience would help to support and even save the institution economically. With no comprehensive plan in place, the institution used a combination of the Faculty Knows Best approach to the development of courses and programs and a Father Knows Best approach to the choice of courseware the faculty would use. One department, after receiving some training from us, began offering a series of courses and experienced some success at drawing students from the local geographic region. When the department decided to expand its reach, however, the institution was unable to support it. For example, when students at a significant distance attempted to register for online courses, they were told that they needed to come to campus in order to do so. Despite intervention from the department, the registrar's office refused to budge. The obvious result was that the students did not take the courses. A comprehensive plan, wherein all departments and units in the institution were represented, would have avoided this situation.

Thinking through all aspects of the implementation of an online program or even a few online courses is critical to the success of that effort. Furthermore, the technology plan for the institution should not stand alone but should be embedded in the strategic plan of the institution. Bates (2000) notes the outcome of a benchmarking study describing best practices in the use of technology on campus. The results of the study were not surprising and echo the best practices that we have been and will be encouraging throughout this book: the development of a strategic plan in which the implementation of technology in teaching plays a prominent role; investment in the technology infrastructure needed to support such an effort; support by senior leadership for the use of technology; support for those faculty who use technology in their teaching; and support for students through access to computers, courses, and the Internet.

The best practices relate to the activities of teaching and learning, and not to the technology itself. Bates notes that although faculty development in this area is important, it is not the main strategy to be used in successful implementation of a technology plan. We will, however, now return to a discussion of both faculty and student development as important activities that cannot be ignored. But before we do, it is important to share one last thought on planning for the implementation of technology: although it is critical to plan institutionally to create realistic strategies consistent with the institution's mission, strengths, and available resources, it is also important to create plans and strategies that are focused on the future, allowing for growth and change. As with all activities related to the implementation of technology in teaching, balance is the key.

Another Look at Faculty and Student Support, Training, and Development

The benchmarking report that Bates describes noted that in institutions where best practices in the implementation of technology are followed, faculty development focuses on teaching and learning, and not on the technology itself. Certainly, faculty need to develop skills in computer literacy before they can move into teaching online. However, as we have been emphasizing, the focus in faculty development should be on pedagogical methods and not the software in use.

Several authors note that when presented with instructional design principles appropriate to online teaching, faculty often ask, "Where is the lecture?" Clearly, this is an indication of a traditional approach to education wherein lectures have had a place (Farrington, 1999; Lytle, Lytle, Lenhart, and Skrotsky, 1999; Barone and Luker, 2000). However, as Lytle, Lytle, Lenhart, and Skrotsky state, "Lectures are important and certainly numerous in higher education, but are not necessarily any more valuable in the learning process than any other learning tool" (p. 58). Incorporated into faculty training and development, then, should be concrete ways in which content can be presented without the use of lectures. Some of the techniques can include these:

- Creating web pages that contain no more than one screen of text and graphics
- Providing collaborative small group assignments
- Providing research assignments asking students to seek out and present additional resources available on the Internet and in books and journals
- Using simulations
- Asking students to become "expert" on a topic in the scope of the course and then presenting that topic to their peers
- Using asynchronous discussion of the topics in the scope of the course material being studied
- Having students post papers to the course site
- Making limited use of audio and video clips

What is important is to encourage and support faculty in thinking outside the box when it comes to developing creative ways to present course content, keeping in mind the technology to which students are likely to have access.

Students need training not only in the software they will be using to access their courses but also in how to learn in the online environment. If the institution cannot provide training in how to learn or does not see this as a part of its technology plan, then incorporating suggestions for how to learn online becomes the responsibility of the instructors. Instructors can do this in several ways, including the following:

- Holding a face-to-face orientation, if possible, to show students the course site and discuss online learning
- Providing an orientation to the course somewhere on the course site or as a first discussion item
- Providing students with a list of frequently asked questions and responses to those questions
- Placing basic information about how to navigate the course site on the welcome screen or course homepage
- Sending an e-mail message containing orientation information to each student enrolled in the course

Regardless of how student orientation occurs, it needs to be considered an important element in the development of the course, yet unfortunately it is often overlooked. Including information about this in faculty training can create an awareness on the faculty's part of just how important this is.

As was noted in the benchmarking report, support for faculty and students is a crucial element in the construction of a good technological infrastructure. Administrators must keep in mind who their constituents are when a technology plan is constructed, and they must provide the fiscal and staff support necessary to keep an online program alive and well.

Two other issues that are critical to the successful development of an online program relate to the ongoing role of faculty in that program. Just as faculty need to be involved in decisions such as the choice of course authoring software, they also need to be involved in decisions about which courses are to be offered online and how those courses will be developed. We now turn our attention to issues of governance and return to the discussion of copyright and intellectual property issues as they relate to developing a plan to deliver online courses and programs.

Governance and Intellectual Property

Who decides which courses are offered online and which degree programs are worthy of migration to the online environment? Should these decisions rest with department chairs, individual faculty members, the faculty senate, administrators, coordinators of distance learning, or a combination of all of them? Questions of who holds the decision-making power in distance learning, and of equal importance, who owns courses, are becoming increasingly critical as the number and range of courses offered increase. And as with other issues pertaining to distance learning, these are not questions that are normally asked when it comes to traditional face-to-face classes held on campus.

Those who are writing about the impact of online learning on the academy have noted that distance learning has changed the economics of instruction, throwing institutions headlong into a competitive marketplace (Chambers, 1999; Barone and Luker, 2000). "To meet a growing societal demand for higher education at a time when costs are increasing and public support is declining, most institutions have been forced to sharply increase tuition and fees, triggering public concern about the costs and availability of a college education. As a result, most colleges and universities are now looking for ways to control costs and increase productivity, but most are also finding that their current organization and governance makes this very difficult" (Duderstadt, 1999, p. 3). The response of many institutions has been to offer online distance learning programs and courses as a way to extend their reach, attract more students, and control costs. As we have discussed, some institutions are more ready than others to participate in the distance learning market, whereas others have floundered because of a lack of vision or plan for successful entry or unrealistic hopes of "saving" the institution from financial ruin.

Not surprisingly, the economics of distance education have changed the ways in which decisions are made about the offering of courses and programs. On some campuses, departments and their faculty in conjunction with faculty senates are still making decisions about which courses and programs will be offered online. On other campuses, however, these decisions are being taken from faculty and made by senior administrative personnel, chairs of new departments focused solely on distance learning, or continuing education coordinators. The new departments, in many cases, hire their own faculty and develop their own courses to be offered online. In an environment that is already fostering the rift between faculty and administration, dealing with governance issues in this way cannot be helpful.

In response to this situation, institutions such as San Diego State University have engaged in a comprehensive planning process involving the faculty senate and administrators. The result has been a comprehensive and detailed policy covering both administrative and faculty concerns that revisits agreements between faculty and administration and places concern for students at the forefront. The overall spirit of the policy is that distance learning courses should be treated no differently than traditional courses are (Carnavale, 2000d). Quality measures in place for courses taught on campus will also apply to online courses, meaning that the curriculum committees of the university will review all courses; faculty will be hired in ways consistent with hiring on campus; the outsourcing of courses or programs cannot occur without the approval of appropriate university bodies; an adequate support structure will be put in place to assist both faculty and students; and prior to the offering of a course or program, agreements regarding copyright and intellectual property as well as faculty compensation and use of revenue will be completed in accordance with the university's existing policy on intellectual property. The entire text of San Diego State's policy can be found online at: http://www.rohan.sdsu.edu/dept/senate/sendoc/distanceed.apr2000.html.

Policies such as the one adopted by San Diego State are likely to be the wave of the near future. Such policies should include clear rules and guidelines regarding ownership of materials created for online courses. Bates (2000) offers some interesting perspective on this issue. As a matter of course, faculty who are hired to teach on campus are expected to write and publish independently. The university, in general, takes no ownership of or revenue from the materials its faculty publish. But when it comes to creating online courses, the picture changes. "Universities and colleges are now themselves funding the creation of materials and becoming major stakeholders in and *producers* of copyrighted materials" (Bates, 2000, p. 110). Consequently, if the course materials are created as a part of the faculty's regular work responsibilities, then that material may, in fact, belong to the employer—in this case, the university. Complicating this picture is that, increasingly, courses are being created not just by one faculty member but by a team that includes faculty, instructional designers, and programmers. The same, however, could be said for the writing and publication of a book—few faculty self-publish books. The books they write are produced with the help of a team. Consequently, the principle of fairness applies. Hawke (2000) notes that several models of course ownership are being applied by universities. The first assumes that the faculty member owns the work and can assign ownership to the institution or can grant the institution a nonexclusive license to use the work. Profits from it are shared by both the institution and the faculty member who created the course. The second model assumes ownership by the institution as work for hire. In this case, the faculty member may be given royalties and a license to use the materials elsewhere. The third model assumes that the faculty member who creates the work is an independent contractor who has ownership of the work created and can assign or license the work as in the first model.

San Diego State's policy addresses the need to establish agreements—before course development—on the use of intellectual property and the use of the revenues derived from the delivery of courses. Prior agreements that are fair to all concerned can help to alleviate the current concerns that exist in this arena. Such agreements may include royalties to faculty who develop courses, inclusion of the delivery of courses into the standard teaching load rather than treating them as an overload, and revenue sharing once the courses have been delivered. There are no hard-and-fast answers yet. Few cases are being tried in the courts that address this issue. However, the potential for the development of case law in this area exists if universities and their faculties are not proactive about how materials will be developed and used. Once again, good planning is the key.

Student Retention

Another important component of the new economics of distance learning, and one that seems to be consistently overlooked or ignored both in the planning and in the delivery of distance learning courses, is the student. San Diego State's policy does address student concerns. Many plans and policies, however, do not, leading to concerns about attracting students to online programs, and more importantly, retaining them once they enroll. Phipps and Merisotis (1999) note that "a large majority of institutions believe it somewhat or very important that their distance education offerings increase access to new audiences and increase enrollments"

(p. 2). However, according to Phipps and Merisotis, research that has attempted to follow up on the impact of distance education on access, enrollments, and program costs does not conclusively show that if an institution offers distance education courses and programs then enrollment will increase. Complicating this picture is the fact that once students enroll in distance learning courses, the likelihood that they will complete courses and stay enrolled in online programs is lower than in on-campus courses.

There is no research yet to help institutions understand why online students drop out more frequently. However, the reasons generally given for this phenomenon relate to the demographics of the students who enroll. They tend to be older, working adults with family obligations. The life situations that drew them to distance learning programs to begin with may also interfere with their ability to complete them. Others describe the newness of online programs and inexperience of online instructors along with the difference in the mode of instruction as factors (Carr, 2000a).

What cannot be ignored, however, is that often technology plans are created by institutions without exploring their market or asking students what they want or need in an online program. Institutions tend to build online courses and programs based on faculty needs and interests or because some faculty are already versed in the delivery of online courses (Blustain, Goldstein, and Lozier, 1999).

The traditional paradigm of education on college campuses is faculty-centered. As we have argued, in order for online courses to be successful the faculty-centered focus needs to change to a learner-centered focus. The same is true when developing a plan for the implementation of technology into teaching and the construction of online programs: *in order to be successful, plans, courses, and programs must be learner-focused.* To accomplish this goal, institutions need to engage in a planning process that includes good market research to answer these questions: Who are our students? Where are they located? What are their academic needs? How can we meet those needs?

Online distance learning courses and programs will not "save" academic institutions. However, technology in education makes sense when it is used to reach the increasingly nontraditional student body we now see in institutions of higher education and to meet their learning needs and objectives—needs and objectives that are different from the students institutions have traditionally taught.

Some Last Thoughts on Administrative Issues and Concerns

Bates (2000) sums up the issues in the administrative arena well when he states, "Large investment in technology-based teaching can be justified only if it leads to significant changes in the ways we teach" (p. 119). As we have been stressing, using technology to replicate the traditional face-to-face classroom is a waste of time, energy, and money. Technology is and should be used as a vehicle to assist institutions and their faculties in reaching students who might not otherwise be reached because of distance or learning style. It is also a vehicle to assist instructors in achieving learning objectives in new ways.

The introduction of technology into teaching is creating cultural changes in academic institutions that we cannot deny. Faculty and administrators alike are beginning to learn that the development of technology-enhanced or technology-driven courses cannot be accomplished by one person in isolation. It takes a team of committed professionals to develop high-quality online courses and programs. As a result, institutions can no longer do business as usual and must reexamine the ways in which faculty and administrators interact. In our next chapter, we will take another look at technology, particularly as it pertains to the planning process. Our focus is the development of a sound technological infrastructure designed to support the changes we are describing.

Tips for Creating a Technological Infrastructure

- Create an inclusive team or committee to develop policies and plans for the institution regarding online courses and programs.
- Make incentives available to faculty for course development, including release time, reduced teaching load, and grants.
- Provide adequate technical support and training to faculty and students. Faculty not only need to know how to use the technology but also need to be able to explore new teaching methods and techniques. Students need to understand the technology in use and how to learn in the online environment.
- Reconsider agreements with faculty to include provisions related to the use of intellectual property that are fair and equitable for all concerned.
- Limit enrollments in online courses. If enrollments are to be high, provide graders, readers, or teaching assistants to reduce the burden on the instructor and allow the students greater access to the instructor.
- Work toward the development of a shared vision and strategic plan around the use of technology in teaching and learning. Plans should be fluid enough to allow for inclusion of technological developments as they occur and not just limited to what is available at the time the plan is conceived.

CHAPTER FOUR

THE TOOLS OF ONLINE TEACHING

As we stated at the beginning of this book, we expected that the last two years would bring dramatic advances in course authoring software and tools. This has not been the case. Instead what has occurred is that some leading course authoring tools have emerged, such as WebCT™, Blackboard™, Convene™, and eCollege™. The companies that offer them have begun to compete aggressively with one another for the academic market. All of them have developed complete software packages that have become household names on university campuses.

Technology is not the "be all and end all" of the online course. It is merely the vehicle for course delivery. Don Foshee (1999) remarks that the use of the new technologies is only as good as the people and content behind them. He offers some lessons learned from the evolution of technology in education, noting, "Good teaching is good teaching and bad teaching is even worse in a technology-based environment" (p. 26). Foshee warns administrators to beware of vendors that profess to offer "the solution" to the delivery of online courses, explaining that the best technology packages offer choices, flexibility, and the ability to change over time. And finally, he states what we cannot emphasize enough: nothing substitutes for good planning. Planning should cover the technology to be used as well as programs to be developed and courses to be taught.

In this chapter, we will look at new technological developments and courseware applications and discuss how to work within their strengths and limitations, thus assisting in the planning process and providing some suggestions for evaluating good courseware. In addition, we will explore ways in which online courses and programs can be developed and delivered when the institution has limited financial resources and is unable to purchase courseware outright. Also, to help determine their utility, we will evaluate the "bells and whistles" currently being promoted by many courseware applications. We will not tout one software package or one approach over another. Instead, we will offer enough concrete information about what is needed in software so that institutions can make informed decisions about purchasing or using software that meets their needs.

Technology in the Year 2000

The 1999 report of the National Center for Educational Statistics discusses the ways in which distance learning technology has advanced and changed. The report's authors, Merisotis and Phipps, note that the key features of current technology are the increased level of interactivity between students and faculty with resulting ability to exchange greater amounts of information, greater variety in the types of information that can be exchanged, and significantly shorter amounts of time required for information exchange to occur. The types of online technology to which they are referring include e-mail, chat sessions, electronic bulletin boards, video, CD-ROM, audioconferencing, and desktop videoconferencing. The report cautions, however, that the use of advanced technologies does not necessarily mean better implementation of distance learning programs. Technology needs vary, depending on instructional and learner needs. In other words, just because various technologies are available does not mean that they need to be used in the delivery of a course. One course may be delivered using only discussion boards, whereas another might make good use of chat or a whiteboard. However, if chat is inappropriate for a course, it should not be used even if it is available.

Factors besides instructional and learning needs that have been associated with appropriate use of technology in online learning are the ages of the learners, cultural and socioeconomic backgrounds, interests and experiences, educational levels, and familiarity with distance education methods and delivery systems (Sherry, 1996). According to Hazari (1998), instructional design principles should be applied to develop pedagogically effective learning materials, and online instruction must be designed to accommodate individual learning styles. Hazari does not suggest that all available technologies be used to address all learning styles. Instead, appropriate technologies to enhance and contribute to learning should be used.

But as we have been noting and as Sherry (1996) states, "The most important factor for successful distance learning is a caring, concerned teacher who is confident, experienced, at ease with the equipment, uses the media creatively, and maintains a high level of interactivity with the students" (p. 5). The instructor, then, is the key factor in making an online course work, regardless of the technology being used, and the learner must be the focus. "A widely accepted technology is most often defined by a single characteristic: it makes a task rewarding for the user, where the 'user' includes the student first, and the faculty second" (p. 13). Sherry further notes the importance of interactivity in distance learning and states, "Interactivity takes many forms; it is not just limited to audio and video, nor solely to teacher-student interactions. It represents the connectivity the students feel with the distance teacher . . . and their peers" (p. 5).

The technology tools available to the instructor to enhance and create interactivity are varied. Boettcher and Conrad (1999) have determined that there are two types of courseware packages available: those designed only for web-based instruction and those that are considered course management tools. The packages designed for instruction offer the ability to design, develop, and deliver a web-based course. Course management packages make it possible to link to the university's administrative functions. Software is currently being developed that would link any instructional tool to administrative functions.

The very basic tools allow for the creation of web pages in either text or HTML. Most courseware packages allow for creation of discussion boards and have e-mail functions that let the instructor communicate easily with students and students communicate easily with one another. Many packages allow the instructor to create smaller discussion groups in the class, which can then communicate using their own discussion board. Access to the individual discussion boards may be password-protected or instructors may opt to keep all discussions open, allowing students to visit groups other than the one to which they were assigned. Almost all courseware packages now contain the option to use synchronous chat. Most allow for the creation of student and instructor homepages and offer the ability to record and report student grades. In addition, many include some form of student tracking, allowing an instructor to see which students have logged on to the course site or to individual pages or discussion boards on the site and how long they remained on the site. All allow for the embedding of links to outside resources on the Internet. Most course authoring packages allow the instructor to use colors and graphics on course pages to create visual appeal, and many permit institutions to embed their logos and banners on course pages to present institutional identity and to create consistency across courses. Some software programs offer the ability to use a whiteboard, and some allow whiteboard images to be saved or transferred to other locations in the course. Almost all allow for the use of graphics and many for the use of streaming audio and video.

In addition to the course authoring software and course management software on the market, textbook publishers are now offering options to instructors who may not feel ready to immerse themselves completely in the online distance learning arena or who have limited resources and support. Several publishers are offering what are called "companion sites" to accompany or replace their texts. Generally, access to the site is by payment of a subscription fee. The site may contain all of the material found in a textbook or supplemental material such as interactive exercises, quizzes, study guides, video clips, and other activities. Some sites also include communication tools, such as chat and discussion boards, gradebooks, and student tracking tools.

Again, we cannot stress enough that the availability of these tools does not prescribe their use. Instructors should design courses with learning objectives in mind, building learning activities that allow students to reach those objectives. The tools available in an instructional package should be chosen to match the objectives and serve as a vehicle for reaching them. We will now discuss how that might be effectively done.

Matching the Technology to the Course

Don Olcott (1999) notes that the selection of distance learning technologies should involve the assessment of course content, learning outcomes, and interaction needs. He further notes that no one technology is optimum for achieving all learning objectives, and conversely, instructors will rarely have the latitude to integrate all technologies into a course. Consequently, Olcott provides what he calls the five "I's" of effective distance teaching: interaction, introspection, innovation, integration, and information.

Interaction refers not only to the communication that should occur between the student and the instructor and the student with other students but also the interaction between the student and the content of the course. Thus, asynchronous and synchronous communications as well as the presentation of print materials and links to the Internet form the technology needs of interaction. *Introspection* is the interpretation, revision, and demonstrated understanding of concepts. Discussion boards, graphics, and even audio and video can be effective technologies to encourage introspection. Olcott notes, "Regardless of the technology employed, practical examples where students can apply their understanding of the content [are] critical" (p. 38). *Innovation* refers to the ability of instructors to experiment with technologies to address various learning styles. Thus, combinations of audio, video, and asynchronous discussion can provide various opportunities for students to learn. However, Olcott notes that more important than using various technologies is implementing various modes of assessment of student work in a course. Instructors may even choose to offer students choices of ways in which they will be assessed, furthering the goal of student empowerment in the learning process. *Integration* reflects the integration of facts, concepts, theories, and practical application of knowledge. Using case studies, print exercises, and role-play can create a setting in which integration can occur. These collaborative activities can easily be accomplished in an asynchronous environment. *Information* refers to the knowledge and understanding that is a prerequisite for students to move to the next level of learning. Instructors have traditionally thought of the transfer of information that occurs in a lecture situation. Olcott states, however, "Any technology can disseminate information; the instructor must create interactive opportunities and assess whether students have the basic knowledge to move forward to the next level of learning" (p. 39).

Olcott's discussion makes clear that any form of technology can be used to deliver a course. What is more critical to a successful online course is good, learner-centered teaching. Consequently, when choosing the forms of technology to be used in a course, the first consideration should be the outcomes to be achieved as well as the technology used by students. All else should flow from there. In many cases, learning outcomes can be achieved with the least complex technology—readings and discussion boards. This also allows the course to be accessed by the majority of users with little difficulty.

When instructors choose to use other forms of technology—such as audio, video, chat, and whiteboards—they must consider what their students are able to receive. Slow Internet connections and older, slower computer hardware and software prove difficult or impossible to use when attempting to access more complex course sites, causing frustration on the part of both students and instructors. Many campus-based instructors now have the luxury of access to high-speed Internet connections and computers that allow for rapid transfer of graphics and audio and video files. Instructors must not be lulled into believing that because they have this luxury their students will, too.

As Olcott concludes, "Given the diverse range of available technologies in concert with varying instructional goals and objectives, technology selection and use requires careful analysis to balance access, quality, and costs. There is no simple solution to this process" (p. 39). Our rule of thumb is to continue to rely on asynchronous technologies for course delivery. This assures that the largest number will be able to access and benefit from the course. Creating a diversity of learning approaches serves to keep students interested and engaged, even without the use of technological bells and whistles.

Working with the Strengths and Weaknesses of Technology

What happens when an institution adopts a courseware package that an instructor feels is not conducive to the delivery of her course? What can an instructor do if a particular tool is not included in the software package chosen? What if a package is considered too advanced or too basic for instructor and student needs? Can these obstacles be overcome?

The beauty of most course authoring software available now is that instructors can pick and choose among the tools included in the package to create a course that meets the learning objectives they have established, making it easy to work around any limitations the package might have. As Hazari (1998) notes, "The new generation of Web course development tools provide features that let instructors adapt components according to learning outcomes of the course" (p. 4). In addition, other software applications that are widely available but not designed necessarily for academic use allow an instructor who is technologically savvy to add to a package that might be lacking. If a package lacks a whiteboard, for example, and an instructor feels this is a critical component to be used in his course, then a program such as NetMeeting can be used to fill the void. If synchronous chat is not a part of the package, then an instant messaging program such as those now available with most Internet browser software can be used. Some instructors have linked graphics programs from their own websites to their course sites to demonstrate or illustrate concepts. Consequently, adding to existing courseware is a relatively simple matter.

Working with courseware not conducive to meeting learning outcomes provides more of a challenge. For example, one of us taught in an institution using a piece of software that was developed to serve the corporate arena but was difficult to use in the delivery of online courses. Although it worked well in facilitating more general online discussions, when it was applied to courses, confusion was the result. Discussion threads were not easily accessible—sometimes buried four or five levels down from the original post—and it was not possible to view all of the discussion threads simultaneously, either in outline form or in text. Exhibit 4.1 illustrates the difference between a course site where threads of a discussion are visible versus one where discussion threads are buried.

When they are unable to view the discussion threads, it is easy for students and faculty to post in the wrong place. The first example in the exhibit illustrates this problem by showing postings that occurred where the topics of the course should be (posts numbered 14, 15, and 16). The postings were responses to a topic but show up on the course site as a new topic. Although many course authoring packages provide some indication of the number of responses to a topic on a discussion board (the numbers in parentheses following the initial post), this software provided only the number of responses to the top-level topic. Consequently, if responses were posted to another response, it was not possible to note that from the topic level. The second example shows a discussion site where the discussion threads are clearly visible. It is easy to see the responses to an initial post.

Students often expressed dissatisfaction with the first software tool shown in the exhibit; they felt that it was a fairly primitive bulletin board system that allowed

EXHIBIT 4.1. A COMPARISON OF COURSE SITES WITH BURIED AND VISIBLE DISCUSSION THREADS.

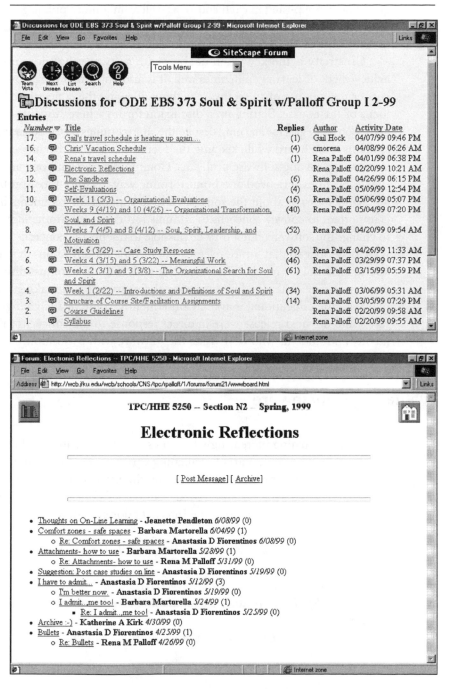

for little else. In order to deal with the shortcomings of the software and to minimize confusion, the faculty decided to create a set of guidelines for its use. The guidelines were posted in each course as well as in a more public gathering place for all students. These guidelines helped to overcome many of the frustrations and make the use of the software more tolerable.

Creativity is the key when dealing with software that does not serve the achievement of learning outcomes well. It is also important to respond to student concerns about use of the software without allowing the concerns to become the focus of the course. Setting up a discussion forum where students can work together on strategies for learning despite the shortcomings of the software can allow students to be heard while keeping the focus on learning. Faculty collaboration is critical to solving software problems. Communicating with one another about the problems experienced and brainstorming ways to solve those problems helps all faculty to learn about the software and to support their students in its use. It is important to convey concerns to administrators as well. It may not be possible to change the software, but it may be possible to discuss the concerns with the software developer so that future releases can include modifications that are responsive to stakeholder needs. This was done with the software just discussed. The developers were interested in improving their product and making it more popular with the educational market. Consequently, some of the changes incorporated into the next release were in direct response to the concerns raised by the faculty and students who were using the software with frustration.

Evaluating Courseware

As distance learning increasingly becomes a fact of institutional life, many instructors who have been part of evaluating various courseware applications have published their experiences and findings on the Internet to assist others in doing the same. The following are three good examples of courseware comparisons and evaluations that can be found at the Internet addresses shown:

- *Evaluation and Selection of Web Course Management Tools,* Sunil Hazari, Ed.D. [http://sunil.umd.edu/Webct/]
- *University of Manitoba Feature Comparison of Web Course in a Box™, WebCT™, Black-Board™, TopClass™* [http://www.umanitoba.ca/ip/tools/courseware/model.html]
- *SCOET/CCIT/OLT Feature Comparison* [http://www.ctt.bc.ca/landonline/]

Including faculty in the selection process is critical. If at all possible, it is help-ful to include students in the process as well. Although these appear to be obvious conclusions, often faculty and students, who are the prime users of the courseware selected, are overlooked in the evaluation and selection process. As Hazari (1998) states, "Very often technology-based decisions are made by technical personnel who base their decision on personal use, attendance at vendor sponsored workshops, reading about it in trade publications, or having used other products from the same vendor. This type of decision-making process does not take into account the needs and capabilities of the customers, users, or client" (p. 5). Clearly, the ability of tech-nical personnel to support the chosen courseware should be one of the criterion used to evaluate the various packages. However, it should not be the only means by which the decision is made. Technical personnel should be only one voice in the decision-making process; the faculty and students who are the users of the soft-ware should hold the majority vote.

Because each institution has its own needs, requirements, and resources avail-able—all factors in the choice of courseware—there can be no standards for se-lection that cut across all situations. However, some common elements need to be considered regardless of the specific needs of the institution, its faculty, and stu-dents. Lawrence Tomei (1999) divides the common elements into three broad cat-egories: use of technology, infrastructure, and instructional strategy. We will consider each category and provide some questions to assist others in establishing their own strategy for courseware selection.

Use of Technology

Simply purchasing computers and a courseware package without a sense of how they will be used either in or to support the work of the classroom is shortsighted. Tomei suggests that understanding instructional technology can assist an insti-tution in avoiding this common pitfall. He defines instructional technology as technology that "combines education technology with learning strategies, devel-opmental principles, and pedagogical ideals to solve educational problems" (p. 32). Consequently, some questions to consider regarding the use of technol-ogy are these:

- How do we envision using technology? Will we consider it to be a support to the face-to-face classroom or will it be used to deliver classes and programs or both?
- How will technology meet instructional needs in our institution?
- What do we see as the implications of technology use in our institution?
- How extensive do we expect the use of technology to be? Will its use be phased

in, or will we move directly to offering full programs that require immediate implementation?

Infrastructure

Unfortunately, many institutions embark on the delivery of online classes without first building a solid infrastructure to support the use of technology. According to Tomei, the critical elements of the technological infrastructure are people, money, and resources, as illustrated in Figure 4.1.

The people who should be considered while the infrastructure is being built are faculty, students, administrators, instructional designers (if the institution uses them), technology coordinators, and support staff. Simply identifying the stakeholders in the technology infrastructure is not enough, however. The training needs of each of them is also an important element here. The people and their training needs have a direct impact on the budget, or the money component, of the technology infrastructure. In addition to training expenses, budgetary concerns should include hardware and software purchase and upgrades, technical support and assistance, and incentives for faculty to develop online courses. The resources component of the infrastructure includes the allocation of time and effort necessary to make the use of technology viable. Release time for course development and delivery as well as time for faculty and staff development are important elements of the resources component. Questions to consider when building a technology infrastructure include these:

- How many faculty are interested in and ready to teach online classes?
- How many faculty will we need to train so that they can begin to develop and teach online classes? What levels of training do we need to provide for users (from novice to experienced)?
- How do we intend to provide training for faculty? What will it cost us to deliver training on an ongoing basis?
- What are student training needs? How will we meet them? What will it cost us to train our students?
- Will we be able to offer faculty incentives for course development? Will faculty be expected to teach online courses in addition to their existing teaching loads or will they be light-loaded in order to teach online?
- How will we provide technical support to both faculty and students?
- What kind of technology budget, in terms of both money and time, can we expect to develop? Will the institution support an expenditure for technology on an annual basis? If so, what will it look like?

FIGURE 4.1. THE TECHNOLOGICAL INFRASTRUCTURE.

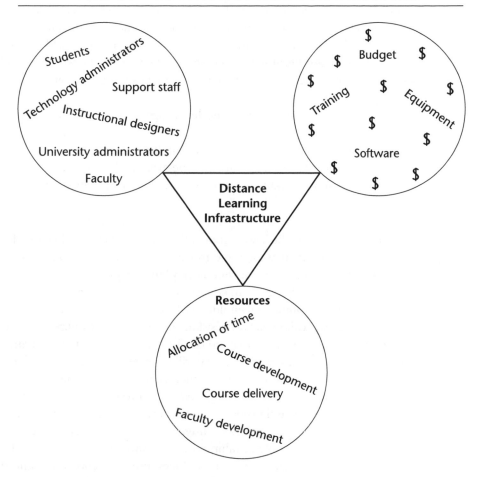

Instructional Strategy

As we have been emphasizing, decisions about curricular direction and learning objectives must precede decisions about the use of technology in teaching and learning. Tomei notes that even when the elements of the use of technology and infrastructure are firmly in place, a viable instructional strategy is pivotal for a successful technology program. If hardware and software are selected without a good sense of the learning outcomes the institution is hoping to achieve, there may be resistance to the implementation of technology in the curriculum and poor use among the faculty for both the creation and delivery of courses. Once decisions about learning outcomes are made, appropriate choices of technology as a tool for learning and a vehicle to achieve outcomes can then follow. Discussion of how students will be evaluated should also be included during consideration of instructional strategy, because that has some influence on the technology chosen. Questions to consider in the area of instructional strategy are these:

- What programmatic, course, and learning outcomes are we attempting to achieve?
- How will technology assist us in achieving these outcomes?
- How will students' learning outcomes be evaluated? How will the courseware selected assist us in evaluating students and their achievement of learning outcomes?

Planning is clearly the key component to an institution's evaluation of courseware. It often appears that the rapid movement in the direction of online learning has sacrificed a good comprehensive planning process. However, nothing substitutes for a well thought out, comprehensive, inclusive approach that allows the time for input from all stakeholders. Many of the institutional concerns that have been expressed about faculty resistance to entering the online distance learning arena can be overcome with good planning processes that allow them to have a strong say in the courseware that they will be expected to use. In addition, planning and budgeting for a strong infrastructure to support an online learning endeavor can help to sustain it. Cutting corners in these areas amounts to nothing less than self-sabotage and needless expenditure of money. "Use of Web course development tools can piggyback on huge investments higher education institutions have made in not only installing the hardware and software but also planning the network infrastructure to link offices, libraries, classroom, and student dormitories for local, wide area, and Internet connectivity" (Hazari, 1998, p. 4).

Obtaining the money to invest in online distance learning is a concern for many institutions. Consequently, we will now turn to a discussion of means by which institutions can enter the online arena when money concerns are very real.

When Money Is an Issue

Many smaller institutions are finding that the purchase and maintenance of hardware and software for online learning can be costly. Although the cost for a license to download and run course authoring software may not be exorbitant, technical personnel are needed to configure and install it and to provide ongoing technical support. Some course-delivery vendors do not offer the purchase of a license, but instead require that institutions pay them a fee for course development and hosting in addition to paying per student. Many institutions simply do not have the budget or ability to purchase servers and licenses for software, hire support personnel, or pay high fees to a company that is willing to host and maintain their courses. How, then, can these institutions offer online options to their students and do so within their means?

Most of the course authoring software companies have come up with a solution. Originally intending to encourage faculty to "test-drive" their software, the companies have given faculty the opportunity to create a course to be housed on that company's server. Should the instructor choose to offer that course, these companies will allow them to do so for a minimal fee—for example, $250 per course per semester. There are no additional per-student charges. In cases where institutions are not planning to deliver entire programs online but want to offer a few courses without making a large expenditure, this can be a good solution. In addition, this allows faculty members to try out various courseware packages for a semester before the institution purchases the software; thus it can be an important component of the evaluation process.

Another solution is one mentioned previously: many textbook companies are providing electronic versions of their texts with accompanying materials and exercises as well as communication tools. Access to the materials is by subscription. If an instructor wants to try teaching online for the first time or if money is an obstacle for the institution, then using an electronic textbook can be another cost-effective solution. Students can pay the subscription fee just as if they were buying a textbook. There would be no cost to the institution.

In order to enter the online arena, then, money should not be considered an obstacle. Faculty members who would like to give it a try only need the moral, logistical, or minimal financial support of their institution to get started.

Access Is a Major Concern

In contrast, accessibility issues are significant in online learning. Access can be a problem for a student who owns an older computer with outdated software installed on it. In addition, accessibility can be an issue for people with disabilities. Many mistakenly believe that computer technology serves all people with disabilities equally well. However, the use of computers is predicated on the ability to read what is on a monitor and type on a keyboard. Not all disabled people are able to accomplish these tasks. Software exists—such as screen-readers or voice-activated software—that assists people with disabilities of varying kinds to use technology and access the Internet. However, this does not ensure that a website or course site will be accessible unless it is constructed with accessibility in mind. "In reality, an increasingly sophisticated Internet, one rich with graphics, multimedia clips and compressed text, has meant a less accessible Internet for the disabled" (Strasburg, 2000, p. B3).

Chisholm, Vanderheiden, and Jacobs (1999) have compiled and made available a set of guidelines to make web content accessible to people with disabilities. They note that the guidelines are intended to promote accessibility. However, the guidelines also make content more accessible to all users, regardless of the hardware and software they are using. One of the problems with accessibility comes from the use of graphics or audio content on websites or course sites. The guidelines do not suggest eliminating images or sound when developing websites, but instead suggest that text equivalents and explanations be added whenever possible. Sometimes, a label or phrase noting that an image is present and describing what it contains is enough. In addition, hyperlinks on a site can be a problem if they have no meaningful description beyond "click here." A better way to provide a link that assistive software would be able to read would be to describe where the link takes the user, such as "link to library resources."

A good way to ensure accessibility by all students is to keep the design as simple as possible, keep the screen relatively uncluttered, and use consistent page layouts (Casey, 1999). To do so means to engage in thoughtful planning keeping learning objectives in mind. Our experience continues to tell us that simple course designs making minimal use of technological bells and whistles allow the largest number of users to access and get the most from a course. A course can be aesthetically pleasing even if it does not have complex graphics; learners can and do meet learning objectives through the use of discussion. We state once again that technology needs to be treated as just another learning tool. Technology is only a vehicle to meet learning objectives. When viewed in this way, the needs of the learners are kept primary—which is as it should be in the learner-centered online classroom.

Tips for Adopting and Working with Courseware

- Choose technology for an online course with the learner and learning outcomes in mind *first*. Instructor needs should come second.
- Do not use various technological tools, such as a whiteboard or chat, simply because they are available. Tools should be used only if they serve learning goals.
- Synchronous chat is neither the best way to deliver content nor the best pedagogical tool. Use chat judiciously, cautiously, and with specific learning goals in mind.

- Evaluate and adopt a courseware package based on programmatic and learning goals, not sales hype. Courseware should be easy to use, transparent, and predominantly in the control of the instructor or an instructional team.
- Be wary of courseware that promises "total solutions." If courseware is not under the control of faculty and the institution, concerns ranging from the ownership of intellectual property to the flexibility of use can arise and become problematic.
- Include faculty, and if possible, students in the evaluation and choosing of courseware. This not only helps to increase a sense of ownership and buy-in but also is more likely to result in a choice that more closely aligns technology use with learning objectives.
- Above all, keep it simple! A simply constructed course site with minimal or no graphics, audio, or video is more likely to be accessible to all users and cause fewer problems in the long run.

PART TWO

TEACHING AND LEARNING IN CYBERSPACE

CHAPTER FIVE

TRANSFORMING COURSES
FOR THE ONLINE CLASSROOM

Frequently, as we meet with faculty around the country, we find that both novices and seasoned instructors struggle with successfully transforming a course that has been taught for years in the face-to-face classroom into one that will work well online. As we have stated previously, simply putting lecture material online is not the answer. Indeed, instead of looking for ways to convert a course that has been successful in the face-to-face classroom, instructors are better served by approaching a course to be taught online as if it were a course to be taught for the first time—which in essence it is—while drawing on content knowledge and best practices. This allows a sense of freedom in the development of the course, without a tendency to adhere to tried-and-true methods that may not work online.

Another issue with which faculty struggle is the degree to use web delivery in a course. Judith Boettcher and Rita-Marie Conrad (1999) suggest that there are three types of online courses currently being offered: *web courses,* or courses in which material is placed on a website, allowing students access at any time during a given period and allowing for larger enrollments per class but little or no interaction between students, much like the algebra class we described in Chapter Two; *web-enhanced* courses, which use both face-to-face meetings and web delivery; and *web-centric* courses, which are interactive courses conducted exclusively using a course site that is housed on the web. Not all classes lend themselves well to web or web-centric delivery, and not all faculty feel comfortable jumping into a class that is completely delivered online. Some classes that may not transfer well are lab sciences, applied art, counseling skills, and speech. Even with these classes, however, creative faculty have found ways to deliver them online.

We have had faculty apologize to us for their use of a web-enhanced approach; they were feeling guilty that they had not moved directly to web-centric delivery. However, a 1999 study conducted by the American Association for History and Computing suggests that the most successful course outcomes are being seen in classes that are small and combine face-to-face with online interaction—that is, web-enhanced classes. Consequently, an important consideration in the development of an online class should be the degree to which technology can and should be used in course delivery.

Boettcher and Conrad (1999) present three questions that form the foundation of good instructional design: Who are my students? What do I want my students to know, to feel, or to be able to do as a result of this course or experience? And where, when, and with what resources will my students be learning? We have incorporated these questions into a series of questions that will assist faculty in translating course material for online work. The questions we address and examine are the following:

- Who are my students?
- What do I want to accomplish through this course? What do I want my students to know, to feel, or to be able to do as a result of this course or experience? What course content will support these objectives?
- Is this a course that will successfully transfer to the online environment?
- What guidelines, rules, roles, and norms need to be established for course completion?
- How do I plan to deliver course material? What will be expected of students in the learning process? Will I offer a combination of online and face-to-face options?
- How comfortable do I as an instructor feel about collaborative learning assignments, personal interaction, promotion of knowledge in learners, and releasing control of the learning process?
- How do I want to organize the course site? How much flexibility will I have in doing so? Do I have the freedom to develop this course in whatever manner I choose?
- How will I assess student performance in this course?
- How will I address attendance requirements?
- How do I define learning and what do I want to see as the learning outcomes for this class?

Each of these questions will be discussed and answered as we guide readers through the process of developing a course. The course we will develop here is an undergraduate course in sociology that we actually taught online: Systems Theories. We will design the course using WebCT™, one of a number of good course authoring tools. WebCT™ is a tool that we find meets the criteria we presented in Chapter Two for good course authoring software.

- *It is functional.* It offers the functions necessary to design and deliver an online course.
- *It is simple to operate for both faculty and students.* Once the users learn the software, it becomes transparent to the course delivery process.
- *It is user-friendly, visually appealing, and easy to navigate* (Palloff and Pratt, 1999).

In Resource B we show pieces of the same course developed with other course authoring tools—CourseInfo™, developed by Blackboard, Inc., and in eCollege—in order to show readers how the course could look using different packages.

Once software decisions have been made, the instructor can turn to the process of developing the course. We will now examine the considerations and decisions that need to be made.

Starting Over: Considerations in the Development of an Online Course

Boettcher and Conrad (1999) suggest that there are two decision levels involved in moving a course from the classroom to the web: first, determining your vision (including the degree to which the class will be conducted using the Internet), and second, envisioning the process. As instructors consider moving a course from the classroom to the Internet and begin to consider the answers to the questions we presented earlier, it is important to maintain a vision of the course as a whole and the desired learning outcomes for students. With this in mind, the instructor can then consider the process to be used to reach the desired outcomes in the context of what is possible online. Although the outcomes of a face-to-face or online course are likely to be the same, the process for reaching them differ in the two arenas. A comparison of two syllabi for a course titled Basic Addictions Studies—one for face-to-face delivery and one for online delivery—appear in Resource A as an illustration of the different processes.

Too often, instructors jump to the online process (that is, posting lecture notes) without having a vision for the course and desired outcomes. Starting with the desired result in mind helps to shape the process needed to get there. We will now illustrate the course development process by presenting and answering a series of questions to consider in course development and illustrate the answers with our course example: Systems Theories.

Who Are My Students?

We were asked to teach a semester-long course in systems theories using three six-hour face-to-face intensive sessions, spaced one month apart, along with online discussion, to a group of ten to fifteen adult undergraduate students in health and human sciences. Although this may seem like a complete enough answer to the question of who we are teaching and how the course will be delivered, other questions about them surfaced, such as these:

- What other courses will they be taking while taking my course?
- Have they had any exposure to the content to be studied in other courses they have completed?
- Where does this course fit in the overall program of studies in which these students are engaged?
- How far away from the institution do these students live?
- Are they all working? Are they working full-time?
- Have they taken other classes in this format or will this be their first online experience?
- What technological capabilities does each student have and what technology is available to them?

These questions were easily answered for us through a brief conversation with the department chairperson. Most students were taking an additional course in physiology, and some were fulfilling undergraduate requirements at other Bay Area schools. We discovered that this would be the first exposure these students would have to systems theory concepts. Although some of their other classes might have touched on the topic, it was not covered to any great degree. All of the students who enrolled in the course were working full-time and most had family responsibilities as well. Many had long commutes to campus, but all lived in the San Francisco Bay Area, where the college is located. None of the students was likely to have had online course experience. Having this information assisted us in determining how much computer training we would need to provide as well as what we might expect from the students enrolled in the course in terms of participation.

In developing a class for online delivery, it is important to get as full a picture as possible of the students to be served by the class before embarking on its development. In the face-to-face setting, an instructor would not design a basic survey class for upper-division students unless, for example, those students were in a degree completion program and had never been exposed to the material before.

Just as we would gather information about the group to be served in a face-to-face class, it is important to do so in an online group. Many institutions are hoping to expand their market and extend their reach by offering online options. As a result, ideas about who our students will be may be speculative. Nevertheless, this is important information to be used in class design. This information also helps us to determine process—if, for example, most of the students who will enroll in the course live a significant distance from the institution, then the use of face-to-face sessions may not be viable. Once the class has begun, if we find that there are some differences in what we expected and the group enrolled in the class, we can adjust as we go to accommodate them.

What Do I Want to Accomplish Through This Course?

Beginning at the end by determining appropriate learning outcomes for a course is the best way to decide what content should be covered. The development of appropriate learning outcomes also begins to give the instructor a sense of what steps might be needed to move a student from the beginning of the course to the end. Instead of focusing on learning strategies first, such as lecture or lecture-discussion, deciding on learning outcomes, including what we want students to know, feel, or be able to do at the end of the course, helps us to determine how we might get there.

Because we had learned that our students in the systems theories class had little or no previous experience with the topic, we established the learning objectives shown in Exhibit 5.1.

Once our objectives were established, we were then able to move on and determine appropriate reading material and assignments to enable students to achieve those objectives. Our course format was predetermined—a web-enhanced format—so we could begin to decide what material to cover in face-to-face sessions and what to cover online. We searched for a text that had what is known as a companion website—a site constructed by the publisher containing supplemental materials and exercises—but found none on the topic of social systems. Consequently, we decided to rely heavily on books we did choose and to provide supplemental material, such as a glossary of systems terms posted on the course site, to convey course content. Weekly online discussions would focus on topics presented in the readings.

Will This Course Successfully Transfer to the Online Environment?

As noted earlier in this chapter, few classes do not transfer to the online environment, with the exception perhaps of applied art classes and the others we mentioned. Even then, however, creative use of local lab and studio facilities and the inclusion of demonstration material using PowerPoint slides or limited amounts of video content that students can access on the course site may overcome the need for face-to-face contact. So the issue usually becomes *how* to transfer the course rather than *if* the course can be transferred.

We felt that there was little doubt that systems theories would do well as an online course, because a reading-discussion format would work well in this case. Content could be delivered through reading assignments and asking students to work on collaborative assignments designed to push them to think critically and to apply what they were reading. Consequently, we decided to use our face-to-face time for experiential exercises, such as case studies, simulations, and student presentations, and to use the online classroom for discussion of reading and other course-related material.

EXHIBIT 5.1. LEARNING OBJECTIVES.

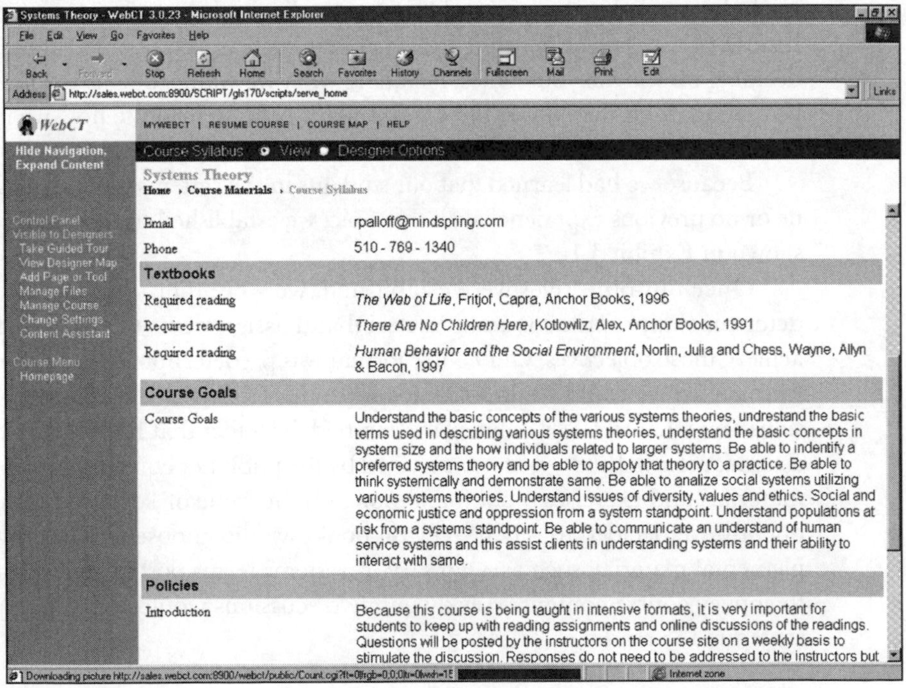

What Guidelines, Rules, Roles, and Norms Need to Be Established for Course Completion?

As we have already noted, we cannot stress enough the importance of developing a good set of course guidelines, including rules for interacting with one another and expectations for receiving a grade. Course guidelines form the structure of the course and create a container within which students can learn together. Exhibit 5.2 illustrates the guidelines we developed for the systems theories class.

The guidelines for this course were loosely conceived, but they created enough structure so that students knew what was expected of them. At the first face-to-face class meeting, which began the class, the guidelines were reviewed and modifications made based on student input. Students felt they needed the structure of knowing when the week's discussion question would be posted along with a day or date by which their first responses to the question were "due." They agreed that they wanted to see the discussion questions on Sundays, with first responses posted on Wednesdays, allowing them to read and reflect for a couple of days before answering.

EXHIBIT 5.2. COURSE GUIDELINES.

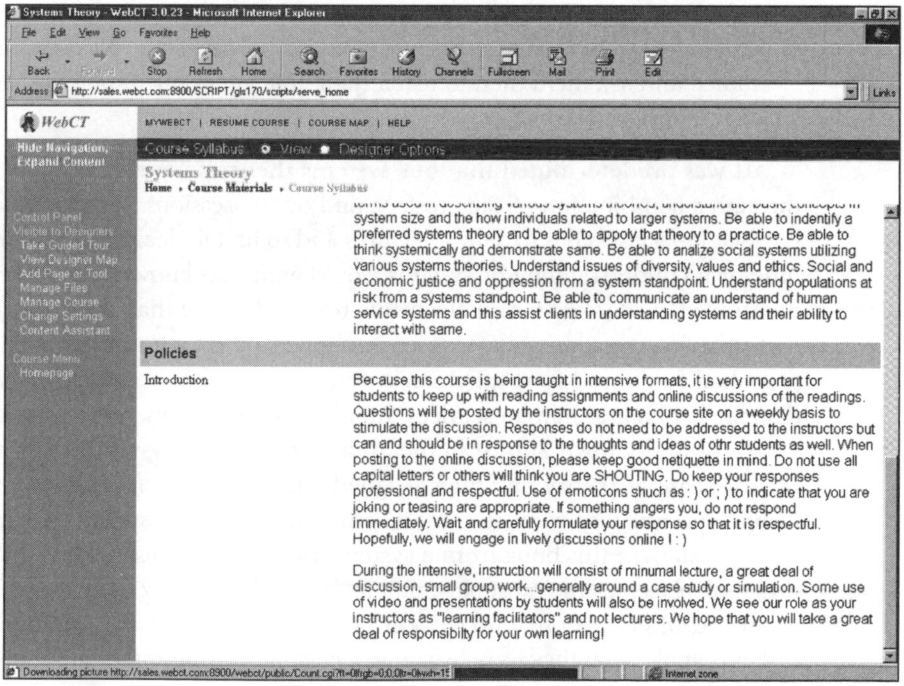

How Do I Plan to Deliver Course Material?

An instructor who is offering a course for the first time may choose to take small steps in online course development by offering a web-enhanced version of a class. In so doing, "lecture" material might be placed on a website along with directions for assignment completion and some amount of asynchronous discussion. Thus the instructor can conduct face-to-face sessions that are made up of active learning activities allowing for application of the theory being studied. Other ways to begin experimenting with online learning are to place course-related information on a website without requiring online discussion or to use a text in an electronic format.

Whether the course is to be conducted completely online or is web-enhanced, the instructor needs to decide how students will acquire their knowledge of the content. If lectures are not the mode of choice for imparting information and content, then how will students access material that will provide them with the same information? Here are a few suggestions:

- An electronic textbook that has interactive study guides and activities
- Assignments that develop research skills and empower students to find articles, websites, and other resources that pertain to the content being studied
- Collaborative assignments that enable students to learn from one another and that serve to enhance and deepen the knowledge acquired
- Assignments that turn students into "experts" in one area of the content being studied and ask them then to teach their colleagues (including the instructor) what they have learned

It was predetermined that our systems theories course would be offered through a combination of face-to-face and online sessions. We chose not to use the face-to-face sessions to deliver lectures and so had to decide how students with little or no understanding of systems would gain that knowledge. As previously mentioned, we looked for an electronic text and found that none was available that suited our requirements. Consequently, we opted for a standard text that approached the subject from a human systems perspective, because these were students in health and human services. In addition, we assigned the work of Fritjof Capra, a well-known author in the area of ecological systems, to give them a broader base of theory, and then assigned a nonfiction book describing a family living in poverty who come in contact with numerous social systems. We asked students to analyze this book from a systems perspective. Discussion of the readings took place, for the most part, online. In the face-to-face sessions, we decided to use video, simulations, and student presentations as learning exercises to help students apply what they were learning. The course assignments are shown in Exhibit 5.3.

How Comfortable Am I in Releasing Control to the Learners?

The success of collaborative assignments in an online course rests with the instructor's willingness to empower students to take on the work with clear expectations for completion and then step out of the way. In addition, because of the amount of work involved for students in completing collaborative assignments online, spacing out the assignments judiciously and using a combination of intensive and less intensive assignments helps with successful completion and meaningful acquisition of knowledge. For example, assigning a weekly group project involving research and compilation of results is likely to be too much, but assigning two to three such assignments during a term is much more doable. These assignments can be interspersed with discussing readings, giving feedback on each other's assignments, alternating facilitation assignments, and using other collaborative processes that keep the spirit of collaborative learning alive.

We consulted with one instructor who complained that her students were unable to complete collaborative assignments online. When we visited her course site, we noticed two things. First, she was involving herself in the small group discussion

EXHIBIT 5.3. COURSE ASSIGNMENTS.

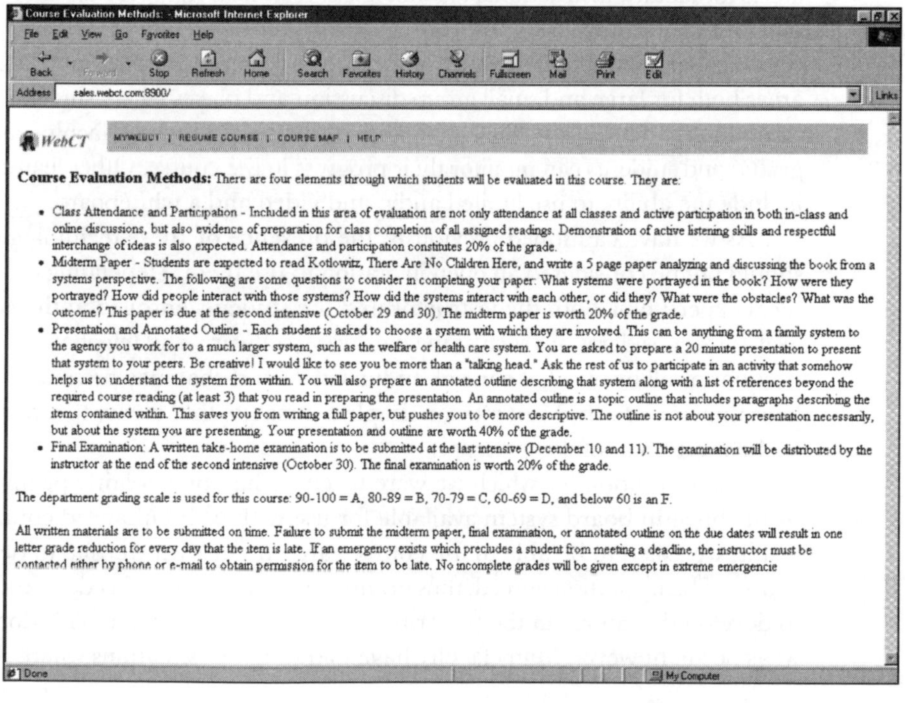

Course Evaluation Methods: There are four elements through which students will be evaluated in this course. They are:

- Class Attendance and Participation - Included in this area of evaluation are not only attendance at all classes and active participation in both in-class and online discussions, but also evidence of preparation for class completion of all assigned readings. Demonstration of active listening skills and respectful interchange of ideas is also expected. Attendance and participation constitutes 20% of the grade.
- Midterm Paper - Students are expected to read Kotlowitz, There Are No Children Here, and write a 5 page paper analyzing and discussing the book from a systems perspective. The following are some questions to consider in completing your paper: What systems were portrayed in the book? How were they portrayed? How did people interact with those systems? How did the systems interact with each other, or did they? What were the obstacles? What was the outcome? This paper is due at the second intensive (October 29 and 30). The midterm paper is worth 20% of the grade.
- Presentation and Annotated Outline - Each student is asked to choose a system with which they are involved. This can be anything from a family system to the agency you work for to a much larger system, such as the welfare or health care system. You are asked to prepare a 20 minute presentation to present that system to your peers. Be creative! I would like to see you be more than a "talking head." Ask the rest of us to participate in an activity that somehow helps us to understand the system from within. You will also prepare an annotated outline describing that system along with a list of references beyond the required course reading (at least 3) that you read in preparing the presentation. An annotated outline is a topic outline that includes paragraphs describing the items contained within. This saves you from writing a full paper, but pushes you to be more descriptive. The outline is not about your presentation necessarily, but about the system you are presenting. Your presentation and outline are worth 40% of the grade.
- Final Examination: A written take-home examination is to be submitted at the last intensive (December 10 and 11). The examination will be distributed by the instructor at the end of the second intensive (October 30). The final examination is worth 20% of the grade.

The department grading scale is used for this course: 90-100 = A, 80-89 = B, 70-79 = C, 60-69 = D, and below 60 is an F.

All written materials are to be submitted on time. Failure to submit the midterm paper, final examination, or annotated outline on the due dates will result in one letter grade reduction for every day that the item is late. If an emergency exists which precludes a student from meeting a deadline, the instructor must be contacted either by phone or e-mail to obtain permission for the item to be late. No incomplete grades will be given except in extreme emergencie around collaborative assignments, and second, she was assigning small group projects weekly. Students were complaining that the workload was too heavy and that they were not getting much out of the assignments. We suggested that she eliminate some of the collaborative assignments, allowing more time for students to complete the remaining assignments. We also suggested that she remove herself from the negotiation and small group discussion of the collaborative groups because we felt that her involvement was actually complicating their group process. Small groups should have the option of asking the instructor to intercede if the group is not working well together. However, the instructor should not make himself or herself an integral part of the group process.

As we have previously stated, in developing our course in systems theories we chose to use our allotted face-to-face time for intensive collaborative work. These sessions were interspersed with online discussion of the readings and other topics related to systems. A portion of the schedule of the discussions developed to coincide with reading assignments is shown in Exhibit 5.4.

How Do I Want to Organize the Course Site?

Many institutions have adopted courseware that they ask faculty to use in order to simplify and unify course management and to minimize technological headaches for faculty, instructional technologists, technical support staff, and students. Current course authoring software generally allows faculty to upload a syllabus that has been created in a word processor and create asynchronous discussion areas both for large and small group discussion and places where students can post assignments. They also offer e-mail and gradebooks, in which faculty can record grades and students can monitor their progress in the course. Other features might include the ability to use limited audio and video and a whiteboard.

As we have cautioned previously, the presence of these technological tools should not be considered an open invitation to use them. Depending on the technical expertise of both the instructor and the students enrolled in the course, as well as on considerations such as the hardware, software, and telephone access connections of all involved, the use of audio, video, and chat may present more problems than it is worth. Most often, a simple course site that is easy to navigate leads to the most successful experience.

The institution for which we were teaching had only a fairly primitive electronic bulletin board system available for use with web-enhanced courses. As a result, we asked to be able to use courseware on our own website to deliver the course. The institution agreed, thus granting us considerable freedom and latitude to develop the course in the prescribed web-enhanced format. This does not always occur, however. Many faculty have told us about situations where they have

EXHIBIT 5.4. SCHEDULE OF ASSIGNMENTS AND DISCUSSIONS.

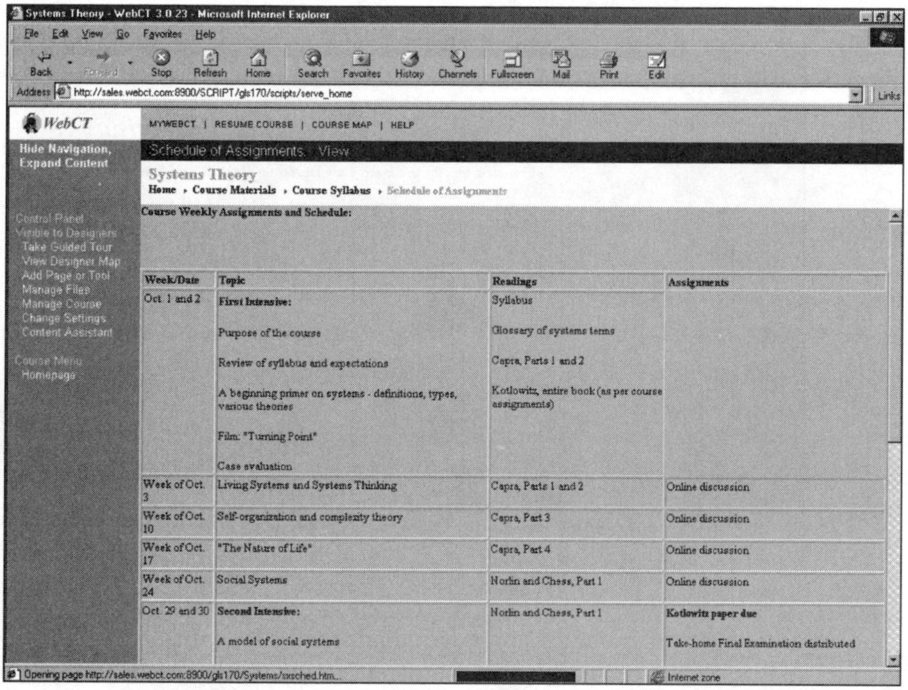

Week/Date	Topic	Readings	Assignments
Oct. 1 and 2	**First Intensive:** Purpose of the course Review of syllabus and expectations A beginning primer on systems - definitions, types, various theories Film: "Turning Point" Case evaluation	Syllabus Glossary of systems terms Capra, Parts 1 and 2 Kotlowitz, entire book (as per course assignments)	
Week of Oct. 3	Living Systems and Systems Thinking	Capra, Parts 1 and 2	Online discussion
Week of Oct. 10	Self-organization and complexity theory	Capra, Part 3	Online discussion
Week of Oct. 17	"The Nature of Life"	Capra, Part 4	Online discussion
Week of Oct. 24	Social Systems	Norlin and Chess, Part 1	Online discussion
Oct. 29 and 30	**Second Intensive:** A model of social systems	Norlin and Chess, Part 1	**Kotlowitz paper due** Take-home Final Examination distributed

been told to use a software package that did not serve their learning outcomes, thus limiting their ability to deliver the course in the way they saw fit.

Through WebCT™, we relied on basic discussion forums as the main means of conducting the class. The courseware allowed us to choose the icons for each area of the course and customize the titles of the links as well as to create as many discussion forums as we needed. Exhibit 5.5 shows the course homepage and illustrates the icons used to delineate each area of the course.

Exhibit 5.6 shows the listing of discussion forums that we created for the class.

How Will I Assess Student Performance in This Course?

Just as in a face-to-face course, decisions about how student performance will be evaluated surface during the planning stages of the course. What is the most effective means of determining how students are mastering content and applying it appropriately? Often in the face-to-face classroom, the instructor uses tests, quizzes,

EXHIBIT 5.5. COURSE HOMEPAGE.

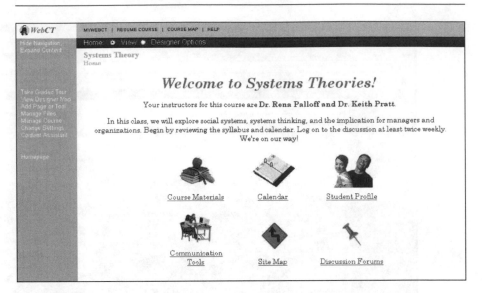

and papers to evaluate knowledge acquisition. There may be additional requirements, such as attendance, that students are expected to meet. In the online classroom, however, there needs to be careful consideration of how well any of the
traditional means of evaluation will work.

Many institutions continue to require that some form of examination be used
to evaluate students. Most of the courseware applications available for online courses
allow for secure administration of tests and quizzes, often with a link to the gradebook embedded in the application. Answers to test questions can be entered into
an encrypted file that is then available only to the instructor. Just as in the face-to-
face classroom, however, the question of cheating emerges when tests and quizzes
are used. However, because students in an online course are often working at a
distance, there are additional concerns. How will the instructor know that the test
answers he or she received were really given by the student whose name appears
on the test? There are some ways to minimize the possibility of cheating. For example, a test might be administered at a proctored site with a requirement that
the student show identification before being allowed to take the test. Students might
also be required to take the test on campus. Although these are not ideal solutions
and may not completely eliminate the possibility of cheating, they do help to reduce that possibility.

The use of a collaborative process in delivering the course, with minimal
use of tests and quizzes, allows an instructor to build trust in students' abilities to

EXHIBIT 5.6. DISCUSSION BOARD.

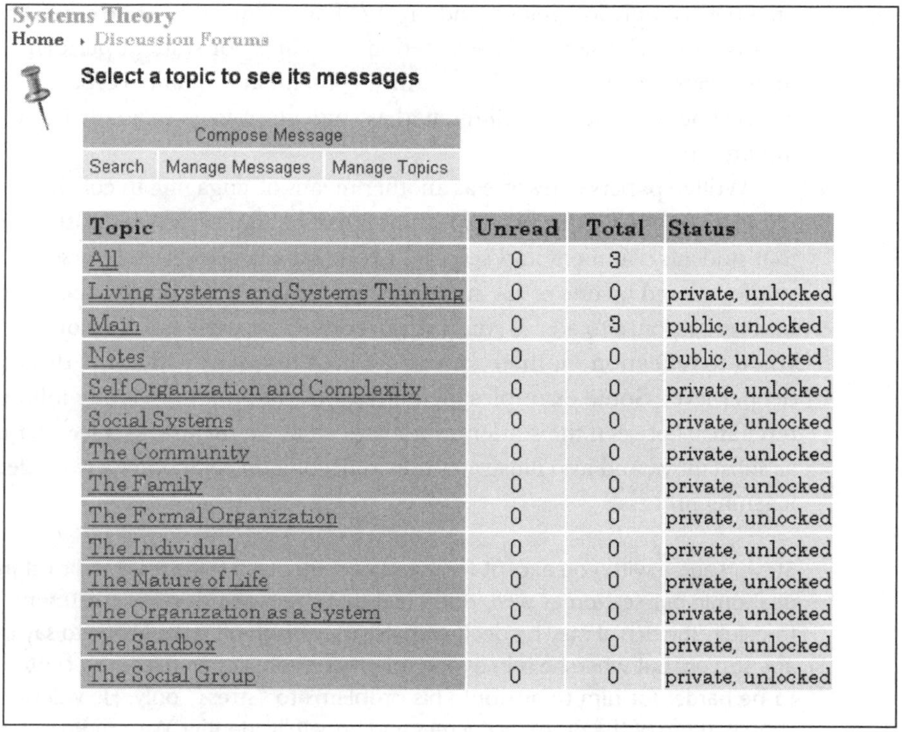

Systems Theory
Home › Discussion Forums

Select a topic to see its messages

Compose Message

Search | Manage Messages | Manage Topics

Topic	Unread	Total	Status
All	0	3	
Living Systems and Systems Thinking	0	0	private, unlocked
Main	0	3	public, unlocked
Notes	0	0	public, unlocked
Self Organization and Complexity	0	0	private, unlocked
Social Systems	0	0	private, unlocked
The Community	0	0	private, unlocked
The Family	0	0	private, unlocked
The Formal Organization	0	0	private, unlocked
The Individual	0	0	private, unlocked
The Nature of Life	0	0	private, unlocked
The Organization as a System	0	0	private, unlocked
The Sandbox	0	0	private, unlocked
The Social Group	0	0	private, unlocked

do the work, gives the instructor ongoing evidence of the work they are capable of producing, and most importantly, empowers students to engage in their own learning process. Instructors are able to recognize the unique writing style of each student. The advantage in the online course is that students not only submit papers but also post written responses to online discussions. Therefore, any variations in a student's writing become more obvious and can be addressed by the instructor.

The online course actually has yet another advantage in evaluating students that the face-to-face classroom does not. In an online course, students must participate in some fashion in order to complete it successfully. This means that the instructor can see on a regular basis how students are analyzing and applying course material, especially if they are being asked to respond to questions that encourage them to think critically. Consequently, a good means of evaluating student performance in an online course is to require a particular number of substantive posts each week. A substantive post responds to the question in a way that clearly supports a position, begins a new topic, or somehow adds to the discussion by critically reflecting on what is being discussed or moving the discussion in a new direction. Simply logging on and saying "I agree" would not be considered a substantive post. Consequently, evaluation guidelines for student performance in an online course can include the quantity, content, and quality of posts. Thus, concerns about cheating are eliminated as students engage in a collaborative learning process.

Written papers can serve as another means of engaging in collaborative learning in an online course. An expectation can be that papers be posted online and that students comment and respond to one other's work. In a course on addiction studies offered by one of us, students were asked to post brief papers on a weekly basis in response to a case study. A portion of the week's discussion was then devoted to reflection on the responses, which frequently took the discussion to a deeper level. Some examples of the responses to one case study follow. The interchange between the students indicates what we mean when we identify a post as substantive and also illustrates how reflecting on each other's work deepens the learning process.

Steve, I agree with you except for your last sentence. I think it's good to start with education in our session as well. But, I feel that the higher level of treatment, the more forcefully the denial may be dealt with. He may brush off what I have to say in the therapy session, but when he is in a room of other alcoholics or in a rehab center it is going to be harder for him to attribute his problems to "stress" only. He will hear his own story in those of the other recoverees and hopefully identify. With more intensive treatment he may be more confronted with the reality of the severity of his problems. Also the PhD in Psychology indicates to me that he may tend to intellectualize, and probably already knows something about substance abuse from this mental level. Ron needs to really get it. *Kathy*

Kathy, I understand your position. But after reading the discussion I think there is a good possibility that his major problem is his PTSD and that the alcohol and marijuana addiction has been his way to deal with it. I think the whole family needs to be brought in so that it can be evaluated in terms of his wife's possible addiction and how to provide support for increased symptoms of PTSD when he detoxes. I meant to also say that with some view of the family situation there will be some possibility of doing a more effective confrontation. There should be more evidence of how the alcohol and marijuana use has been detrimental and how it would be helpful to detox in order to deal with the PTSD more effectively. *Steve*

Steve, I agree with you that the PTSD is also a large problem which he has probably been covering up with alcohol and drugs. And I also agree with you about family involvement. But, for me there was enough evidence in the case study that the alcohol and drug use needed to be treated first or in conjunction with the PTSD. Thanks. :-) *Kathy*

In the interest of learning, can you please explain how you would justify a use of medical monitoring with this guy? I take it you mean level 3.7 or 4, treatment with medical monitoring? The reason I'm asking, is because I didn't see this in reviewing the case study and I don't feel as experienced in making that kind of call, even after reading your comment. Or, do you mean, involve his doctor externally? Appreciate the clarification. *Tasia*

Exhibit 5.3 demonstrated how we decided to evaluate our students in Systems Theories. Because the course was web-enhanced rather than web-centric, we used the face-to-face sessions to initiate, complete, and discuss assignments. Instead of having students post papers online, we determined that they would be turned in at the face-to-face sessions and discussed at that time. We were required to give some form of a final examination for the course. Consequently, we decided to give a take-home essay exam that required students to reflect on the material being studied. Exhibit 5.7 shows the exam we developed. We determined that the exam would only account for 20 percent of the total grade because the ongoing online discussion would provide us with a good idea of how well students were understanding and applying systems theories.

How Will I Address Attendance Requirements?

Accounting for attendance becomes to some degree more difficult online. Yet many institutions are requiring faculty to account for attendance just as they would in the face-to-face classroom in order to meet guidelines for state, federal, and financial aid. So we have established a rule of thumb for our online classes. In order to meet attendance requirements, students must log on and post something to the discussion an equivalent number of times to that which the class would have met on a face-to-face basis. For example, an undergraduate class that would normally meet three times per week then equates to at least three posts per week. A graduate level class that would have met once per week for two hours requires two posts per week to the online discussion.

In a web-enhanced course, accounting for attendance becomes an easier task because there are required face-to-face sessions. Some web-enhanced classes may require one in-person session each week, with additional work online. However, it is still a good practice to mandate a certain number of posts to the online component of the course weekly. Our web-enhanced class required three weekend

EXHIBIT 5.7. SAMPLE FINAL EXAM.

Take-Home Final—Systems Theories

Please briefly, but thoroughly, answer the following three questions. Your answers should be typed and double-spaced. If you use references, please cite them and include a reference list at the end of each question. There is no page expectation for your answers, but please don't submit a 20-page paper! You should be able to answer each question in 2 to 3 pages. Your take-home final is due on Saturday of the last intensive, which is December 11. No late papers will be accepted. Please feel free to contact us if you have any questions, problems, or concerns. Good luck and try to have some fun with this!

1. During the first week of the online discussion, we asked you to describe the most influential system in your life. Looking back over the reading and discussions for this course, talk about all (or as many as you can think of) the systems you encounter on a typical day. What are they? What do they look like? How do they interrelate, or do they? (Remember—there are virtual systems, too!!)

2. Think about a system that bothers you. This could be the political system, the healthcare system, the education system, or any that comes to your mind. Describe and analyze it. What is it about this system that disturbs you? What changes would need to be made in this system that would make it less disturbing? When talking and writing about the system, make sure you discuss the participants, make-up, boundaries, etc.

3. Briefly answer the following:

   What did I know about systems when I entered this course?

   What have I learned?

   Has my learning changed me in any way? If so, how? As you identify the changes, try to identify them with the system that might have influenced that change.

sessions and two online posts per week. Regardless of the configuration of sessions, attendance in a web-enhanced class is usually made up of a combination of presence at required meetings on campus coupled with presence online.

How Do I Define Learning and What Do I Want to See as the Learning Outcomes?

Although this question appears to be a reiteration of the questions asked when beginning to plan for the course, it is actually an important reflection on the overall process. How will I know that I have met the objectives I have set for students? What does learning look like to me?

In a collaborative learning environment, learning and learning outcomes are much more than simple acquisition of knowledge. The co-creation of meaning and knowledge that can occur in the collaborative online classroom can serve to create a level of reflection that results in what is called *transformative learning*. In transformative learning, students are able to begin to reflect on the following question: How am I growing and changing as a learner and as a person through my involvement in this course? If the course has been designed to incorporate and invite real life experience into the classroom, students can begin to explore the material being studied not just from an academic standpoint but through the personal meaning they derive from it. As facilitators of the online classroom process, instructors can encourage students to engage in this level of reflection by creating assignments and asking questions that allow students to apply material to their work or life situations. The following student quote from Systems Theories illustrates a successful learning outcome, the generation of transformative knowledge. It illustrates this student's ability to begin to reflect on what was being studied and apply it to his own life. David came into the course stating that he had little to no understanding or much interest in studying systems. However, as the course progressed, he became intrigued with and excited about the number of systems he saw and interacted with daily. This brief quote begins to capture what he learned:

It seems that upon inspection, all systems have influences over others at some point. The weather (ecology system) or traffic (transportation system) could impact my work or family system, living in the Bay Area (community) may influence my being politically active affecting the government, etc. . . . There is no end! *David*

Beginnings

Now that we have moved through the planning process to create an online course, we can begin to consider the process of the course itself. How do online courses actually work? What does the process look like? Once a syllabus has been created and posted to the course site, how do we get started?

Before the course begins, students need to be introduced to the software in use. Some courseware applications, such as Blackboard™ and WebCT™, offer their own orientations to their software on their websites. Some academic institutions have created their own online orientations, which help the student understand not only the software they will be using but online learning itself. Distance Learning 101, created by Pennsylvania State University, is a good example. When an instructor does not have an orientation program available to students, one can be created in the course. The syllabus should contain tips for successful completion of the course, along with guidelines for completion and guidelines for respectful interaction, also known as *netiquette*. Some instructors post a document on the course site containing frequently asked questions in order to easily provide an orientation for students. A portion of the syllabus for Systems Theories as it appears on the course site can be seen in Exhibit 5.8.

Once the orientation has been developed and delivered, there are two important steps to take at the beginning of an online course. The first is to create a welcome message that repeats some basic orientation information for students and remains on the course site. Some courseware applications allow the instructor to place a welcome message on the course homepage, as we were able to do in WebCT™. When that function is not available, a welcome message, such as the one that follows, can be posted as a first discussion item on the course site.

Hello all! I'm excited to begin this exploration of groups and group process with you all. As many of you may know, working with online groups is not only my interest but my passion—particularly groups who come together online for the purpose of learning together. We have the opportunity here to act as our own "laboratory" if you will— we can learn about online groups by forming our own. My hopes for this term are that we all will learn something about how groups form, develop norms together, and work together online. But more importantly, I hope we all can learn something about how we as members of that group and how we as individual members contribute to that process. I also hope that we all will be able to apply this new knowledge and skill development in the workplace and certainly in your other classes. What we're doing is groundbreaking stuff which has tremendous implications for networked organizations and in team building. I'll post more of an introduction later. Just wanted to say hello and that I'm looking forward to taking this collaborative journey with you—I hope you're all willing to join me and have some fun in the process! *Rena*

Instructors can also send an e-mail or hard copy instructions for course completion. The best option is to hold a face-to-face session with students to orient them to the course and the software in use. Because our systems theories course

EXHIBIT 5.8. COURSE SYLLABUS.

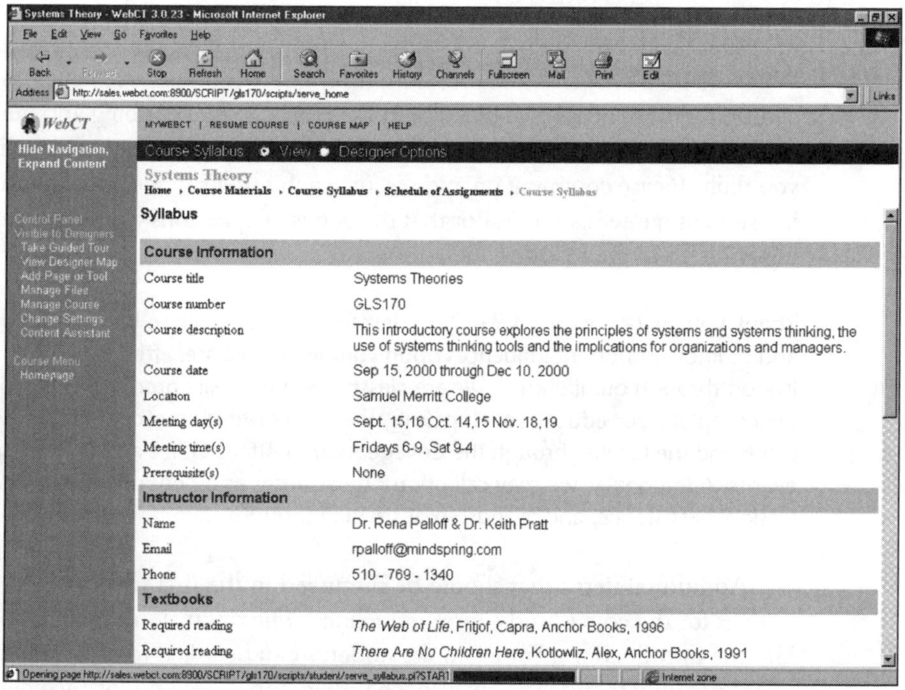

was web-enhanced, we were able to use the first face-to-face session to introduce students to the course and courseware.

Posting introductions is the second important step to take when a course begins. Most courseware allows both students and the instructor to create simple homepages, often including a picture, that remain on the course site. We have heard students and instructors comment on how useful this has been to them. These pages serve as an initial way to get to know one another, and because they remain on the site, students and instructors find themselves visiting the homepages frequently as a reminder about what students look like or what they said about themselves. In addition to being a good community-building tool, this helps everyone involved with the course understand why someone else might be coming from a particular place or take a particular position in his or her postings.

It is not uncommon for us to set aside the first week of an online class to get to know one another. In addition to asking students to create their homepages, our first questions for the course generally involve stating their learning objectives for the course or beginning to discuss the course as it relates to their lives outside of the online classroom. For example, our first question in Systems Theories was, "Following up on our discussions in class about the fact that all of you know more about systems than you think, we'd like you to think about all the systems you come in contact with on a daily basis. What are they and how can you describe them? What are their elements and the relationships between those elements? What constitutes their boundaries? Think about the reading you are doing and our analysis of *Dead Poets Society* and then describe in some detail the system that most influences you daily. Please comment on and discuss each other's descriptions." The following student quote is an indicator that this series of questions was successful in helping students to get to know one another:

Thank you everyone for your system descriptions. It is nice to know more about you and to know important influences upon your lives—we are, after all, a system that will live on through our lifetimes. We are classmates who will enter new professions once we complete our education. Hopefully, we will continue our connections with each other and the faculty through the College Alumni Affairs Office and College-sponsored events. Additionally, we may call upon one another as a network of knowledge, professional assistance, and friendship. It's a nice thought. *David*

Additional items that should be discussed in the first week are learning objectives for the course and course guidelines. The discussion can be incorporated into the introductions. For example, students can be asked to present information about not only themselves but also what they hope to get out of the course. They can also be asked to comment on course guidelines to determine if they will assist them in reaching their learning objectives. This should not be the only time that the guidelines are discussed, however. If students find that the guidelines are not meeting their needs in some way, they should feel free to raise this as a topic of discussion and the guidelines can be renegotiated at that time. We generally do not change guidelines until we hear from all of the students involved with the class to make sure that all will benefit from the change. The following is an example of such negotiations:

Now that we are only responding to the week's case study and we are about halfway through the term, I thought I'd clarify academic expectations (I am nothing if not prompt:-}). We each have used varying styles in posting responses to the case studies. Some have followed the more traditional format noted in the guidebook, others have shared their thoughts that the case study brought up for them, while others have answered discussion questions noted at the end of the case. I haven't noted any performance feedback from you (either positive or negative) on the way you would like to see these postings continued. Is there a particular style you would like to see? Is there a way you consider best or most appropriate in how we approach the cases for the rest of the term? *Jane*

Thanks for asking this question, Jane. It's been kind of a free-for-all up until now due for the most part to the confused discussion expectations to begin with and for that I apologize!! As for the remainder of the term, what I'd like to see is for you to use the case study guidelines I posted in the beginning of the term if they work for you—for this week's case, they may not. If not, use what seems appropriate from those guidelines and rely on the questions at the end of the case. Whether you use the guidelines in whole or in part, the questions should be somehow addressed in your response. Have I muddied the waters even more, or does this make sense??? *Rena*

Clear as mud!:-) No, that's great. It sounds like we should first use the guidelines unless another approach makes more sense. If another approach makes more sense, you would like us to ensure that we work to include all applicable facets of the case study guidelines in our response. Is this close? *Jane*

You got it, Jane!!!:-) *Rena*

Rena, Thanks for the clarification (and thanks to Jane for asking the question). Sometimes the case method works (especially if it is a case versus an article) and sometimes it is a stretch to get a reply in that format. I just noticed that Liz posted a discussion question and a case. I thought we were going to modify our original course and only post cases and the discussion will occur thereafter. What is the latest on this? *Lynn*

Lynn, In answer to your question, we are only required to do a case study now. Liz simply went above and beyond the call of duty. *Jane*

What this bit of discussion illustrates is that clarification of guidelines is an ongoing, important process in an online course. All students need to accept the guidelines in order for the course to progress smoothly. These students clearly felt empowered to raise the issues that were important for them and to clarify issues for each other. At times, revisiting the guidelines is helpful in order to assure that learning objectives are achieved.

Once the Course Has Started

Once introductions have been made and the course has begun, how does the instructor move into course content and stimulate participation? The key to good participation and dynamic discussion is asking open, expansive questions that promote critical thinking and analytic responses. Once students begin to work with expansive questions, they also learn to ask questions of each other in the same way. The momentum generated through lively discussion of the topic being studied generally can be carried through the remainder of the course.

There is a difference, for example, between asking, "Give three examples of systems in your life" and the questions we used to begin our systems theories class, which were, "Think about all the systems you come in contact with on a daily basis. What are they and how can you describe them? What are their elements and the relationships between those elements? What constitutes their boundaries? Think about the reading you are doing and our analysis of *Dead Poets Society* and then describe in some detail the system that most influences you daily." The first question will encourage students simply to generate a list of systems with little or no reflection about what that means. The second series of questions encourages students to reflect more critically on the systems they encounter daily and to describe and analyze them using material they are reading for the course. The second approach not only expands the thinking process of the group but also begins to get the students in this particular course to engage in systems thinking, a learning objective for the course.

Often we have found that when instructors worry about lack of participation in an online course, one of the problems stems from the way in which they are asking questions. When instructors learn to reframe their questions to be more expansive and to include real examples from the students' lives, participation increases dramatically. The course becomes more relevant as a result.

In order to move the process along, students should be encouraged to bring real life into the online classroom as much as possible. Asking questions that relate the course material to their lives or asking them to engage in real-life research—such as, "Analyze your work or school organization using chaos theory. Would you describe your work organization as a self-organizing system? Why or why not?" or "We'd like you to go to your local Wal-Mart. From a systems perspective, what did you see there?"—helps students to begin to make sense of the material on a very personal level.

In addition, as the course progresses it is important to continue to pay attention to the development of the learning community. Allowing for the sharing of important personal events helps students and the instructor to bond as people, builds trust among them, and serves to enhance the collaborative process. For example, while Systems Theories was in progress, one of us reunited with his son, whom he had not seen in many years. He shared that information with the group. The following is an example of discussion surrounding that event:

Just wanted to let everyone know what a great weekend it was for me even though the Raiders lost the football game. Both my sons arrived and in good condition. We spent the weekend getting to know one another and just all-around having fun. We were on the front page of the *Fremont Argus* on Monday and they told the story pretty well. Its really scary how much we all are alike, not being together for 26 years. Hugs, *Keith*

Keith, That is so awesome! Congratulations!!! I'm sure it was a weekend you will not soon forget.:) *Polly*

Many heart felt congratulations to you!! It was nice to hear all went well. Take care you Proud Dad! *Sabrina*:)

That's great! I 'm going to have to get a copy of the Monday's paper so I can read the story. *Gracie*

The comments are brief but supportive. The emoticons—symbols used to convey emotion online—help to convey a sense of warmth and the happiness the students were feeling about this event. Although not related to the academic material being studied, this event helped this group to coalesce into a learning community. They had shared something important on a deeply personal level, which served to assist them in working more closely together in the learning process.

Endings

As we discussed in Chapter Two, as a course draws to an end it is important to allow time for reflection on what has been learned and whether learning objectives have been met. If there is a final face-to-face meeting, some of that time can be devoted to discussion of this topic. If not, allowing time for closure online is important. Frequently, we use the last week of the class for online discussion of learning objectives and an evaluation by the students of how they experienced the course. We also post some feedback to the group as a whole on how we thought the course went and send individual e-mail messages to students to give them feedback on their work and contribution to the course. We may also ask the students to send us private e-mails evaluating their own work and that of their student colleagues.

Because we met face-to-face with the Systems Theories group at the end of the course, we used some of that time for an evaluation of the experience. The following, then, is an example of closure in another online course:

Hello everyone and welcome to the end of our time together for the term! As you think about what you've learned and gained from this class, I wanted to post a thank you to all of you for your enthusiastic participation. All of you have been thoughtful in your responses and have done a wonderful job of responding to one another. The dialogue has been lively and definitely interesting!

Leo, thanks for usually being first out of the box with beautifully thought-out and written responses to the cases. I continue to appreciate your ability to think in metaphor and your ability to weave that in as appropriate.

Mike, thanks for your sense of humor, responsiveness to your team-mates, and wonderful ability to think critically and to analyze material. I enjoyed working with you for yet another term!

Jane, it was a pleasure meeting you this term! I appreciate your critical thinking skills, your warmth, your willingness to engage in dialogue and to pursue points that needed pursuing! Your papers were always well written and thought-provoking—looked forward to reading them!

Liz, I enjoyed working with you in another context! It was great to see your confidence grow this term and to see your willingness to offer another viewpoint that might not agree with the others. Good for you! Don't lose that courage!

Lynn, Again, a pleasure to work with you! I enjoy your sense of humor immensely! Coupled with it is your ability to think deeply and critically and to respond in a creative and sound way to the material we've discussed.

I also want to express my appreciation to all of you for hanging in and renegotiating the course design when it looked like it wasn't working. It is always difficult as an instructor to take over somebody else's course and to try to get into their logic of design and material. All of you helped me do that and I thank you! *Rena*

Hi everyone, Thanks for your assessment of everyone Rena. We think the same pleasant thoughts about you too! The following are my ending thoughts on our learning experience. Thanks again everyone for your sharing, caring, and insights! Virtual Leadership was the name of the course but we really covered the gambit, didn't we? I believe what we learned followed a natural progression for subject matter that broke new ground for all of us. In an effort to learn how to lead in a virtual environment we first had to understand the idiosyncrasies of that environment. Going back through some of our postings it seems that all of us at one time or another referred to a self-revelation that opened our eyes to both the similarities and the differences found between our normal work environments and our virtual environments. . . . I appreciate the idea of learning how to be more flexible and adaptable by understanding our strengths and being aware of our weaknesses. I do believe that all of us are very optimistic concerning the relationships and level of friendships that can be created and fostered within the virtual environment. I think in our organizations that we need all the help we can get in evolving a friendlier and a happier work environment. Maybe this medium offers an aspect that can propagate the idea of improved and enhanced social connections and interactions. . . . Even more than leading though, are the aspects of all of us "being" a part of this environment and the recognition of our own "doing" as we participate within this environment. What then is this virtual environment and what of those relationships created from within? Turkle (1995, 269) suggests that, "The imperative to self-knowledge has always been at the heart of philosophical inquiry." And "we work to know ourselves in order to improve not only our own lives, but those of our families and society." Rena and group thanks for another great learning experience! *Mike*

Mike's assessment of his learning experience demonstrates not only that the learning objectives for this course were met, but that transformative learning occurred for him. Others in the group shared similar observations and reflections, indicating that the course was a successful learning experience for them and that they felt they had created an effective learning community.

I wanted to take another opportunity to thank each of you for your participation in this course. I remember when I first joined the program . . . [other students] talked about the importance their colleagues played in their success in the program. I had no idea of the significance of those statements, or the degree to which they were true, until I experienced it for myself. Thank you all for this tremendous contribution to my development. Take care, colleagues. May our paths cross again. I thank you all for your participation and commitment to our group this term. *Jane*

The ending reflections shared by this group of students are what we hope to see. They are an indication that the planning and delivery of the course was effective in moving students not only toward their learning objectives but also toward what we view as real learning.

The end of a course is also the time to communicate grades to students, although it is preferable for students to have a sense of how they have been doing throughout the course. Many courseware packages now allow for the use of a gradebook on the course site. The gradebook is a private way of communicating progress to a student during and at the end of a course. Any exams, quizzes, or grades on papers can be recorded in the online gradebook by the instructor. The instructor has the ability to see the grades for all students in the class. But the student can only see his or her own grades when accessing the gradebook on the course site. When a gradebook is not used, progress and grades can be communicated via e-mail. Regardless of how the communication of grades occurs, it should be private between the instructor and the student. Grades should not be posted publicly on the course site.

In this chapter, we have reviewed and described with course examples ways in which to take an existing course and move it to the online environment. A growing phenomenon among institutions, however, is to hire faculty to develop courses that other faculty will teach or to purchase already-developed courses for the same purpose. In the next chapter, we will examine this phenomenon in more detail and suggest ways in which instructors who are charged with delivering courses they have not developed can do so effectively.

Tips for Successfully Moving a Course from the Classroom to Cyberspace

- Develop as comprehensive a picture as possible of the students who will be enrolling in the class.
- Begin with the end in mind by developing learning objectives first.
- Determine the best fit between the course and the degree to which technology and online delivery will be used.
- Develop a good set of initial guidelines to create a container in which all participants can interact.
- Include collaborative learning assignments, the ability for students to interact on a personal level, and other means for developing a learning community.
- Give as much control of the learning process as possible to the learners themselves. Be creative in developing means by which content can be delivered without the use of lectures.
- Provide clear expectations for performance in the course, including how assignments will be evaluated, the degree to which participation will be evaluated, how attendance will be taken, and how overall evaluation of student performance will be conducted.

CHAPTER SIX

TEACHING COURSES DEVELOPED BY OTHERS

An increasing phenomenon in online distance learning is faculty being asked to deliver a course they did not develop or design. There are several reasons for this trend, but the main one is that institutions are discovering that creating an effective online course requires more than just transferring classroom materials to the web. Creating online courses that are high quality and promote the achievement of learning outcomes is time-consuming and expensive. Many instructors on campuses today do not have the time or expertise to develop a good online course, even with the help of a course authoring package such as WebCT™ or CourseInfo™. Some institutions are offering training and incentives for instructors to develop courses. However, once the course is developed, the faculty member who designed it may not be the one to teach it.

Instructors are teaching courses designed by others for a number of reasons:

- A faculty member may be asked to develop a course for online use and then leave the institution. Another faculty member may then be asked to take over the course and teach it as it has been created.
- Institutions are hiring faculty as content experts specifically to design—but not deliver—online courses. This may be done to create a uniform look and feel to all courses delivered by the institution or in order to save money on costly course development time.

- Institutions are purchasing or licensing courses from another organization whose business it is to develop courses for online use.
- Instructors are opting to use electronic textbooks, which provide text material, exercises, quizzes, a gradebook, and the ability to hold discussions on a website that belongs to the publisher.
- Some institutions are contracting with organizations that specialize in what are termed "total solutions," where faculty submit material to the company to be converted into an online course. The course is then installed on that company's server and can be used by other instructors from the academic institution.

Regardless of how the course is created, many instructors now find themselves being asked to deliver such a course to students. The issues that emerge for these instructors include how to build community into the process as well as how to add material that they deem to be important and work with material they consider unimportant.

In this chapter, we will explore these issues and make concrete suggestions about how instructors might work with and personalize the material. In addition, we will consider ways to evaluate good course material and packages. We will present course material developed by Quisic (formerly known as University Access), an organization devoted to the development and licensing of business courses for use in schools of business. We chose material developed by Quisic because it offers the flexibility that we feel is important when working with a course developed by another entity. The courses allow instructors to:

- Use the material they feel is most important
- Omit material they feel is unnecessary
- Include collaborative activities
- Promote interactivity and community-building

A Focus on Content

Often when an online class is developed by an instructor who will not be teaching the course, the focus is on content rather than on pedagogical process. We have made the case that teaching online requires another form of pedagogy, one that is more focused on the facilitation of a collaborative process than on the delivery of content. Thus, simply hiring a content expert to develop a course will not address the issues involved with online teaching. Pairing the content expert with an instructional designer, who understands electronic pedagogy and can assist in the course development process by asking questions that are central to good course design, can help to alleviate the problem. An instructional designer might move the subject expert away from a focus on content by asking how to achieve learning outcomes for the course. In other words, what exercises, readings, case studies, and so on, would be useful to students in gaining an understanding of the material being studied? If the content expert can be coached to focus on ways to apply the material online, then he or she is more likely to develop a course that can be transferred to another instructor.

Because many instructors do not receive training in electronic pedagogy, when they create an online course it may not be built with that form of pedagogy in mind. Furthermore, the receiving instructor is frequently not privy to the thought process and logic used to develop the course. In addition, the receiving instructor may not know how to deliver a course using methods appropriate to online teaching. Because the receiving instructor may not have online facilitation skills either, the importance of good training once again becomes an issue.

One of our former supervisors once remarked that a good instructor can teach almost anything if he or she has good preparation. Thus, a receiving instructor who is practiced in delivering an online course can make it work.

Parker Hudnut, formerly of Quisic, recently remarked that his experience has shown that a course can be beautifully constructed but if the instructor does not teach using techniques appropriate to the online classroom, the course experience will not be a good one for either the instructor or the students. Instructors can be given all the resources they need to teach the course, but a successful outcome comes down to the pedagogical approach they use.

Ability to Adjust the Course

The initial reaction of an instructor who is being asked to teach a class he or she did not create is often, "How much can I customize it?" Consequently, the most critical issue in the use of a course created by another instructor is the ability to adjust it. With an activity as new as customizing online courses, there are no commonly agreed-upon experts or guidelines to which an instructor might refer in customizing online courses. Furthermore, there is not yet a widely accepted standard for what constitutes a good online course. We have had success in using the framework we have developed in creating and delivering online courses. However, ours is not the only model. The central issue, then, in customizing an online course is knowing what is involved with its successful facilitation and what elements should be considered when revising and adapting it. Adjustment, therefore, may take the form of adding discussion forums for the purpose of building community. The receiving instructor may decide that some material included when the course was developed is unnecessary, or he or she may choose to add more collaborative activities or change the suggested assignments for the course.

We recently had the opportunity to talk to an instructor who teaches science and whose institution had purchased an online science course that he was asked to teach. His first reaction to the course was to express dismay that there were no labs. The first adjustment he made was to add labs by asking students to conduct simple lab projects at home and report the results, make arrangements to visit the science labs at a local university to conduct some of their work, or come to campus to complete lab assignments. The lab work he assigned was simple enough that students could complete it on their own, but it added a practical element to the class that assisted with the achievement of learning outcomes.

The need for adjustment may not be initially apparent to the receiving instructor. Therefore, the ability to make adjustments as the course progresses is also critical to successful delivery. An important consideration, then, is the flexibility of the software in use. Does it allow for the insertion of topics not originally included in the course? Can topics easily be deleted? Can the discussion board be modified in any way? The instructors who are teaching the course must also have enough knowledge of the software to be able to make these changes should they so desire, or have support staff available who can assist with this. Many courseware applications allow for changes submitted in text or HTML (hypertext markup language) and most word processing software programs now allow for the conversion of text files into HTML, making it relatively easy for instructors to make the changes they wish to make. Consequently, training the instructors may be as simple as teaching them how to upload HTML files into the courseware. This type of flexibility in the courseware allows instructors to adapt the course in whatever way they see fit, and makes the use of another instructor's course more manageable.

Examples of Customization

One of us was asked to teach a course created by another instructor when that instructor chose to leave the institution two weeks before the start of the term. Students were already enrolled and had received copies of the syllabus, and books had been purchased. The course site had not yet been established, however, allowing for a significant degree of customization in the delivery of the material. The possibility of adding reading material in the form of journal articles and book chapters also existed. However, the department chair asked that all else remain the same if at all possible, including the topics to be discussed.

At first, the task appeared relatively easy because delivery could be altered to fit the instructor's usual teaching style. However, after reviewing the assigned readings, course assignments, and topics for discussion, the instructor found the course to be somewhat confusing, and it did not cover many topics that would have been included had he or she created it. The task, then, became how to include relevant readings and topics without confusing students in the process. But the course design as it was originally configured proved confusing for the students. They were asked to work with a case study every week, and in addition, to respond to a set of discussion questions. Having two types of collaborative assignments weekly was burdensome, and the students kept asking which set of questions they should focus on—the ones included in the case study or the separate discussion questions based on the readings—because the questions focused on related issues. Around the third week of the course, students asked that the course design be reconsidered. This request from the students actually came as a relief to the instructor. It then became necessary to renegotiate the way in which students were proceeding, and it was decided that they would prepare and respond only to case studies that they themselves developed. Once that adjustment was made, the course proceeded smoothly.

Working with a course created by someone else offers additional challenges as well. But if it is constructed with customization in mind and if training is provided to the instructor, then the challenge is lessened and the instructor can focus on delivering a course more in line with his or her own style of teaching. The following are some pages from courses developed by Quisic that help to illustrate this point. We also had the opportunity to talk with two instructors who delivered Quisic courses about their experience. Following presentation of the exhibits, we will review what they told us.

First, Exhibit 6.1 shows the course index for a course in macroeconomics as it is delivered to the instructor. The instructor is able to choose, through a course building tool, which lessons he or she feels should be presented to students by inserting the lesson into the course. Likewise, if an instructor feels a lesson is unnecessary, that lesson can either be removed or made unavailable to students.

Instructors delivering a Quisic course can also build their own quizzes through a quiz editing function. Exhibit 6.2 shows the quiz building function. Instructors can remove or reorder questions, choose to use the quiz associated with a particular lesson, or omit the quiz altogether.

Exhibits 6.3 and 6.4 show the results of the course building process. The first exhibit is a lesson in accounting and the second an interactive quiz exercise in macroeconomics; both are shown as a student would see them.

Once a course is delivered to instructors, they are invited to participate in an eight- to ten-hour online training course (that is, approximately two weeks) designed to help them navigate and teach an online course. They are taught techniques for customizing and there is also a focus on pedagogy. Both of the instructors we interviewed participated in the online training course and found it to

EXHIBIT 6.1. COURSE BUILDER.

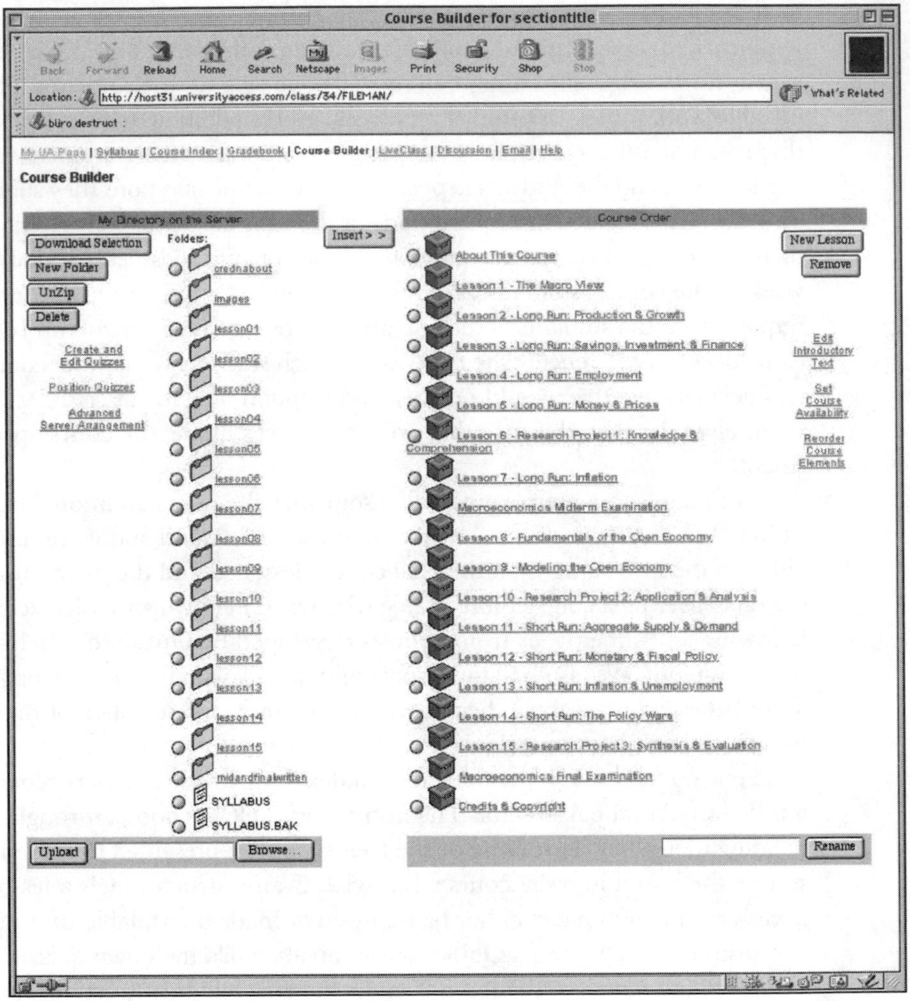

EXHIBIT 6.2. QUIZ BUILDER.

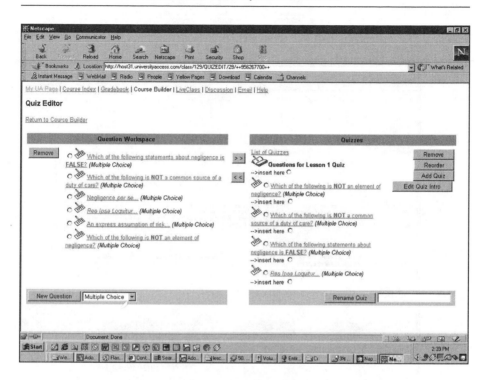

be extremely helpful. One felt that it gave her a good start and enough confidence to continue learning through trial and error.

The instructors also customized the courses they taught—one in macroeconomics and one in business communication—by adding assignments to those provided, modifying quizzes, and adding some of their own content. They felt that this was easy to do with the format they had been provided and that using a predesigned course did not inhibit them in any way from addressing what they saw as the learning needs of their students. One instructor commented that she felt it was an advantage to have already-prepared online course materials for her first online course experience.

When Customizing Is Not Possible

What happens, however, when an instructor is unable to customize a course to any significant degree? There are many times when an institution will ask an instructor to teach the course "as is," at least the first time it is offered. The request to do

EXHIBIT 6.3. SAMPLE STUDENT LESSON.

Netscape: University Access – Principles of Accounting I – Summary

Back | Forward | Reload | Home | Search | Netscape | Images | Print | Security | Shop | Stop

Location: http://host31.universityaccess.com/class/103/Lesson02/02_06sa.htm?++950113783++   What's Related

büro destruct :

My UA Page | Course Index | Gradebook | Course Builder | Edit Page | LiveClass | Discussion | Email | Help

Previous | Next | Lesson Contents

PRINCIPLES OF
Accounting I
Double-Entry System of Accounting

The Schedule of Accounts

The fact that increases in assets are entered on the debit side and decreases are recorded on the credit side is based on accounting convention and has become the standard practice. Once the rule for how debits and credits affect assets is established, it follows that the effect of debits and credits on liabilities and owner's equity is the opposite. This is because liabilities and owner's equity are on the opposite side of the equal sign in the basic accounting equation.

Directions

Click on the START button to listen to an explanation of how debits and credits effect different accounts and to learn how the double-entry system of accounting effects the basic accounting equation.

Start   **The Schedule of Accounts**

Assets		=	Liabilities		+	Owner's Equity	
DR	CR		DR	CR		DR	CR
+	-		-	+		-	+
						Drawing	Capital (Add'l Inv's)
						+	+
						Expenses	Revenues
						+	+

Transcripts

Previous | Next | Lesson Contents

UA Web Course

EXHIBIT 6.4. SAMPLE STUDENT EXERCISE.

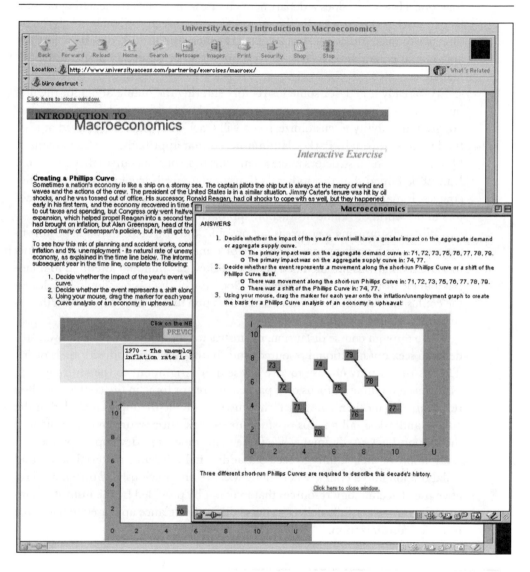

University Access | Introduction to Macroeconomics

Back Forward Reload Home Search Netscape Images Print Security Shop Stop

Location: http://www.universityaccess.com/partnering/exercises/macroex/   What's Related

büro destruct :

Click here to close window.

INTRODUCTION TO
Macroeconomics

Interactive Exercise

Creating a Phillips Curve
Sometimes a nation's economy is like a ship on a stormy sea. The captain pilots the ship but is always at the mercy of wind and waves and the actions of the crew. The president of the United States is in a similar situation. Jimmy Carter's tenure was hit by oil shocks, and he was tossed out of office. His successor, Ronald Reagan, had oil shocks to cope with as well, but they happened early in his first term, and the economy recovered in time for him to cut taxes and spending, but Congress only went halfway expansion, which helped propel Reagan into a second term had brought on inflation, but Alan Greenspan, head of the opposed many of Greenspan's policies, but he still got to

To see how this mix of planning and accident works, consi inflation and 5% unemployment - its natural rate of unemp economy, as explained in the time line below. The informa subsequent year in the time line, complete the following:

1. Decide whether the impact of the year's event will curve.
2. Decide whether the event represents a shift alon
3. Using your mouse, drag the marker for each year Curve analysis of an economy in upheaval.

Click on the NE
PREVIO

1970 - The unemploy
inflation rate is

Macroeconomics

ANSWERS

1. Decide whether the impact of the year's event will have a greater impact on the aggregate demand or aggregate supply curve.
    o The primary impact was on the aggregate demand curve in: 71, 72, 73, 75, 76, 77, 78, 79.
    o The primary impact was on the aggregate supply curve in: 74, 77.
2. Decide whether the event represents a movement along the short-run Phillips Curve or a shift of the Phillips Curve itself.
    o There was movement along the short-run Phillips Curve in: 71, 72, 73, 75, 76, 77, 78, 79.
    o There was a shift of the Phillips Curve in: 74, 77.
3. Using your mouse, drag the marker for each year onto the inflation/unemployment graph to create the basis for a Phillips Curve analysis of an economy in upheaval:

Three different short-run Phillips Curves are required to describe this decade's history.

Click here to close window.

so raises some important questions: Is this a violation of the instructor's academic freedom? How often does a department chair ask an instructor teaching face-to-face to teach a class in exactly the same way it was taught by someone else? The directive to make no changes in a course is generally considered to be objectionable in academia. Nevertheless, it is a request that is frequently made in the online arena.

As already noted, for some instructors entering the online arena for the first time it can be a relief to receive a course that is already developed. Even when they are given the ability to customize, some will teach the course as received at least the first time through. Parker Hudnut noted that approximately 60 percent of Quisic's receiving instructors make no modification of the courses they are given. It must be hoped that this indicates that they are well-developed, high-quality courses. It may also indicate, however, the tentativeness with which new instructors in the world of online instruction approach their first experiences.

When customizing a course is not possible, the instructor may still be able to use discussion boards or make good use of e-mail. Both can help point students to material that was not included or suggest they pay minimal attention to material that the instructor feels is irrelevant. Good use of discussion should help lessen the confusion while moving students in a direction that is more in line with the instructor's orientation.

Also through course discussion, the instructor should be able to empower students to seek out additional resources and share what they find with their peers. The instructor may choose to give a research assignment to the entire group, asking each member to focus on a particular area or topic in the course and then report to one another. Another technique is to divide the topics included in the course and ask small groups of students to seek out resources on a topic and then report back. Assignments like these help students to develop their research skills, improve their ability to seek out additional reference material, and build collaboration into a course where none was present previously. If they make creative use of technology resources that may not be provided by the institution, instructors can successfully deliver a course that at first glance appeared to have little room for customization.

Building Community into the Process

A more critical factor in teaching a course that another instructor has created is building community during the process of delivering the course. Because most courses developed by another instructor or entity focus on content rather than process, the development of a learning community is often neglected. Yet as we have consistently stated, it is a key component in the successful achievement of learning outcomes. How, then, can an instructor build a learning community into a course from which it is absent?

By using discussion boards in the course, or even using e-mail if necessary, the instructor can encourage students to begin communicating with one another on a personal level. For example, the instructor may ask all the students to create an e-mail list for the class in their electronic address books and use that list to share introductions, reflections on the readings, resources they might find on the Internet, and so on.

An instructor contacted us because she had been asked to teach her first online course using a website on which another instructor had placed course content. She had no ability to create a discussion board associated with the course or to customize it in any way. She decided, after talking to us, not only to use e-mail in the way we just described but also to create subgroups of students for the purpose of collaboratively working with case study material. Although she found this approach cumbersome and a bit primitive, she was able to create a more collaborative approach to the course and received feedback from students that the outcome was successful. Based on that first experience, she has since requested her institution to allow her to make significant changes in the way in which the course is constructed using a different course authoring software package so that collaboration and discussion can be built into the course site.

Evaluating a Course Developed by Another

An important focus of research on online courses is an attempt to create a list of quality benchmarks by which to measure them. Toward this end, the Institute for Higher Education Policy recently released a list of twenty-four quality assurance benchmarks for online education. Funded by the National Education Association and Blackboard, Inc. and authored by Jamie Merisotis (2000), the list is the result of a survey of six academic institutions with significant experience in online education. Although the quality assurance benchmarks cover all aspects of online education, a number of them pertain specifically to course development and delivery. Quality benchmarks would be important when deciding whether to adopt a course developed by another entity. However, in and of themselves, benchmarks mean nothing; they must be couched within a good planning process for an overall institutional online program. The benchmarks related to online course development and teaching and learning make common sense and reflect the practices we have been promoting. They include the following:

- Learning outcomes, not the availability of existing technology, determine the technology being used to deliver course content.

- Instructional materials are reviewed periodically to ensure they meet [institutional] program standards.
- Courses are designed to require students to engage themselves in analysis, synthesis, and evaluation as part of their course and program requirements.
- Student interaction with faculty and other students is an essential characteristic and is facilitated through a variety of ways, including voice mail or e-mail.
- Feedback to student assignments and questions is constructive and provided in a timely manner.
- Students are instructed in the proper methods of effective research, including assessment of the validity of resources.
- Students are provided with supplemental course information that outlines course objectives, concepts, and ideas, and learning outcomes for each course are summarized in a clearly written, straightforward statement.
- The program's educational effectiveness and teaching-learning process are assessed through an evaluation process that uses several methods and applies specific standards.
- Intended learning outcomes are reviewed regularly to ensure clarity, utility, and appropriateness [Merisotis, 2000, pp. 2–3].

It is important to note that all of the quality benchmarks related to course development and delivery have little to do with content. Instead, the benchmarks focus on constructing the course in a way that facilitates good delivery—in other words, on the process of online teaching and learning. Consequently, when evaluating a course for possible adoption, institutions and faculty should be concerned first and foremost with how well the process of the course will assist students in meeting learning objectives. Although both content and process can be customized, if the basic structure of the course allows for an interactive, learner-focused delivery process, it will provide a solid foundation on which to customize content.

Issues of Intellectual Property

Intellectual property issues, or the debate about who owns online courses, have been getting increasing attention as the phenomenon of online learning grows. This is particularly so when institutions ask faculty to develop and teach a course online for the first time but then switch the teaching responsibility to another member of the faculty, or when they adopt courses developed by other entities that they then modify. Intellectual property issues do not belong entirely in the realm of administrators and their lawyers. Faculty also need to be concerned with the ownership of intellectual property, and as they create courses for online delivery, with a number of other questions, including these:

- Is there an agreement in place between faculty and administrators that spells out who owns courses housed on the university's server?
- If one faculty member develops a course that another member of the faculty teaches, is there a provision for royalties or has the developing faculty member been adequately compensated for "work for hire?"
- Do faculty members own the courses they develop and can they use those courses in other ways, such as teaching them at other institutions, placing them on their own private websites, or selling them to a private entity for delivery elsewhere?
- If the institution has an agreement with a course developer and a member of the faculty is asked to submit course material to be placed on that company's website, does the faculty member still own the course material?
- If the faculty member leaves the institution, does the course he or she has developed go along or does it remain on the institution's server and become the property of the institution?

Unfortunately, at this point in time there are no hard-and-fast answers to any of these questions. Nor are these questions applicable to the face-to-face classroom. The American Association of University Professors issued a statement regarding distance education and intellectual property in its May-June 1999 issue of *Academe*. It noted that online education "invariably presents administrative, technical, and legal problems usually not encountered in the traditional classroom setting" (p. 41), which result in difficult issues of ownership of materials designed for distance education.

The issue, then, is that faculty need to be aware of and ask the questions presented here as they move forward with course development, rather than move blindly into uncharted territory. It is dangerous to assume that intellectual property issues will not apply to the work being created or modified. Consequently, faculty and their institutions need to come to an agreement about how courses will be used, and most importantly, who owns them.

Final Thoughts on Teaching a Course Developed by Another

Our discussion of the use of courses developed by another entity or faculty member is not intended to suggest that the practice be inhibited, but rather that good planning is needed when moving in this direction. Given the amount of time for training, development, and support that is needed to develop a new course, the use of predeveloped courses can be cost-effective. Building an online course is similar to writing a textbook and developing associated learning materials—it is a process that takes a tremendous amount of time and energy.

When predeveloped courses are well designed and focus on the process of delivering the material rather than the content, they can be a high-quality means of moving into the online arena. As with any other online course, however, the focus must remain on faculty and student training in order to be able to move through the course successfully and give support when problems occur. Purchasing courses does not relieve the institution of its obligation to provide a strong infrastructure for its online program.

With these thoughts in mind, we now turn our attention to the learner, who should be the central focus of all online efforts. In the next chapter, we will explore the roles of the learner in the online learning process as well as what learners need in order to become successful online students.

Tips for Successfully Teaching a Class Developed by Another

- Evaluate the material in the course to determine its relevance for students. Do make modifications as needed. Add material through readings, Internet research, lab assignments, fieldwork, or any other creative means in order to customize the course if so desired.
- If the original course includes little or no interactivity, add a means by which interactivity between students can be enhanced—through the use of discussion boards or e-mail lists, for example.
- If the original course includes little or no interactivity, add a means by which students can collaborate with one another through assignments and discussions.
- Facilitate the building of community among the students by encouraging personal interaction such as sharing introductions and by creating a social space either on the course site or through the use of e-mail.
- Get training in online teaching and ask for help when necessary. Don't feel you need to just "muddle through."
- When developing a course that another faculty member is likely to teach, ask questions about intellectual property and the ongoing use of the course.

CHAPTER SEVEN

WORKING WITH THE VIRTUAL STUDENT

Successful learners in the online environment need to be active, creative, and engaged in the learning process. In other words, they need to be "noisy learners" (Nipper, 1989), or learners who are visibly engaged with one another and with the generation of knowledge. Some students who are not noisy learners in the face-to-face classroom can flourish online because they have the luxury of time for reflection and response and do not have to compete with more extroverted students in order to be heard. However, it cannot be assumed that students will engage with one another in the learning process; this must be taught. Preparing students to enter online distance learning courses will be the focus of this chapter.

If We Build It, They Will Come

As academic institutions rush headlong into online distance learning, at least two key assumptions are being made. It is assumed both that teachers will know how to teach in the online environment and that students will instinctively know how to manage the learning process. Our experience in teaching online courses and in consulting with faculty, faculty developers, and administrators across the United States is that the opposite is true. Faculty need training and assistance in making the transition to the online environment, and students also need to be taught how to learn online. Learning through the use of technology takes more than mastering a software program or feeling comfortable with the hardware being used. Students in online learning situations need to come to an awareness that learning through the use of technology significantly affects the learning process itself. Furthermore, they need to realize that the online learning process occurs, for the most part, through the formation of a learning community and is reflective in nature.

Students may enter an online course expecting to be educated by a content expert, just as in a traditional classroom. When they discover that the most profound learning in an online course comes through interacting with other students, they may become confused and sometimes feel "cheated" by the process. Our culture has led students to believe that education happens through exposure to "the sage on the stage," as many might describe the traditional academic. In the online environment, in contrast, the instructor acts as a facilitator, or a "guide on the side," enabling students to learn collaboratively from one another. For many students, this is a significant shift, and one for which they need to be adequately prepared.

As we consider the collaborative learning process that occurs online, some questions emerge. What are the characteristics of the successful learner in the online environment? What is the role of the learner? How do instructors facilitate online courses in order to maximize the potential of the online learner? And finally, how can instructors teach their students to use the online environment effectively for learning? We will explore each of these questions in an attempt to provide instructors with ideas and suggestions to assist them in working more effectively with the virtual student.

The Successful Learner in the Online Classroom

Some students take to the online classroom easily and successfully. For others, it is a struggle. Some students feel that the online classroom more closely supports their learning style than the face-to-face classroom, particularly if they need time to think and reflect before responding to questions and ideas. Some may find that they express themselves more effectively in writing than verbally. For them, the online environment, because it is text-based, may be more appropriate too. The following are comments by two students addressing this issue:

I am . . . fairly introverted, and I find that I spend a good deal of face-to-face meetings as a listener. In virtual discussions, however, listening is implicit, and all contributions to such discussions are extroverted by definition. Thus, I appear more extroverted than I actually am. I am also more comfortable expressing myself in writing than in speech. *Liane*

I, too, am an introvert so I am not able to speak up for the "extrovert" perspective of this. However, my experience in virtual medium is very similar to yours. I am much more "outspoken" through the written word than through speaking. In part, I think this has to do with my more reflective nature. Written communication provides me with the opportunity to reflect, collect my thoughts and respond before the topic has changed like it often does in face-to-face communications. *Jane*

Much of the research done on successful students in distance education programs suggests that students who are attracted to this form of education share certain characteristics, including that they are voluntarily seeking further education, are motivated, have higher expectations, and are more self-disciplined. They tend to be older than the average student and to have a more serious attitude toward their courses, education, and learning. They are what most would consider to be nontraditional students. We have found, however, that this description does not and should not exclude traditional undergraduate students, particularly when we realize that few of today's undergraduates can truly be considered traditional. It is estimated that only one-fourth of our undergraduate population is made up of eighteen- to twenty-two-year-olds who are attending school full-time and living on campus. Most of our students today are older, are working, and need more flexible schedules. They are not necessarily looking for campus-based educational and social opportunities. Consequently, they bring with them a different set of assets and expectations to the learning process.

Several attributes make a student successful online when he may not blossom in the face-to-face classroom. There are also means by which instructors can enable these attributes to emerge. The successful online student tends to enjoy learning for learning's sake. He or she becomes energized by the ability to be set free to explore a topic with peers. Successful online students demonstrate good thinking skills, an ability to work and do some amount of research independently, and an ability to work with a minimal amount of structure.

In general, distance education has been applied to and seen as most successful in the arena of adult and continuing education. However, more universities are using this delivery method with all groups of students regardless of age or level of educational experience. Our own experience with younger undergraduate students has shown us that the students in that age-group who do well online are looking for more flexibility in their busy schedules, are more independent than the average undergraduate, and may feel lost in large face-to-face classes. The online classroom allows them to express themselves in ways that the traditional classroom does not.

In our experience, computer-mediated distance education can successfully draw out a student who would not be considered a noisy learner in the traditional classroom. It can provide an educational experience that helps to motivate students who appear unmotivated in another setting, because they are quieter than their peers and less likely to enter into a discussion in the classroom. We are also discovering, however, that the interactive skills learned in the online environment can be carried over to the face-to-face setting. In other words, once students are acknowledged for their contributions to the class, their thinking skills, and their ability to interact, they gain confidence in their ability and tend to use these newly discovered skills in other settings. A student recently enrolled in one of our online classes makes this point by stating:

I have found through the learning environment that I have somewhat changed personally and continue to develop another side of myself. Most explicitly, confidence continues to develop within. Also, because I am more of an introvert, I tend to be more direct with my staff and peers. Yet, as I communicate online, I don't have to worry and do find myself toning down at work. I am not as impulsive and I tend to think more before I speak. *Liz*

The online classroom can provide an alternative that may be quite useful for some students. However, all students must not be forced into the online classroom because it is not effective for all. Understanding different learning styles can help illustrate why that is the case.

Addressing Different Learning Styles

Litzinger and Osif (1993) define learning styles as the ways in which children and adults think and learn. They break down thinking and learning processes into *cognition,* or the ways in which people acquire knowledge; *conceptualization,* or the ways in which people process information; and *motivation,* which includes decision-making styles, values, and emotional preferences.

A number of authors have attempted to further categorize the ranges of learning styles people possess based on the basic processes. Probably the best known is Kolb (1984), who determined that there are four predominant learning styles. *Convergers* like to reach closure quickly by finding concrete solutions to problems and making decisions; *divergers* have an awareness of meaning and values and enjoy brainstorming and imagining alternative solutions; *assimilators* like to take in lots of information and build theoretical models based on that information; and *accommodators* are more action-oriented, taking risks and teaching themselves through trial and error.

Although from our description thus far it may appear that accommodators are most suited to the online classroom environment, the reality is that all learning styles can work well there. Kolb described a cycle of learning that begins with one's own experience, followed by observation and reflection on that experience, leading to the formation of abstract concepts and generalizations, which leads to the development of hypotheses to be tested in future action, leading to new experiences. Everyone develops a learning style that has some strong and weak points. For example, a person might jump into new experiences without taking the time to reflect on the lessons to be learned from those experiences. Because all students move through this cycle in the learning process and embrace parts of it to a greater or lesser extent, all learning styles can be adequately accommodated online. Creating learning experiences that allow students to experience all portions of the learning cycle enables them to develop more fully in areas where they might be weak, and thus develop a new learning style. Knowledge generation through interaction with peers plus the development of a more reflective approach to learning as influenced by the use of technology further influences this process. Figure 7.1 illustrates this concept. The result of the process is a more reflective style indicating that the transformative nature of online learning has taken hold. We thus refer to this new learning style as *reflective transformative*.

   To complicate the understanding of learning styles further, it has been theorized that people tend to learn predominantly through one of their senses; that is, they are auditory, visual, or tactile (Barsch, 1980). Auditory learners tend to retain more of what they hear, visual learners tend to retain more of what they see or

Figure 7.1. Different Learning Styles and Online Learning.

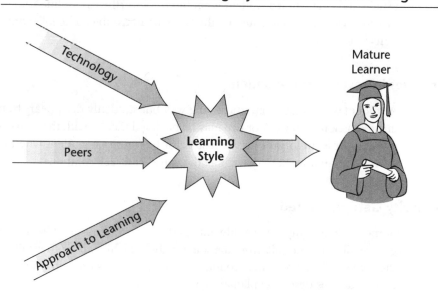

read, and tactile learners tend to retain more when they are using their sense of touch—when taking notes, for example. Many published articles seem to indicate that in order to accommodate various learning styles in the online classroom, various forms of technology must be used. But an online course that uses different types of assignments and approaches to learning can accomplish the same objective without using more complex technologies, such as audio or video. For example, in addition to asking students to read and engage in discussion online, if instructors use simulations, case studies, Internet research, and collaborative group experiences they help broaden the learning experience and accommodate various learning styles. Because it is difficult for an instructor to know the learning styles of his or her students in advance, creating a course that is varied in its approaches can help to motivate all students and keep them involved.

Recognizing and Working with Those Who Do Not Succeed

Should we expect all students to succeed in this environment? Although a student who might not be successful in the face-to-face classroom may do well online, it is unrealistic to expect that all will do well in this environment, just as all faculty will not be able to adapt their teaching styles to fit the medium. How does an instructor determine when a student is not doing well in the online classroom? This is a more difficult question to answer when the instructor cannot see the nonverbal cues that usually indicate when a student is confused. Nevertheless, online students do still provide evidence to indicate that they may be in trouble. The following are some signs to look for.

Changes in Level of Participation

A student who had been participating well but suddenly disappears from the online discussion for a week or two may be having difficulty with the course or course material. It is important for the instructor to contact a student who drops away for more than a week to determine the cause and seek solutions.

Difficulty Getting Started

Some students simply have difficulty getting started online. The instructor may get e-mail or phone calls from the student about technical or other difficulties with the course. The student may continue to express confusion with course procedures and guidelines despite explanation by the instructor.

Flaming

When students are frustrated or confused, they may inappropriately express these emotions by lashing out on the course site. The instructor needs to respond quickly to an outburst online, just as he or she would do in the face-to-face classroom. We will return to the topic of dealing with disruptive behavior in the next chapter.

Dominating the Discussion in Inappropriate Ways

Some students will attempt to dominate the discussion, moving it to personal or other concerns that have little to do with course material. Again, as in the face-to-face classroom, the instructor should attempt to work with the student on an individual basis to redirect this behavior.

When students do not do well online, as evidenced by any of these behaviors, they should be given the option to return to the face-to-face classroom. Their performance should not be considered a failure, but simply a poor fit or perhaps an indication of a different learning style or preference. Not all students do well online and may simply need more structure and face-to-face contact with an instructor and other students in order to succeed. Once again, this approach to participation problems differs significantly from the traditional way in which these issues might be resolved. In the traditional academic setting, a student might be asked to drop a course or transfer to another section. Flexibility in moving that student to a completely different learning environment simply did not exist until the advent of online instruction. Consequently, the online environment provides the instructor with a new means by which to assess and work with student capabilities, learning preferences, and performance.

The Role of the Learner in the Online Learning Process

One of the hallmarks of the online classroom, and one that differentiates it from face-to-face learning, is the need for students to take responsibility for their learning process. In so doing, students play various roles and take on various functions. All the roles are very much intertwined and interdependent. They are knowledge generation, collaboration, and process management.

Knowledge Generation

The instructor in the online classroom serves only as a gentle guide in the educational process. Consequently, the "recipient" of that guidance, the learner, has a responsibility to use that guidance in a meaningful way. Learners in the online classroom are responsible for going beyond a summary of reading or information contained in the subject area under study to analyze the material critically and present it to their peers and the instructor in ways that demonstrate critical thinking, analytic, and research skills. Thus, the learners in the online classroom are together developing original thought and realizing the preferred learning outcome: the construction of their own knowledge and meaning. Students may express their thoughts tentatively at the beginning of a course, as the following student post illustrates, and should become more assertive as a course progresses.

This assignment has me baffled and I hope that you can help me. I have not enjoyed the readings by Negroponte and haven't been able to tie in his readings with this assignment. I then began the readings by author Jackie Kostner and found her readings notably enjoyable and easier to tie in to this assignment. I am somewhat baffled because I don't quite know what the realm of virtual media is. I picture virtual media as a form of electronic communication through computers. Do I have a limited perception? *Liz*

Liz was tentatively expressing an opinion that was different from that of her peers. The response she received from them was warm and supportive, encouraging her to become more confident in her opinions as the term progressed.

The following post, which appeared toward the end of a different course, illustrates the level of assertiveness that students can attain. Although it may be difficult for some to read, it illustrates the level of comfort in a learning community that this student was experiencing. He knew, because of the interaction with his peers, that his post would be received in the spirit with which it had been created. Steve did not post this material in an attempt to upset his colleagues. Instead, he demonstrated a willingness to question long-held beliefs and go beyond assigned course material to analyze information and present an opposing viewpoint. This post is also not atypical of those that an instructor might see in an online course, because the relative anonymity of the medium allows students the freedom to express what they might not in a face-to-face setting.

NOW's (The National Organization of Women) slogan for breast cancer is "If breast cancer targeted men, emphasis on research leading to a potential cure would have taken on an added sense of urgency." The National Cancer Institute reports that there were 180,200 new cases of breast cancer in 1996/7; there were 334,500 new cases of prostrate cancer. In 1996/7 43,900 women and 290 men died from breast cancer. In that same period 41,800 men and 0 women died from prostrate cancer. The American Cancer Society estimates they will spend $12,547,500 on breast cancer research, $5,576,000 on prostrate cancer and $875,000 on testicular cancer in 1997. [I feel] the NOW slogan slanders men, accusing them of not caring about women where as in reality women receive the vast majority of benefits in our society especially in the important areas of emotional and psychological care. Take a look around you at JFK, who are the minorities? What group is the most under represented in psychotherapy, if you guessed men you guessed right! Think about it!!! *Steve*

Collaboration

Students in the online learning environment should not feel alone and isolated but instead that they are a part of a learning community that is working together to achieve learning outcomes and generate knowledge. The failing of many computer-mediated distance learning programs stems from the instructor's inability or unwillingness to facilitate a collaborative learning process. A recent study conducted by the Sloan Center for Asynchronous Learning Environments at the University of Illinois (Arvan and others, 1998) suggests that if the course material is simply placed on a website for students to access, the course will not provide increased contact with professors and peers or lead to better learning outcomes.

In the online environment, students should be expected to work together to generate deeper levels of understanding and critical evaluation of the material under study. They should also be expected to share the resources they are finding with the other members of the group. For example, an instructor might consider creating a space on the course site to house the material that the students are discovering. It might be called a "web-liography" or simply "resources." Providing assignments that encourage students to seek out additional resources is a good way to increase their research ability and knowledge of how to use the Internet as the vast source of information that it is. Some discussion of or information about search and research skills and techniques can be included on the course site to assist students in this process.

One joy we have found in working with faculty as they explore the medium is their discovery that the online classroom is the perfect environment in which to encourage collaborative learning. Including collaborative assignments in an online course helps facilitate the development of a learning community and enable achievement of the goal of generating new knowledge and deeper levels of meaning. The mistake that some instructors make is that, as a result of their excitement about collaboration, they may include too many collaborative assignments in a course. Students find collaborative work time-consuming as they strive to "meet" together in creative ways and negotiate the roles and tasks necessary to complete this kind of assignment. Consequently, an instructor should allow some "breathing room" between collaborative assignments. If a term is fifteen weeks long, then a maximum of three collaborative assignments might be about right. In an eleven-week quarter, one to two may be all there is time for.

Students should be encouraged to use creative means to communicate with one another while completing a collaborative assignment. They might use synchronous discussion, or chat, to work together on an assignment or to have a question-and-answer session with the instructor. They might be encouraged to make extensive use of e-mail, have a whiteboard session, or have a designated site in the course site for their discussions. The instructor should relinquish control over the learning process during the time when a collaborative assignment is in progress and not feel the need to be a part of all of the discussions that occur. Students should be empowered to get the job done and report results to the instructor and the rest of the online class.

In addition, students should be guided and encouraged to give one another meaningful feedback on their work. When a collaborative assignment has been completed, they should be encouraged to evaluate their own and their teammates' performance. Evaluations can be shared privately with the instructor so that students feel more comfortable completing them.

Another means by which to achieve collaboration is to have students post all written assignments to the course site and ask them to provide feedback to one another on that work. The feedback, however, needs to go beyond a pat on the back for good work done; instead, it should comment substantively on the ideas presented and question any gaps, omissions, or inconsistencies. Providing feedback to one another helps students develop the critical thinking skills necessary to engage effectively in their knowledge generation role.

One of the advantages to working over the Internet is that groups of students working together in a class do not need to be isolated. They can engage in dialogue *between* learning communities. By this we mean that instructors who are teaching like courses either in the same or different universities can encourage and even facilitate discussion between the participants in those classes. Instructors may even consider team-teaching through this approach. As students gain confidence and ease in their ability to study online, their interest can be stimulated in doing additional collaborative work. Students may connect, using the Internet, with experts in their field of study, other universities and learning communities, or discussion groups that have formed around interest in the area under study. As they do this, their ability to use these skills while working in other course areas also increases.

Process Management

Faculty members frequently ask us what the process manager's role looks like. It is the student role that most significantly sets this form of learning apart from the face-to-face classroom, and it is also the most difficult for many faculty to accept. Students as active learners are expected to participate with minimal guidelines and structure. We also expect them to interact with one another and take responsibility for the direction of their learning as well as the formation of the online learning community. In order for this to happen, the instructor must empower them and then step out of the way to allow them to do their jobs—much as a business manager would empower employees. All students have the ability to become process managers in an online course. The reality is that one or two of them will step up to this role. Once that happens, the other students in the group are likely to look to the student leaders to assist them in managing the learning process. Evidence that the process management function has emerged exists when one or two students begin to answer questions that might otherwise be directed to and answered by the instructor.

The instructor's response to the development of the process management role needs to be a willingness to leave behind the traditional power boundaries that exist between instructor and student. This medium has been described as the great equalizer—essentially eliminating the boundaries that exist between cultures, genders, ages—and also eliminating power differences between instructors and students. Greg Kearsley, in his "A Guide to Online Education" (1997), suggests that the discussions that occur in the online classroom are as free of sociocultural bias as is possible. In order to achieve this state, however, faculty must be able to relinquish their power over the educational process and let the learners take on their process management role. Clearly, instructors hold the extra edge in the process because they assign a grade for the course. However, in the area of process management, instructors can and should play an equal role. The following student's post illustrates her understanding of the process management role:

Virtual leaders have less managerial authority than face-to-face leaders. Earlier I wrote about the lack of control faced by virtual leaders and how it is best to embrace loss of control rather than fight it. I think that roles in virtual teams are also more flexibly defined. Authority can more easily be distributed in a virtual team. I think this flexibility results from the looser dynamic. When a leader is in a face-to-face meeting, subordinates expect the leader to assume an authoritative role throughout. In a virtual meeting, those expectations are less strong, because the leader's loss of physical control is a given. The virtual leader's power, so to speak, comes from her ability to keep the team connected, because that is essential to the team's success. The focus on connections is much more facilitative than managerial, I think. At least in the conventional sense.

I think that's why teachers act much more as facilitators online than they do in a face-to-face learning environment. In a face-to-face environment, students primarily address themselves to the teacher/professor and not to their peers. And it's hard to break that, because of the physical location of the teacher at the head of the class, etc. Conference classes do that to some extent, but the teacher is still obviously the authority. *Liane*

By relinquishing our traditional power role as teachers, we frequently find that we learn as much from our students in an online course as our students learn from us. Recently, in a workshop we were presenting, an instructor stated, "I'm an expert in my field. What could I possibly learn from an undergraduate student?" Our response to him was that we hoped he was not serious. When instructors participate in learning communities, they must be open to the promise that learning can and will emerge from multiple sources, and furthermore, that learning is a lifelong process.

Flexibility, openness, and willingness to relinquish control are characteristics that, when shared by both instructors and their students, make for a successful online learning experience. If we all can maintain an attitude of "being in this together," with instructors holding an equal role in the learning community that has been created, the ability to create deeper levels of meaning and knowledge exists. Faculty, then, must be willing and able to empower students to take on the roles they need to take on to facilitate educational success in the online classroom.

Maximizing the Potential of the Virtual Student

Even when students are empowered to take on the necessary roles, they may not assume their responsibilities unless they are prompted and encouraged. In addition, some students in the group may take on more responsibility than others. Instructors must take steps to draw out students who are not fully engaging with the course and the other students. Just as an instructor might spend additional time with a student who is not responding well in the face-to-face classroom, he or she needs to spend additional time motivating learners to join the online learning process. The following are some suggestions that instructors may take to maximize the potential of all learners enrolled in an online class:

Use Best Practices from the Face-to-Face Classroom to Promote Participation Online

Instructors need to assess the tricks of the trade that have served them well in motivating students and working with problem students in order to find those that might work online as well. Asking "What would I do in this situation in the face-to-face classroom?" is the best way to do this. If, for example, an instructor has traditionally set up a private tutoring session when a student is struggling, she should do the same with an online student. The session might occur through synchronous discussion online, a telephone conference with the student, an intensive e-mail exchange, or a face-to-face session if distance allows. Nothing should be left to chance or assumption, because of the flat nature of the medium. Consequently, in teaching an online course, instructors need to stay actively involved, diagnose problems as they occur, and seek solutions to keep the course moving and students motivated.

If a Student Is Absent for a Week, Contact Him or Her to Determine Why

Just as in the face-to-face classroom, attendance and presence should contribute
to the grade in an online class. In a large face-to-face class, a student's absence
may go unnoticed. But in the online classroom a student's absence is quite no-
ticeable and also has a detrimental effect on the other members of the group. Instead of assuming that a student's absence is the result of lack of motivation,
instructors need to investigate the reason for the absence and attempt to bring students back into the online classroom as quickly as possible. Sometimes a simple,
brief e-mail message or phone call can make all the difference for students who
may be struggling with the technology in use, the material under study, or other
life issues and concerns, allowing them to reenter the learning process without los-
ing significant ground.

If Students Have Technical Difficulties, Offer Support or Connect Them with Tech Support

Instructors need to be knowledgeable enough about the technology in use for an
online course to be able to answer basic questions for students in their classes. In
general, students may struggle a bit during the first few weeks of a class as they
acclimate to the technology and to learning through the use of technology.

An instructor with whom we were consulting sent us an e-mail requesting our
assistance because he was unable to generate a sufficient degree of discussion in
his online class. He asked us to "lurk" in his classroom to see if we could help him
diagnose the problem. When we visited his class, it became immediately apparent that part of the problem was the technology.

The instructor was using a good courseware application, but he had constructed his course and was asking questions in such a way that students were required to move forward and back continually in order to read and respond to what
was being posted. Some were finding that simply reading what was there was taking them more than an hour before they could think about or post their own responses. The instructor in this situation was able to respond in two ways. First, he
modified how he was asking questions in order to minimize the need for students
to look in several places before they determined what they needed to respond to;
second, he became more familiar with the application so that he could instruct his
students on the best ways to use it and minimize their time online.

If Conflict Hurts Participation, Intercede with the Students Involved

Disagreements and differences of opinion should not interfere with good participation. However, nothing stifles good participation in an online course like
unresolved conflict. Just as in the face-to-face classroom, if a student is acting out
other students may fear becoming the object of that student's negative attention
and will withdraw. In the online classroom, the fear of being attacked is likely

to result in reduced participation and reduced interest in the class itself. The experience of one of us, which we described in Chapter Two, is a case in point. Flaming occurred early in the learning process and the instructor was unable to resolve it satisfactorily. Consequently, students were reluctant to engage with one another for fear of reprisal and they felt unmotivated to participate. The result was dissatisfaction with the entire learning experience for all involved.

Again, this is a situation where "best practices" should prevail. Instructors should determine how they feel most comfortable in dealing with conflict in the classroom and with students who are acting out. Just as in the face-to-face classroom, if conflict resolution assistance is available through the institution, the instructor should make use of it. If all else fails, the student or students involved should be asked to withdraw from the class so that the learning process can continue for the others. When this happens, however, it is advisable to have an online discussion with the remaining students so that they can understand the attempts that were made to ameliorate the situation and why the final decision was made.

If Security Breaches Cause Nonparticipation, Report Them Quickly to Reestablish a Sense of Privacy

We have found that as students form their learning community online, they create for themselves a false sense of privacy. They believe that because the class is password-protected, others will not be able to access their discussions. Although this is generally true, there are times when other students might "hack" their way into a course or it may be discovered that others are "lurking," or observing what is happening, in the online discussions without making their presence known. This can be upsetting to students participating in an online discussion, particularly if they have been sharing material that is sensitive or of a personal nature. Consequently, every attempt to maintain security should be made. If an unauthorized person or persons gain access to the course site, students should be notified and new passwords issued. The instructor should also alert the institution immediately.

Students should also be informed if there will be observers in the classroom and what the nature of their presence might be. In a course we recently taught, the discussion turned to the institution in which the students were enrolled. One student posted a message asking who had access to the discussion forum, because this would significantly affect the nature of her participation. When she was reassured that no one from the school had access to the discussion, she expressed her relief and felt that she could freely express her opinions without fear of repercussion. Had she not received this reassurance, or if someone from the school was observing the class, she would have felt betrayed. Trust is an essential element in the building of a strong learning community. There should be no surprises where privacy is concerned.

Log On to the Online Classroom Three or More Times a Week to Keep the Discussion Moving

Logging on often allows the instructor keep up with the discussion as well as to deal with any problems and move the discussion in another direction should that become necessary. The importance of an appropriate level of instructor participation should be obvious. By providing a good role model, the instructor demonstrates what is meant by acceptable participation. In addition, we have found that students voice anxiety if the instructor is not obviously present. Regardless of the "student centeredness" of this mode of education, students still seek guidance and approval from the instructor as they move through the course. If that guidance is not forthcoming, they begin to worry that they may be headed in the wrong direction. We let our students know at the beginning of a class that we intend to log on daily. We may not post a comment daily, but we want our students to know that we are there.

Many times, the instructor may log on and find that there is no need actually to participate in the ensuing discussion. Nevertheless, making some comments at least a couple of times weekly reassures students that all is well and that they are on track. Comments should be made on a regular and consistent basis.

Learn How to Ask Broad Questions That Stimulate Thinking to Promote Participation

Knowing how to ask good, expansive questions is an art. However, it is an art that can be developed with practice. There is a difference between a question like "Name and describe three social systems theories that apply to community development" and "What theory of community development did you find yourself relating to most? Why? How would you apply that theory to our learning community?" The response to the first type of question will simply yield a list and require little critical thinking ability on the part of students. The second series of questions requires that students evaluate the theories about which they are reading and apply them to the context in which they find themselves. It also has the potential to stimulate discussion among the students as they find themselves agreeing or disagreeing with the choices their colleagues make. As we demonstrated in Chapter Five, when instructors find a discussion falling flat, it is important to reassess the question that has been asked to begin the discussion and either refine that question or ask another one that might serve to stimulate more discussion.

Include Humor in Your Posts to Help Students Feel Welcome and Safe

Although many believe that the text-based nature of the online classroom creates a flat medium in which little emotion is apparent, an increasing body of literature points to the ability to communicate emotion online (Menges, 1996; Pratt, 1996; Palloff and Pratt, 1999). In addition, adults tend to learn best in situations where they can relate what they are learning to the life they are living (Brookfield, 1995; Knowles, 1992).

Therefore, instructors do not necessarily need to feel that teaching online is a completely serious business. It is important to create a warm, inviting course site where students can feel comfortable expressing themselves and relating course material to their everyday lives. Just as in the face-to-face classroom, humor can add personal warmth to the online experience. When students feel comfortable expressing who they are without fear that this might not be relevant to the course, the likelihood of developing a strong learning community is greater.

Furthermore, instructors need not fear sharing themselves in the service of developing a learning community. When students are able to see the instructor as a real human being, their willingness to explore and bring in new ideas increases.

Post a Welcoming Response to Student Introductions to Help All Join More Successfully

We strongly believe that an effective way to begin any course is to have students post an introduction along with their learning objectives for the course and any experience with the subject matter that they might have. Some courseware applications allow students and instructors to create their own homepages within the course. Having students create a homepage is an effective first assignment. It is also important, however, to acknowledge the posting of introductions.

The instructor can be the first to welcome students as they enter the class, once again providing a model for other students to follow. This may well open up ways in which students can connect with one another around common interests and can be a first step in the creation of a learning community. In addition to welcoming students individually, most courseware applications allow the instructor to create an introductory message to the course site on the homepage for the course. Once again, this invites students to participate in the course by presenting a small amount of information about it and making them feel welcome. The instructor should also post his or her introduction and bio as a way of presenting himself or herself as a real person, thus taking the first step to creating a warm, inviting course atmosphere.

Although these suggestions may sound time-consuming for the instructor, it will be time well-spent if it results in active participation and the achievement of learning objectives for all students enrolled in the online course.

Teaching Students to Learn in the Online Environment

Students are, for the most part, unaware of the demands that will be placed on them as learners when they opt to learn online. They may enter a nontraditional learning setting with traditional expectations—that is, that the instructor will "teach" and they will "learn" from the material provided. They do not understand why the instructor is less visible in the learning process and that the instructor's role is one of facilitator rather than traditional teacher. They do not understand that the online learning process is less structured and requires significantly more input from them to make it successful. All of these concepts must somehow be conveyed to students before they embark on an online course. Many times difficulties emerge when teachers and students have differing expectations and no attempt is made to clarify at the outset.

The transition to online distance learning, therefore, is bringing to the fore some new issues for administrators as they field concerns and even complaints from the students enrolled. Students enter an online course with the expectation that the course will be more attuned to their needs as learners. This may mean that the course is more convenient for them because of distance or because of work and family demands. Or it may mean that they do not like large classroom situations and prefer the increased instructor-student interaction that the online classroom has the potential to provide.

Some institutions, such as Pennsylvania State University, are creating online courses to teach students about online learning. They are mandating that students complete the online introduction before embarking on online classes. Others are incorporating mandatory face-to-face orientations in online programs and courses. Regardless of the approach used, the idea is the same: *we cannot assume that learners will automatically understand the new approach to teaching and learning that the online classroom exemplifies.* In order to realize the educational potential that the online classroom holds and ensure that the learners are given the best chance of becoming empowered learners, we must pay attention to teaching our teachers how to teach and our learners how to learn when teaching and learning are virtual.

As with online faculty training, online student training allows students to experience this kind of learning before they take an actual course. But regardless of the means by which the training is conducted, the following should be included in a student orientation to online learning:

- The basics of logging on to the Internet, including use of a browser, accessing the course site, saving and printing material found online, basic Internet searching, and e-mail
- What is required to become a successful online learner, including time requirements and time management
- The differences between face-to-face and online courses, including the role of the instructor and the roles of students, as well as expectations about how students will be evaluated

- How interaction between the instructor and student and between students occurs
- How to give feedback
- What is considered appropriate interaction and communication, including the rules of "netiquette"
- How to get help when needed

Providing an online orientation course may not resolve all of the issues for students as they make the transition to the online classroom. But it certainly can help to give them a leg up and a clearer understanding of the differences in the type of educational experience they are about to undertake.

Tips for Successfully Working with the Virtual Student

- Do not assume that students will automatically *know* how to learn online. Do welcome them to this new learning experience and create a warm, supportive environment in which they can learn.
- Provide some form of orientation to students as they embark on an online learning experience. If the institution does not provide an orientation course for students, an instructor can include some tips and guidelines for success on the course site.
- Construct a course that is varied and addresses different learning styles. This does not mean using complex forms of technology, but instead designing assignments and approaches that require both action and reflection.
- Encourage and empower students to take charge of the learning process. Provide them with assignments that allow them to explore, research, and work collaboratively.
- Pay attention to changes in participation levels and address them promptly.
- Stay present and be responsive to student needs and concerns. The instructor should engage in a balanced level of participation so students know that he or she is there.

CHAPTER EIGHT

ONLINE CLASSROOM DYNAMICS

As we work with instructors in online teaching, a question we are frequently asked is why some online classroom groups seem to flourish while others flounder—despite their best attempts at community development, the students never seem to achieve a rhythm with one another or with the instructor. The same, of course, might be said about face-to-face classrooms. The answer lies in the classroom dynamics, and more specifically, in the group dynamics. With increased knowledge of online group dynamics, instructors can more easily adjust their strategies for dealing with problems such as difficult students or waning participation.

Clearly, a classroom, be it face-to-face or online, should not be viewed as a forum for group therapy. However, the need to develop a strong team, focused on learning collaboratively and completing collaborative assignments, promotes the need to understand team or group development. An instructor's knowledge of group dynamics might not be important when teaching a subject such as accounting in the face-to-face classroom unless collaborative small group work is being used as a learning technique. Online, however, where much of the work is collaborative, observation and knowledge of the dynamics of the group become more critical even in courses such as accounting and the sciences.

In this chapter, we will focus on the nature of groups in cyberspace, examining theories of group formation and development and how they apply when the group is virtual. We will consider formation issues, stages and process of group development, and leadership issues. In so doing, we will review the importance of working with conflict when it arises. In addition, we will explore why some virtual classroom groups work and others fail. We will also discuss working with difficult students in the online environment.

Group Dynamics and Online Classroom Dynamics

Until recently, the literature on group development has focused on stage theory. The most accepted of the stage theories is the one proposed by Tuckman and Jensen (1977). Stage theory states that groups go through five distinct stages in a relatively linear fashion: forming, storming, norming, performing, and adjourning. We have seen all of our online groups go through the stages that Tuckman and Jensen describe. However, we have not seen it happen in that exact order. Frequently in the forming stage, online classroom groups will discuss the guidelines for the class, especially if encouraged to do so by the instructor. This may or may not lead to a storming stage, otherwise known as conflict. We find that conflict arises at varying points in the development of the group, and it is not uncommon for it to occur almost immediately. One of us had an experience with an online group that entered into a heated conflict in the second week of the class because two members felt that the expectations for course completion were unclear. In other classes, conflict occurred later in the group's development, once members were feeling more comfortable with one another. All of our groups have performed to a lesser or greater extent throughout the course. The adjourning stage in online group development is also not distinct. We find that some classes end with no formal good-byes, and particularly if the group will be interacting with one another in other classes, either face-to-face or online, the group interaction continues, in essence "re-forming" to suit other circumstances.

Our experience, then, is more in line with more recent work that is focused on the integration of systems theory into group development and has begun to question the linear nature of Tuckman and Jensen's model. McClure (1998) proposes a seven-stage model of group development. The stages he outlines are pre-forming, unity, disunity, conflict-confrontation, disharmony, harmony, and performing. He organizes these stages into a model of descent toward conflict and then ascent out of conflict with pre-forming, unity, and disunity as descending stages, conflict-confrontation as the apex of group development, and disharmony, harmony, and performing as ascending stages.

> In small groups, individuals come together, create a purpose, and forge a collective identity. Initially in that process, individuality is constrained as a group identity forms. The descent represents the collective forging process. The vertex

depicts the crucial conflict stage. This is the turning point in groups where responsibility is shifted from the leader to the members. Once a strong bond is established, responsibility assumed, and a group identity emerges, individuality can be reclaimed, asserted, and expressed. The ascent signifies that reclamation process [McClure, 1998, p. 39].

McClure views group development as chaotic and self-organizing. Therefore, the movement between stages is not linear. In order to move from one stage to another, he proposes, the group must enter a chaotic phase that results in agreement—in verbal or nonverbal terms—by the majority to move to the next phase of development. He does not address the termination phase of the group because he believes that most groups rarely successfully negotiate all of the ascent stages. Instead, he proposes that groups move back and forth between harmony and disharmony, rarely achieving a true performing stage.

McClure also proposes that groups experience six issues of concern as they move through the phases of development, although as with the stages they may not experience the issues in order. The issues are safety, affiliation, dependence, independence, intimacy, and risk taking. We have certainly seen all of the issues of concern emerge in online classroom groups and believe that they are influential in the development of a good learning community. They emerge in the following ways:

• In order to feel comfortable in participating in the online class, students need to feel safe. The instructor's responsibility is to create a safe container by providing guidelines and expectations that create a structure for the course and by encouraging students to express themselves in whatever way seems appropriate to them within that structure. In addition, the fact that most online classes are password-protected allows for a sense of privacy that encourages students to feel safe in the knowledge that their posts will not be read by people outside of the class.

• Affiliation is a key to the development of a learning community. Students need to feel that they are a part of something greater than themselves. They belong to a group that is engaged in working together to achieve a goal.

• Dependence on one another is an important by-product of affiliation. In order to sustain the learning community, students need to feel that they all can depend on the others to hold up their end of the bargain, so to speak. They need to know that they can count on their peers to provide feedback to them in a timely manner, contribute to online discussions, and do the work that is expected of them.

• Dependence on one another should not come at a price, however. Students in an online group need to feel that they can maintain their independence in the form of independent thought and feeling. Instructors should be on the lookout for "groupthink"—when students appear to feel pressured to express the same opinions as others—and intervene if this occurs to move the discussion back to a place where independent thinking is the norm.

• Many instructors have commented on the level of intimacy that online classroom groups can and do achieve. The relative anonymity of the medium seems to free students to express thoughts they would likely not express face-to-face. Consequently, it is not unusual to see members of online groups sharing very intimate details of their lives. In addition, students in online classes tend to form intimate bonds with one another that frequently extend beyond the online classroom. Another way in which intimacy might be expressed is when students who are geographically dispersed get together with each other socially when visiting the area where another student lives. It is also not unusual to see conversations about meetings such as this occurring in the social area of the course site.

• Because of the sense of intimacy that members of online groups feel with one another, members feel comfortable taking risks and expressing ideas that may be controversial or less than "politically correct" because they have a sense that they will not be rejected by the group for doing so. Steve's post about breast cancer research, which we presented in the last chapter, is an example of the type of post an instructor might see when students are engaging in risk-taking behavior. Risk-taking behavior might also take the form of confronting a member who is not participating or who has flamed another member of the group. We tend to see risk-taking behavior increase as the class progresses.

Because McClure's model has been developed in working with face-to-face groups, it raises some questions. How does a model like his apply to online groups? The preceding paragraphs described how the six issues of concern might emerge. However, do all groups we work with in online classrooms experience the six issues of concern? When and where do these issues occur? How might the issues be addressed and encouraged? To explore these questions and gain further understanding of McClure's model, let us look at the development of one online group.

Applying What We Understand About Groups to Online Classes

The following is a description of one group of students in an online class. We will view their development as a group using the stages proposed in McClure's model and provide examples to illustrate their movement through each stage.

Pre-forming

Many of the students entering this class had never met one another previously and the instructor had not met any of the students face-to-face before the start of the class, which was delivered completely online. All had taken at least one on-line class previously. The course was an elective titled The Search for Soul and Spirit in the Workplace. Students were drawn to the course by their interest in the subject matter. Coincidentally, the instructor was working with two of the students in another online class simultaneously. The class began with the posting of in-troductions and learning objectives for the class. The instructor responded to each introduction, welcoming the students to the class. Following the instructor's lead, students then began to respond to one another, connecting with elements of the posted introductions. The following are some examples of the type of connection that began to occur early on in the course.

Hi Shannon:

Thanks for your introduction. Sounds as though you are involved in some very creative and innovative projects. I am interested in reading your article regarding the common threads in all religions. The power of religious writings, I think, do come from the stories, examples and metaphors. Let me know when and where it will be avail-able. It is interesting how each member of this group has expressed a delightful cu-riosity about spirit and soul. It should make for some great dialogue. And, hopefully it will help you in your search along your life path. Thanks for the intro. . . .

Take care,
Karen

Hi Shannon,

Glad you looped back for the introduction! We have at least three things in com-mon: the Midwest (Kansas, in my case), an interest in San Diego (you're there and I'd like to be) and a healthy suspicion of work environments that try to entice people to buy into the illusion that everything they need as an individual can come from the work experience. I'm looking forward to more conversation with you! *Laurie*

Unity

As part of the course design, students were asked to take responsibility for facili-tating one week of the discussion for the course based on their interest either in the topic for the week or in some of the assigned reading. The group was able to complete this task with only minor difficulty. Following the negotiations, discus-sion of course material began. Discussion was lively and active. The following are a couple of bits of discussion from the first week of the class, illustrating the group's attempts at coming together to achieve their learning objectives. The dialogue is supportive and professional, expressing slight disagreement but avoiding any areas of controversy. The avoidance of conflict or controversy is typical of a group in the unity phase of development.

Thank you Peter for getting us started. I agree with what you have put out here for us to consider. I especially liked where you said "I think one way organizations could help their employees bring their soul and spirit into the workplace would be to start examining what's enough, and to relax some of the incessant pressure that seems to permeate today's workplace." I think this is a huge leap though. . . . You are right on when you said "A more likely strategy would be for individual employees, you and I, to start asking that question in our own personal lives. Once we've got enough, we're free to choose whether we'll work those extra hours or not. It really frees you up from your work; it provides the space required to restore a balance in your life—the space required to nurture your body, mind and spirit." I have a friend that works four weeks on and then has two weeks off. This R&R he traveled, leaving the day he got off work and returning home the day before he flies out for work again. Next time he is taking three weeks off and is basically doing the same thing. This means that he will be away from his home for 3 months straight. All of a sudden he is feeling like he is never at home and the house is suffering. Today I asked why he scheduled his travel so tightly? Then I asked why when he travels he insists on packing the vacation with something to do every minute of the day. I always try to include one or two days of doing nothing. No wonder he is stretched to the point of breaking. He has not learned to say enough! *Sharon*

Pete:
     I think you have asked an important question, "why is it that everyone feels compelled to work so hard at their jobs?" Perhaps, this is the type of culture organizations have fostered and encouraged? Over a period of time it becomes an explicit or implicit expectation. People get caught on the treadmill and consider long hours normal behavior. Fortunately, there are people who are more reflective and mindful of the need for balance and harmony, both personally and professionally. Yesterday I was working with a group of young professional people in a relatively large organization. It is not unusual for most of these people to routinely work 60–70 hours a week. One of the people described his work as being like "a rat in a maze". None have them have a sense of joy or contentment, yet, they continue putting in the hours with little (if any) quality of life. The good news Pete, is they are starting to independently ask the very question . . . when is enough, enough? This type of dialogue is beginning to become more common place in organizations. People are truly searching for something more meaningful. I sense people have a lot more questions to these type of issues than they have answers. I am not sure the answers are as simple as taking more vacation time or more time off. Thanks for the conversation, *Karen*

Disunity

This group showed great interest in the topics discussed and actively engaged in conversation weekly, far exceeding the twice-weekly required number of posts. One member tended to hold divergent opinions from the rest but felt comfortable expressing them, and by two or three weeks into the course she had no difficulty entering into disagreement with the other members. The risk-taking behavior and ability to disagree both with the instructor and with each other, with no apparent repercussion, created an atmosphere of safety in the group that allowed the group to begin to move into the first of the conflict phases: disunity. Shannon's contributions never went unacknowledged. At this phase of group development, whenever she posted a message, such as the one that follows, one member of the group would support her willingness to speak out without contradicting her opinions.

Sharon—

Oh yeah again! I love this interaction and these challenges to my thoughts. I have commented by each of yours below:

"I do believe that they can be instrumental in helping a person find it for themselves." Note my comments to Rena and Karen earlier about how an organization is only a structure with out its members. It's the members that form a chain to create the organization in the first place. And if the organization is it's individuals then yes the organization is instrumental in the influence of spirit and soul. But again what you refer to as the organization is then synonymous with the individuals, rather than the structure. Also refer to my comments to Karen about the chain effect of organizations. "How many times do we hear someone say "I have the greatest job in the word because I get to do what I love most" and we think "wow they sure are lucky"? I never say this. I would never (never say never though) stay in a job that I did not thoroughly love. This life is precious to me, each moment counts. There is absolutely no reason to do anything short of what I love. But yes several other people do feel this way. I think this is an effect of not following their truth, or more often not knowing what their truth is. [truth is often used by me in the same frame as spirit—as I have here] What if "what they are" is not something that they can use to feed, cloth and house their families? Here is one of those reasons everyone is going to reply with why they do not follow their truths or stay in jobs they do not enjoy. I say this is a lack of responsibility to their spirit. They are not honoring their spirit, they do not have faith. If you do what you love, live your truth 100% the rest will follow. How many times have people finally stepped out of that comfort zone, said enough is enough and found that they are 500% better off than they were before. Often—but not always—this means making more money, etc. . . . Where there's a will there's a way. No one said it was easy—but it does work! . . . I attempt to live my truth, I love what I do, I wake up happier than the day before everyday and I would say I am doing pretty good in all aspects of my life so far. . . . So idealistic or not, if I don't think them they will never be. If I do think them, they may be. I like my odds better in the latter. Combined with my experience with it—it works for me and that's all I can say. *Shannon*

Thanks for going out on a limb, Shannon. . . . it's something I could have done more of throughout all of my courses. In response to your point that it isn't the organization's responsibility to bring spirit or soul into the workplace but it is their responsibility to allow it, I think I agree. I also think it is the organization's responsibility not to stifle it or destroy it. Maybe that means there is an omission and commission aspect to this. What do you think? I also agree with your idea that you either know that an organization lives it's truth or doesn't, although I don't think you can see that as easily from the outside (and when you're inside it may be too late!) The way I think of that the organization is dysfunctional because it is out of integrity with itself, much like your description. *Laurie*

Conflict-Confrontation

Unlike other groups with which we have worked, this particular group never really experienced a strong confrontational phase. They continued to disagree with one another and felt safe voicing that disagreement. Their disagreements continued to be professional and related to ideas, rather than becoming personal. They continued to remain supportive of one another throughout. This may be because the group was enrolled in a graduate-level seminar. All were adult students who were working full-time. Consequently, their level of maturity and professionalism as individuals was greater. They were able to create a safe atmosphere of healthy disagreement that did not result in confrontation. An unspoken norm of acceptance of all opinions was established by the group early on and maintained throughout the course.

Disharmony

As the group moved toward the performing stages, participation remained strong for all but Shannon, whose participation became slightly spotty. Shannon, the student who tended to voice the most disagreement with the opinions of others in the group, dropped away for a short time, claiming that she had first, a computer virus, and then later, a troubled friend who needed her attention. Other students expressed some concern about her absence and welcomed her return when she rejoined the group. Although she described some personal issues in her life that had drawn her away, it is possible that she felt somewhat uncomfortable with being the group member to spark conflict and give voice to different and dissenting opinions and thus withdrew for a short time to allow the group to move beyond the conflict phases. Even in face-to-face groups, this is not unusual. A vocal and more opinionated member of the group may not show up for a few sessions, leaving the other members to wonder why. The shift in group functioning and norms causes a sense of unease or disharmony that frequently results in a reexamination of norms and expectations.

Harmony

As we usually do when we create the course site for an online class, we included a social area—named The Sandbox—on this one. About midway through the quarter, the group began making extensive use of The Sandbox. One student posted a work problem with which she was dealing and several students jumped into a discussion on virtual leadership that was unrelated to the course material. Another student experienced a health scare during the term. He posted this in The Sandbox and was given extensive support from the others in the group. Simultaneously, the nature of participation in the course discussions became more harmonious. Shannon completely reengaged with the group and continued to feel safe expressing her opinions. The following is an exchange illustrating her reentry into the group:

I find this a hard question for some reason today. I have been grappling over these questions for hours, days it seems like. Had they been asked merely 6 months ago, last term for example, I could've popped up with a brilliant answer of my leadership gifts. I am left wondering if I can't find the answers today because I am in a transitionary period. Transitions seem to clear the slate for me. They remind me of what I do not know, of what I have not grasped yet. They are the moments when I first begin to step out of that comfort zone I have been hiding in. . . . I think the biggest gift I offer people these days is power, personal power. I left my previous company because it misused power, stole power, misunderstood power and in the end lacked the power to achieve it's dream because of it. In my choice to leave, combined with the dive I took into the dark sea of myself, I found my own personal power. Through that I found the ability to lead others to their own. I have a blessing in the ability to see the true spirit shining through people, past the [facade] we offer or the image we provide. When I was a social worker people always praised my ability to give great feedback. In business people always praised my ability to see the talents in others whether they exemplified it or not. That ability to bring others to fruition. *Shannon*

Your reference to being blessed was a good reminder to me, Shannon, that a lot of who we are was a gift to us! I, too, feel very blessed in the wonderful family of people I was born into. The gift of personal power and authorship that you offer people is truly a great one—a most significant way of enabling people and, by doing that, helping them create their own significance. *Laurie*

Shannon: I want to echo Laurie's response to you. I found your comments exceptionally powerful and thought provoking. What a wonderful gift of insight you have into your own behavior. It sounds as though you are really going through a wonderful and fascinating period of growth? And, the benefit is you have a better sense of yourself and what you want (at least for this moment in time) is that a correct assumption? *Karen*

Performing

As the term progressed, this became a high-performing group. Despite earlier disagreements, group members developed significant regard for each other, their ideas, and their work. They began to reflect on their learning experience and commented that it was unlike others they had experienced, either online or face-to-face. Participation levels throughout the term were extremely high. It was not uncommon for this group of seven students to generate somewhere between 110 and 150 postings per week. Despite personal issues that periodically interfered with the ability of a couple of students to participate at the same level as the others, overall participation was relatively evenly dispersed across the group. The learning objectives for the course, as described by the instructor, were these: "This course will explore recent writings on the search for soul and spirit in the workplace, as well as how it affects the notions of meaningful work, leadership, and organizational change. We will also explore these concepts as they pertain to your personal search for meaning in the work you do."

The following are some student reflections on the achievement of learning outcomes in this course:

As many have mentioned, this particular virtual environment has been an exceptionally open, engaging process. Jointly, we have raised thought provoking questions, responded to one another with care and respect and we have encouraged one another to reflect and think. I have routinely enjoyed logging on to Felix and reviewing the ongoing conversations and comments. Whatever the topic, some humorous, some serious, some soul-searching, I always felt we sincerely listened to each other. Our entire learning community contributed to the development of incredibly rich and stimulating ongoing conversation. It seems as though we discovered a common ground for learning and we were willing to openly trust each other to honor our thoughts and our feelings. Perhaps for a brief moment in time we found a safe harbor, where it was acceptable to be vulnerable. I know I will reflect on our conversations as I continue to work through some of these issues of soul and spirit. It is an never ending process of discovery. I feel exceptionally blessed to have been surrounded by six talented and gifted learning partners in this journey. You hold a special place in my heart. *Karen*

My learning objective for this [seminar] was to gain some new insights and strategies I could use with myself and others to bring more soulfulness and spirit into the workplace. Our dialogue over the past 10 weeks has exceeded my expectations. . . . I think it's amazing the way this group came together and shared such intensely personal information. With the exception of Shan and Karen, I didn't know anyone else in the group at the outset of the EBS, and yet now I feel as if I know you better than many people I'm in contact with every day. I feel very safe with you. I'm sure, one reason is that we've engaged each other at the level of our soul and spirit. *Pete*

Concluding Thoughts About the Soul and Spirit Group

As previously mentioned, the members of the group enrolled in The Search for Soul and Spirit in the Workplace were mature, professional working adults. Their experience with online classes varied but all had taken at least one online class previously. Not all of the students had worked together previously, however. The class was an elective, not a required course. Consequently, all students were there voluntarily. All of these factors contributed to a very positive group experience.

The group did, however, move through conflict on its way to the harmony and performing stages of group development. Early on, they worked hard to get to know one another and establish unspoken norms of open, accepting participation. Active participation also became a norm for this group as they far exceeded the mandatory guideline of two posts per week.

This may appear to be an ideal group experience, yet it is one that we have had often as we teach online classes. Allowing space for the group to move through its developmental phases contributes positively to the achievement of learning objectives. What would have happened if the instructor had stopped the emergence of conflict by silencing the dissenting voice? Most likely, this would have become what McClure describes as a regressive group, never able to move to the harmony and performing stages.

What this example does tell us is that it is important for an instructor to look for signs that the group is moving through stages of development. It is not necessary to comment on this to the group, but it may become necessary to facilitate movement to the next stage if the group becomes stuck in the conflict phases.

Other Ways of Looking at Online Groups

McGrath and Hollingshead (1994) have focused their work on the study of online work groups, attempting to establish the impact of technology on team development. Rather than looking at online groups as moving through various stages, this model looks at the numerous factors that lead to successful or unsuccessful outcomes when online groups come together to perform various tasks.

The essential elements of McGrath and Hollingshead's model can be distilled down to three that have equal influence over each other: people, tasks, and technology. McGrath and Hollingshead further argue that there are three functions that online groups strive to achieve:

- *Production,* or the ability to complete a tangible task
- *Well-being,* or a sense of individual satisfaction and that individual needs are being met through the group
- *Member support,* or a sense that a safe space has been created through which members can support each other in achieving their collaborative task

Online groups attempt to achieve these functions through four modes of operation:

- *Inception,* or what McClure would likely call pre-forming, during which group members begin to work together to understand their common task
- *Problem solving,* which is considered to be the main reason why task-oriented groups come together online
- *Conflict resolution,* a critical factor in successfully completing tasks together
- *Execution,* or the completion of the task

McGrath and Hollingshead argue that, rather than moving through the modes in linear fashion, online groups may move back and forth between each mode, with each function manifested in each mode. The example of the Soul and Spirit group we just presented illustrates all aspects of the McGrath and Hollingshead model. Certainly, the group completed their task together, felt good about what they were able to accomplish in the process, and supported one another throughout. They were able to discuss and solve problems together, resolve conflict easily, and perform well as a group.

Schopler, Abell, and Galinsky (1998), with yet another way of observing online groups, note the importance of looking at the differences between online and face-to-face groups from three system levels: individual, group, and environmental. They state that on an individual level, members may feel freer to be more independent, set their own pace in asynchronous discussion, and try out new roles and behaviors. Because of the absence of social cues, such as facial expression and tone of voice, it may be more difficult for members to assess the mood or intent of other members and thus communications may be more easily misinterpreted. In addition, because of the relative anonymity of the medium, members may have fewer inhibitions, leading to more impulsive responses. Posting reminders of guidelines and norms of behavior may therefore be necessary.

Pratt (1996) adds to our understanding of the individual level with his description and discussion of what he terms *electronic personality.* He proposes that when individuals enter the online environment, they allow parts of their personalities that are not seen face-to-face to emerge. Introverts tend to flourish online because of the absence of the social cues and body language that are somewhat inhibiting to them in face-to-face situations. They therefore tend to become more extroverted in their participation in online groups. Extroverts, in contrast, have more difficulty establishing a "presence" online. Because they tend to be more verbal in face-to-face situations, extroverts can easily make social connections and let others know who they are. This is more difficult for them to do in the flat, text-based medium. The ability to free up parts of ourselves online helps level the playing field in online groups, allowing for more even participation from all members regardless of their introversion or extroversion. It also allows people to try out new roles and behaviors.

On a group level, Schopler, Abell, and Galinsky note that the pacing of responses makes for time gaps, which can be both positive and negative in terms of group development. The time gaps can promote reflection but can also create uncomfortable feelings for members who feel their needs and concerns are not being addressed by the group. Some researchers, however, support our own experience that it is possible to develop greater group cohesion in a shorter period of time in technology-based groups (Mennecke, Hoffer, and Wynne, 1992). The ability to engage in informal discussion unrelated to the task that brings the group together assists with this process. In other words, groups need to be given a space in which they can connect with each other on a social level and begin to know each other as people apart from the task that brings them together. In face-to-face teams or groups, informal connections happen outside of the classroom and may be encouraged by the instructor or facilitator. The same opportunity needs to be provided for online groups in order to allow for group cohesion and more satisfactory task completion. The Soul and Spirit group made good use of the social area created for their course. They supported one another through life and health crises, discussed work issues, and also discussed issues of intimacy as a group.

Finally, the environmental realm is clearly made up of the technology that is used. The technology should be a vehicle that ensures clear, unrestricted communication in order to support good group development. In addition, group members need access to technical support should anything occur that interferes with their ability to communicate with the group.

Figure 8.1 summarizes the theories of group development as they relate to online groups. It shows the connections between the individuals, the group, the facilitator, and the technology as these elements relate to the completion of a common task. The list in the center of the diagram describes the activities through which online groups become unique and illustrates how all the elements overlap.

In *Building Learning Communities in Cyberspace,* we offered a diagram that we labeled "The Learning Web." That web, to us, illustrated the interrelationships between the elements involved in the creation and delivery of an online course. We offer that diagram again here as Figure 8.2 to show the relationship between the theories of group dynamics and development that we just presented and the dynamics of the online classroom.

If we combine the elements of effective online groups with the web of learning we can begin to see the roles of the individual, group, facilitator, task, and technology as they relate to online classes.

Student

Students enter online classes with a concern about the task to be accomplished. In other words, they hope to complete the course in which they have registered with a minimum of difficulty and to feel good about the outcome. What attracts individual students to the online environment is the ability to work at their own pace using asynchronous communication. What is often a surprise is the ability to engage with the material and the instructor in a different way. Students are sometimes surprised by the more facilitative role of the instructor, the directive to function both more independently and collaboratively at the same time, and the need to become good managers of their own time given the demands of online classes.

Peers

The role of the group is critical to the success of the online class. A well-designed online class will intentionally build a learning community by providing opportunities for teamwork, the completion of collaborative assignments, and the ability to reflect on the process and the learning. Working with an online group can serve to reduce the sense of isolation that some students have described in taking online classes that lacked interaction. Encouraging students to become part of a whole by joining an online classroom group increases the likelihood that they will stay involved and motivated, because successful completion of the task (in other words, completion of the course) is a collaborative effort.

Another reason why a learning community is important is because it provides social connections that allow students to get to know one another as people. This too increases the likelihood that students will want to stay involved. They will be

FIGURE 8.1. THE ELEMENTS OF EFFECTIVE ONLINE GROUPS.

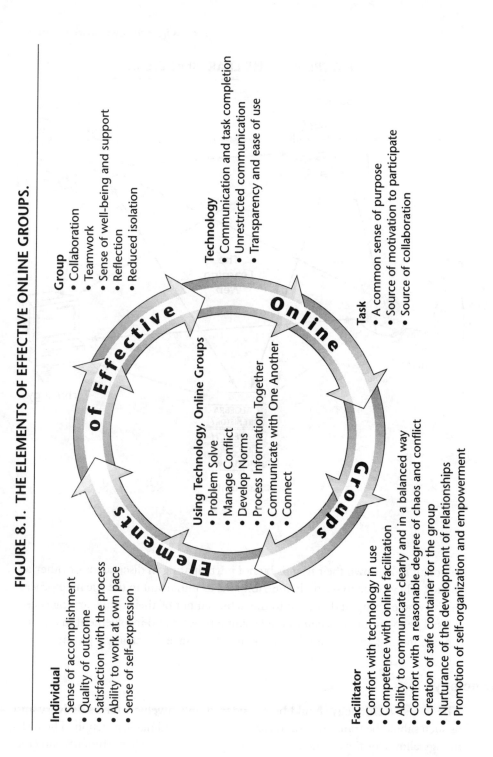

Individual
- Sense of accomplishment
- Quality of outcome
- Satisfaction with the process
- Ability to work at own pace
- Sense of self-expression

Group
- Collaboration
- Teamwork
- Sense of well-being and support
- Reflection
- Reduced isolation

Technology
- Communication and task completion
- Unrestricted communication
- Transparency and ease of use

Task
- A common sense of purpose
- Source of motivation to participate
- Source of collaboration

Facilitator
- Comfort with technology in use
- Competence with online facilitation
- Ability to communicate clearly and in a balanced way
- Comfort with a reasonable degree of chaos and conflict
- Creation of safe container for the group
- Nurturance of the development of relationships
- Promotion of self-organization and empowerment

Using Technology, Online Groups
- Problem Solve
- Manage Conflict
- Develop Norms
- Process Information Together
- Communicate with One Another
- Connect

Elements of Effective Online Groups

FIGURE 8.2. THE LEARNING WEB.

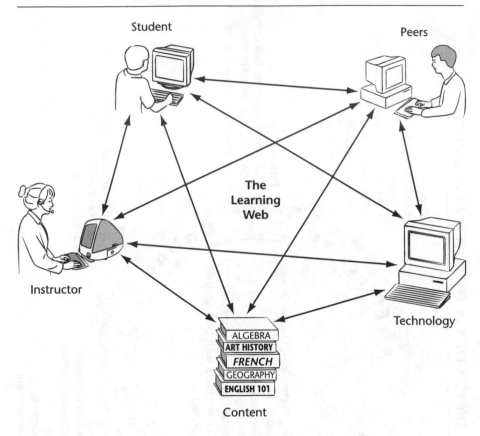

reluctant to let down their friends by not participating in discussions or other activities. They come to see their contributions as important to the learning process of the whole group and not just to the achievement of their own learning objectives. The focus, then, becomes the learning process and involvement in a learning community, and not simply completing the course or earning a passing grade.

Technology

The course technology should be considered only a vehicle for its delivery and as such should be transparent and easy to use with minimal instruction. The technology allows for the creation of a meeting place online where students can connect with one another for both social and task-oriented reasons. The technology itself should not be the reason a course is offered, but rather an important supportive factor in its success.

Task

Clearly, the task that brings students together is to complete the course. In that regard, the task creates the sense of purpose for both the students and the instructor. A well-developed course should motivate students. If the material presented is relevant and the task is structured to empower students to take charge of the learning process, they will be more likely to stay with it through successful completion. Multiple opportunities for teamwork and collaboration will reinforce the sense of common purpose and provide opportunities for students to take charge of their learning.

Instructor

We have already discussed some of the critical characteristics of a successful online instructor, including flexibility, responsiveness to students, a willingness to learn and a self-perception as a lifelong learner, an ability to balance amount of participation in the group, and most importantly, comfort with and the ability to facilitate the development of an online learning community. Instructors who are flexible, open, and willing to go with the flow of an online class are likely to have a successful experience. They must, however, be prepared to deal with the conflict that will inevitably emerge in an online group and develop a means by which to work with it successfully so that the group can move on to achieve its task together.

Conflict Revisited

McClure (1998) states that conflict is a central feature of all groups. It is not a feature that should be feared but instead welcomed, because the presence of conflict indicates that the group is developing successfully. McGrath and Hollingshead (1994) also note that in online groups the ability to resolve conflict is one of the central tasks to be accomplished in order for the goals to be achieved and the tasks completed.

Frequently, the word *conflict* brings to mind an all-out struggle, complete with anger, hurt feelings, and a win-lose outcome. In the online group, however, conflict may simply take the form of disagreement with the instructor or between students. At times it may become heated and be perceived as an attack. When this happens, the instructor should step in to resolve it. However, in many cases students can resolve these disagreements for themselves. Sometimes, resolution may take the form of agreeing to disagree.

Asking students to reflect on the conflict and its resolution can add an element to the learning experience that can be extremely useful to them in their overall reflections about online learning and how it differs from the face-to-face classroom. The following example of conflict and confrontation over the spotty participation of a group member is one that demonstrates growing understanding on the part of students about the need for all to be involved if learning online is to be successful. Although the tone is somewhat harsh, it reflects these students' strong feelings about their dependence on one another in order for their learning objectives to be achieved.

You [Phillip] have mentioned on 3 or 4 occasions, how busy you have been, sleepless nights, coming into this process late, an outcast, x number of consulting proposals. . . . Focus on the participation, learning and the contribution. Let this other stuff go. We are all extremely busy and quite frankly not interested in being reminded how overwhelmed we all are. The boat we are in is the same. The waters are equally turbulent, only our perspectives differ. . . . You are always selling! Seek to understand first. *Larry*

I want to "jump" in here and offer some observations on things that I have seen. I agree Larry, that asking questions is paramount to understanding. I can see that you are striving to "read between the lines" and understand all that is being said. I appreciate this endeavor very much. However, I also agree with Allison's statement: "Not EVERYthing can be answered with another question.—I'm really worried that this is coming out whiny or out of line, but I wanted to state an observation of mine . . . a personal opinion (I don't think that was whiny at all, by the way). In my opinion Larry, I also agree with her that you seem to be a little defensive . . . and I will even add . . . sometimes it comes across with a little bit of an "attacking" feeling to me. Perhaps this is simply your pure desire to understand. I know that this is what you are constantly seeking to teach me. . . . "Seek first to understand." I appreciate this very much and will strive to do so. I also am reminded of a proverb, which basically says, "people often teach what they most need to learn." Just food for thought. Asking the kinds of questions you tend to ask are extremely important and I am thankful for your insight and attempts to clarify and hope to be able to ask such penetrating questions myself. However, there seems to be something missing in your responses and I think that there is not very much sharing of something deeper . . . no collaboration. You mainly just respond by asking for further clarification or with a reason for you previous response. It's a real cognitive approach. I wonder how do you "feeeeel." That is what I want to know, instead of always being asked another question. So I will ask you now, how do you feel about me, what are you so angry with me about? *Phillip*

What might be interpreted by some as petty bickering actually signals the presence of conflict. In fact, this exchange opened the door for others in the group to begin discussing what they saw as appropriate participation. Although Larry and Phillip settled their difference easily once the conflict surfaced, the issue of levels of participation continued well into the course and resurfaced involving other students. They soon began to realize that their expectations of one another and their need to rely on one another for their learning was the issue. Important learning about the process of an online class was gained overall, beginning with this exchange.

A good rule of thumb is for students to wait twenty-four hours before responding to a post they feel is negative. This allows for a cooling-off period and a time to reflect. When a student returns to a post that was initially seen as offensive, he or she may find that, on second reading, it is not so bad. This time-out also gives students a chance to respond from a place of reason rather than anger, thus helping to reduce the possibility that the conflict will escalate. In the previous series of exchanges, Larry is asking Phillip to do just that—wait and reflect rather than react. Phillip is asking Larry to look at the way in which he approaches not only him but also the rest of the group. The students involved are demonstrating the ability to manage their own conflict situation. The instructor intervened only to ask the students to reflect overall on the process, but waited until the conflict had abated before doing so.

Just thought I'd stick my nose in for a second—several of you have been commenting about the need for Phillip to get involved with this process and fearing that he would not. He did—in a big way, in my humble opinion—in his last post by opening himself up to the group in a rather courageous way, I thought, and contributing his thoughts on the task and process. The response was nothing, nada, zilch! I thought it was interesting to note, and thought it was important for all of you to reflect on it a bit. *Rena*

Rena, you are right, Phillip did jump in and no one commented. I thought that it was great that Phillip is back in the game. But, as Stasi said, wasn't going to applaud until I see results over time. It is sort of like making friends. It is not difficult to be nice, witty, thoughtful, etc. for one day. . . . I am looking for a commitment to the group. That commitment means more than popping in once a week on the weekends. *Michele*

Like Stasi, I too am confused by your comments regarding Phillip. He posted a long time ago (under group discussions) . . . and, yes, it was long and philosophical . . . and was a response to Michele and Stasi, so I didn't think it was right for me to get in the middle of it. I was hopeful that after that posting he would get much more involved on a day to day basis. Instead another week lapsed and now we have the one he just posted today. So, after reading it, I don't see where it needs a response either. It seems as though he is giving Larry feedback and then entering into our group process just as the rest of us have. I am hopeful that this is a sign that he's back in to help us. . . . *Allison*

I really think, gang, that you need to take a look at the role that Phillip is playing in this group and your responses (or lack thereof) to him. I also need to say that if it weren't Phillip, it would be someone else. I just noticed something that clearly the others of you didn't based on your confusion in response to my post—you've been asking him to jump in and some have expressed concern that he wouldn't. When he did, you just kept on rolling like nothing had happened. . . . Again, I'm not blaming, shaming, defending, or anything else like that—just asking you to reflect on your own process and dynamics. . . . I have noticed, and there's no judgment intended with this comment—again neutral observation—that everyone is fine with the level with which Chad is able to participate (which is low compared to others) and yet when Phillip participates at actually a higher level, it's his participation that gets questioned. I'd like you, once again, to simply reflect on this. Maybe no comment is even necessary—just notice and reflect. *Rena*

The response to the instructor's observations in this case was a series of "aha's" for the group's members. They began to recognize what conflict looks like. They also began to understand the roles that various group members were playing and their responses to their own expectations about other group members. The following posts reflect the changes that occurred as a result and indicate that the group is beginning to move out of conflict:

I am feeling particularly disappointed and frustrated. I would not say that my experience with teams, in general, has not been totally gratifying. There are probably several reasons for that, partly due to what may be unrealistic expectations on my part and partly due, in my opinion, to others not fulfilling their obligation to the group or the agreed upon norms or rules. I guess that I am trying to understand where Phillip and Chad are coming from and I am frustrated because I can't seem to engage Chad in dialogue and Phillip doesn't seem to get what people are saying. I take participation and leadership on a team very seriously. In regard to my participation, I have had to work very hard to meet the norm of reading once a day and posting every other day. And, I have tried to provide something in the posts that would add or expand the group's work, help move the group forward, and/or encourage and recognize group members. Maybe this is the norm I have established for myself and it is unrealistic to expect it from others. . . . This is the part that feels like the groups I have been part of before. Some people actively participate and add, some hang back and observe, various levels of trust and individual interpretations of the information at hand, individual interpretations of the appropriate levels of commitment to self and commitment to the group. *Michele*

I have read your comments pointed to Chad and Phillip as well as the other Cohort member's comments and have decided not to play in this arena, until now. I am clear that norms have been established and I am also excited with the participation from the group. I look positively at the direction we have taken, the progress that we have made and value everyone's input. My focus remains on what we are accomplishing collectively as well as what I am learning through this process. I am delighted with the results. There is so much stuff that goes on in other people's lives that I try (not always successful) to give them the full benefit of the doubt. I am still learning to hold everyone legitimate and sometimes it is not easy for me. Rena's posting with regard to the group's lack of response to Phillip's posting helped me advance my understanding in this regard even more. This group has dealt with a lot. I have learned so much in such a short time and I am grateful. There will never be a group where there is "equal participation" in everyone's eyes and the value of the individual contribution is the real jewel. *Larry*

It is best, then, for instructors to take a position of noninvolvement and observation when conflict first surfaces. Often students are very capable of working through the issues and achieving successful resolution. However, if the conflict escalates, interferes with progress of the class, or turns into personal attacks or flaming, then the instructor must intervene. Things often begin to quiet down after a post by the instructor setting a limit or asking students to take the conflict offline, or after the instructor has individual conversations with the students involved. If, however, these actions do not work, or if the conflict is perpetuated by a difficult student, it may become necessary to take additional steps.

Working with Difficult Students

Just as in the face-to-face classroom, difficult students appear in the online classroom. The difficulty can take many forms: being unable to adjust to the technology; dominating the conversation; refusing to participate at an adequate level; blaming the instructor, other students, or the program for their lack of satisfactory progress; and bullying other students or the instructor through flaming. In the face-to-face classroom, an instructor may become quickly aware of the presence of a difficult student. But in the online classroom, difficulties may not show up as quickly or may be unrecognizable at first. For example, it is common for students new to the online arena to experience some problems with the technology. Some may require the assistance of the instructor or other technical support staff to resolve their technical difficulties. When difficulties go on for several weeks, however, red flags may start to go up for the instructor and the other students: Is this someone who truly is having difficulty or is this a smokescreen for refusal to participate at the level required?

When instructors diagnose a difficult student, it is important to take steps that they would also take in a face-to-face situation. For example, if an instructor would schedule an individual conversation with a student who is causing problems such as dominating classroom conversation or being argumentative, she should do so with the online student as well. The conversation might take place via e-mail, or the instructor may choose to have a telephone conversation or face-to-face meeting with the student. It is important to recognize that not all conversations need to happen on the course site. Sometimes taking the problem off-line can be more helpful than trying to confront or deal with the student publicly. Regardless of how and where the conversation occurs, it is important for the instructor to provide concrete examples of the behavior in question. The beauty of the online environment is that asynchronous discussion is archived on the course site. Therefore, it is relatively easy for the instructor to point out where and how the problem occurred and give specific suggestions for improvement.

If a problem student is unresponsive to instructor intervention, then once again best practices should prevail. Perhaps the student's access to the course should be suspended until the problem is resolved. The instructor may need to request help from department or program administration if an administrative solution, such as permanently removing the student from the class, becomes necessary.

As we've noted many times, successful achievement of learning outcomes is dependent on the creation of a learning community. Students depend on good participation from one another to build that community. Consequently, an instructor cannot afford to take a passive stance or wait too long when problems are spotted. Decisive action must be taken and limits set when behavior is unacceptable in order to salvage the learning experience for the majority.

When It Simply Isn't Working

There are times when, despite our best efforts, we are unable to facilitate successful formation of an online learning community or create a sense of group among the learners. It is easy for an instructor to blame himself or herself when this occurs, saying, "Surely there is something else I could have done." However, when we have experienced this phenomenon, there is usually a student who offers "a voice of reason" by giving us some feedback that offers clues to what went wrong. The following story of such an experience includes excerpts from an online conversation between one student and the instructor after the class ended during an attempt to discern what transpired in an unsuccessful online learning experience. Interestingly, the class in question was another section of The Search for Soul and Spirit in the Workplace offered at a graduate level.

The class began in fairly typical fashion with the instructor asking that introductions be posted online. This was not the first online class taken by this group of students. Due to the nature of the program in which the students were enrolled, the participants had met one another at a face-to-face session to kick off other classes taken before this one. However, the instructor was not present at that session. Because of this, the instructor faced an immediate challenge of establishing a relationship with and presence in the group. What became apparent to the instructor rather quickly was that there were two subgroups in the class, based on the grouping of the students when they met face-to-face. In addition, there were other concerns about the nature of the group.

As you know, I was so inspired by the course topic and drawn to the class, I had high hopes for rich dialogue and learning. The class size was small, and all female. I remember making an early comment on that and asking if people thought it was significant that we were all women. The answers that came back were just more questions. I do wonder if the balance in the class would have been different if we had some male participants. *Beth*

Although a problem for the group, the concern about group composition was put aside when students began complaining about a lack of clarity in the course design and an inability to determine what was expected of them. This proved confusing to the instructor, who had used the same course design very successfully several times previously.

Unfortunately, we had some early disconnects in the class—in the first week. People were unclear about the assignments (which is normal and has occurred in every class. We simply then post for clarification). One participant was particularly harsh and caustic in the tone of her writing. She was upset that you [the instructor] needed to travel for two or three days in the first week of the class and that you had some trouble connecting online (from Norway, was it?) A second participant joined in the disappointment. What I remember most was the tone of the exchange. It was accusatory and very judgmental, non-forgiving. I think we never fully recovered from this exchange that occurred so early in the class. *Beth*

Once the instructor was able to rejoin the class, after only two days of absence, she was surprised to find the level of confusion and upset present in the group. Quickly, this group had entered a phase of disunity and conflict from which it was difficult to recover. The conflict not only was directed toward the instructor but also occurred between the two subgroups within this small group of six students. The instructor expressed her concern and confusion over the level of hostility in the group. But any attempts she made to intervene in the conflict and reduce it were met with resistance and anger.

I would bristle whenever I read what the "toxic" participant would write. It was harder to log on and less rewarding than other classes I have been in where the exchange and discussion is so rich and supportive. I would come downstairs after doing schoolwork and debrief some of the things this one participant said and how she said it with my husband. I thought they missed a big point of the learning. *Beth*

Because participation continued to be poor and interchanges between the two students and the instructor and a few of the students with one another often bordered on flaming, the instructor attempted to have individual contacts with all of the students in the group, both via e-mail and phone. One student refused all contact with the instructor, whereas others responded fairly favorably to these exchanges. The instructor also enlisted the aid of the program chair who, when she attempted to intervene, also met with resistance and challenge. The difficult student withdrew from the class for a period of time and eventually made a decision to withdraw from the program, returning only to complete the class. Overall, students never fully participated in this class or achieved their learning objectives due to the early problems in the group.

I . . . observed how hard it was for you to try to mitigate all this online. It was helpful when you all would report that you had a conversation. If I recall, we had some improvement after that, but never a full recovery. . . . My approach was to stay focused on the reasons I was in the class, continue to respond to everyone and try to foster dialogue, and to rise above what I saw as pettiness and lack of maturity. . . . It was interesting and puzzling how individuals drawn to the topic of soul and spirit in the workplace spent so much time and thought on the dark side of spirit. Maybe they showed us the dark sides of their own spirits. Maybe they felt they had permission to do so, given the topic. I don't know. At the end of the class, I remember thinking, for a class on soul and spirit, we didn't have very much soul or spirit in our learning community. How sad. *Beth*

What are the lessons learned from working with a group such as this one? What can an instructor do when, despite all efforts at intervention, a learning community fails to form? The following are the key issues as they relate to these questions:

- The group in question contained not one but two difficult students, and the instructor was not clear about the programmatic guidelines in dealing with a student who is inappropriate in the online classroom.
- Decisive action was not taken with the difficult members, thus giving them "permission" to continue to act as they had. In hindsight, both the instructor and the program administrator agreed that had decisive action been taken early on,

such as setting clear limits on acceptable behavior in the class, the learning experience might have been saved.

- The makeup of the group was a problem from the beginning (small numbers, all female, all with the same level of online experience). McClure (1998) notes issues that emerge when a group is all female with a female leader and describes them as follows: "The early stages of group development are further complicated by member reactions to the female leader. These reactions range from ambivalence to confusion and rebellion" (p. 100). When debriefing this experience with administrative staff, it was noted that this fact should have been caught during registration and an attempt made to balance the group's gender composition.

- The group was what McClure (1998) would refer to as "regressive." In other words, it resisted movement out of conflict into harmony and performance. Some group members were intent on "killing the leader," in McClure's terms. When other group members refused to join them in their stance, the dynamics spiraled further downward.

The important thing to learn from a group that fails to establish itself successfully as a learning community is that often more than one factor contributes to the problems. It is rarely just the instructor and his or her facilitation techniques; we have seen good outcomes with inexperienced instructors who are just finding their way in online instruction. What is most important is for the instructor to try everything in his or her bag of tricks: openly discuss concerns about poor participation on the course site; contact students individually; if possible, have meetings with students; and when necessary, contact department or program administration to take decisive action with difficult students and consult with peers or colleagues for advice. The instructor must do *something*, and never simply allow students to flounder. Once the experience has ended, it is essential to review it in some fashion, preferably with supportive colleagues or a willing student participant, in order to glean the important lessons that will assist in avoiding the same situation in the future.

In this chapter and Chapter Seven we have discussed the critical importance of looking at and working with student issues in the development and delivery of an online course. Although we have repeatedly described this form of education as learner-centered, we have been as guilty as our colleagues in forgetting that the student is and should be the central focus of all online programs and courses. Focusing on the student and avoiding assumptions about what they know about online learning, how they might work through the process of the course, and why they may or may not be successful online has been a crucial piece of our own learning as online instructors. With this in mind, in our final chapter we will summarize the lessons we have learned in working in the cyberspace class-room and take a look ahead not only at new developments in online learning but also at the impact of online learning on education as a whole.

Tips for Working with Online Classroom Dynamics

- Be clear about the instructor role as a facilitator. Making this explicit at the beginning of an online class can prevent confusion and create agreement between the instructor and students about expectations.
- Be clear about group tasks and expectations. The clearer the instructor is about what is to be accomplished in the course, the less likely that students will become confused and flounder.
- Expect students to move through phases as they develop their working group. Asking questions about group development—such as, "How comfortable are you feeling with one another as a group?"—as well as about their comfort level with the process can help.
- Facilitate the process. Although we strongly support the empowerment of students to take on their own learning process, instructor guidance and intervention is necessary to keep things moving and on track. Chaos can ensue when students lack appropriate instructor input.
- As Howard Rheingold (1993) states, always assume good intent. If a student flames another student or the instructor, assume that it is inadvertent and came out of good intentions, and respond accordingly.
- Wait twenty-four hours before responding to what you may consider to be a personal attack; advise students to do the same. The intensity of the message always seems to wane with time.
- Always address flaming. A skilled online facilitator put it well: "One voice can be much louder online than off-line. . . . As a facilitator one must decide if they will protect the right of anyone to say anything, or to draw a line or embrace a certain set of norms which, at some point, pulls that one voice back out of the spotlight to allow others back in. For me, this balance between control and emergence is the most difficult, artful, and when it happens, glorious moment for an online group facilitator when they can hold a space for both" (White, 2000).
- Expect conflict. Instead of viewing it as unhealthy, welcome it as a sign that the group is developing. Facilitate movement through conflict so that students can create norms for working with one another and successfully complete their tasks.
- Don't mistake confusion for conflict. Sometimes students do become confused about course expectations, guidelines, and assignments, and a simple explanation on the part of the instructor is all that is needed to move the process forward.

- Ask for support and help when necessary and especially when dealing with difficult students. We have no problem doing that when teaching face-to-face; the same should be true online. Having individual meetings, by phone or in person, are appropriate when dealing with a difficult student. It is important also for instructors to know that they have the support of the administration to remove a difficult student from their online classes should that become necessary.
- As an instructor, use sidebar conversations carefully to avoid having all communication move through the instructor. Encourage students to use sidebars only for personal exchanges unrelated to the course. Concerns and comments about the course should be made on the course site, and whenever possible, conflict resolution with difficult students should occur there as well.

CHAPTER NINE

LESSONS LEARNED IN THE CYBERSPACE CLASSROOM

What key lessons have we learned in our exploration of all the myriad issues and concerns involved with the design, development, and delivery of online courses and programs? In this chapter, we will review the most important lessons from the cyberspace classroom and then take a look ahead into the near future of online education. Changes are occurring rapidly, making it almost impossible to see very far into the future of distance learning. However, some predictions are being made based on current developments that are encouraging yet also indicate a need for caution and measured action.

Lessons from the Cyberspace Classroom

The following, then, are the lessons that may be taken from the cyberspace classroom.

Course Development Needs to Focus on Interactivity, Not Content

The key to success in an online class rests not with the content that is being presented but with the method by which the course is delivered. To reiterate a point we made earlier, the most beautifully designed course—complete with audio, video, and other graphic and multimedia tools—can fail dismally if the instructor is not a skilled online facilitator working to build a learning community among the learners. A well-delivered course provides multiple means by which students and the instructor can interact, including e-mail, discussion boards, and careful use of synchronous discussion. The effective use of the means by which interactivity is enhanced deepens the learning experience and creates a more satisfying outcome for everyone. Content can be creatively delivered through facilitation of effective discussions, collaborative assignments that promote teamwork and interaction, Internet research, and companion websites both on and outside of the course site. When content is delivered in multiple ways, it also addresses different student learning styles and creates a more interesting course overall. But it is the interaction and connections made in the course that students will remember as the keys to learning in an online course. It is pedagogy and not technology that is critical to the success of an online course.

Faculty and Student Roles Need to Change

In order for a high degree of interactivity to occur in an online course, the roles of faculty and students need to change: faculty need to be willing to give up a degree of control and allow the learners to take the lead in learning activities. Although this sounds easy, both faculty and students bring previous educational experience and expectations to the online classroom. Students expect to be "taught" and faculty expect to "teach." Consequently, students need to be oriented to their new role and the ways in which learning occurs online. A formal training program can assist in this process. However, when a training program is not available, instructors can get students started by posting material to the course site in the form of an initial discussion item, static information that students can access at any time, or a frequently asked questions file about the online learning process.

What is most important is to encourage faculty to move away from the lecture mode of teaching and toward the use of more active learning approaches. Faculty should be encouraged to take stock of their pedagogical approach and ask themselves: How do I see myself as a teacher? How do my students respond to my teaching style? What types of learning activities do I currently incorporate into my classes? What changes in those activities do I need to make to move into the online environment? Many faculty—ourselves included—have found that the changes required to deliver an online class successfully also work very successfully in the face-to-face classroom. Our own face-to-face teaching has changed as the result of our experiences online. The use of the collaborative, interactive, active learning techniques we have described can thus enhance the learning experience of students in the traditional classroom. Once again, learner-centered pedagogy is everything when it comes to teaching online or face-to-face.

Both Faculty and Students Need Training

In order to understand the key lessons of the need for interactivity and the changes in faculty and student roles, both faculty and students need training. Training for both currently focuses on technology. However, that needs to change to focus on what it takes to teach and learn online successfully. Other faculty development concerns include the importance of customizing an online course developed by another entity or faculty member, dealing with students and student problems in the online classroom, working with online classroom dynamics, and matching the ways to use technology and approaches to teaching in order to address student learning styles. Both faculty and students will certainly need training in the technology they will be using in online classes, but this should not be the primary concern.

Faculty Who Teach Online Need to Feel Supported

Just as when facing difficulties in the face-to-face classroom, faculty teaching online need to feel supported in dealing with course and student issues. An instructor trying to deal with a difficult student needs to know the parameters within which he or she can operate in order to handle the situation with minimal disruption to the rest of the group. Faculty orientation to the online environment in a given institution should offer policies or at least some discussion of resources that can be used if a difficult situation is encountered. Instructors teaching online can feel isolated from the institution. If the instructor's ties to the institution are strengthened in any way, it will result in an overall online program that appears cohesive and well-planned. Furthermore, in order to build a learning community faculty need to be able to create a safe container within which the learning community can flourish. To do that, faculty need to feel supported by the institution, meaning that the institution must deal swiftly and fairly with the student problems they encounter. When student problems are not adequately addressed, a sense of safety may not prevail.

Based on our own experience, we can say that when an instructor does not feel a sense of institutional support for the action he or she needs to take in the online classroom, the results can be almost disastrous—students may leave the course or program; they may become very vocal in expressing their dissatisfaction with the way a situation was handled; and most importantly, learning outcomes for the entire group may not be achieved. Our students are our customers. Providing them with a successful learning experience takes more than putting a course online, training an instructor to deliver it, and hoping for the best.

Institutions Should Develop a Strategic Plan

Institutions need a strategic plan that is focused on technology as well as policies related to course and program development, ownership, and governance. Rather than muddling through in order to get courses online and compete with other institutions that are doing the same, institutions are better served to use a strategic planning process. The process should include discussion and development of policies related to course and program development, course ownership, and governance issues including decisions about which courses and programs should be placed online, faculty compensation, faculty teaching loads, and enrollments.

Furthermore, in preparation for the development of such a plan, a realistic market assessment should be conducted. Too often assumptions are made about the students who are likely to enroll in online programs without any research to validate those assumptions. If online courses and programs are offered, which students is the institution likely to attract? Would such offerings serve on-campus students in addition to extending the institution's reach off-campus? Answering these questions should help to determine which courses to offer and which programs to develop in response to student needs. Including faculty in this process is critical in order to move these decisions through the institution's regular governance process. In addition, an inclusive process can help to alleviate disagreements over course ownership and intellectual property issues. The key to success in this area is reaching agreement on issues of governance, ownership, and faculty compensation *before* embarking on the development of courses and programs.

Institutions Should Develop an Infrastructure First

Faculty and students need both administrative and technical support in order to teach and learn online effectively. When institutions decide to put a course or two online, making use of faculty who are early adopters of technology, they often do so without first creating an adequate structure for faculty and student technical support. Significant problems may be the result. How will students register for online courses? How will faculty receive enrollment information? Will faculty be expected to enter student information into their courses, or will that be done by someone in registration or instructional technology? Who responds when students or faculty encounter technical difficulty? What happens when and if the server crashes and both faculty and students are unable to access the course site? What happens when hardware and software used for online courses becomes outdated? How do decisions about hardware and software purchase and upgrade get made? These are but some of the questions that need to be adequately answered in order for online courses and programs to be delivered smoothly and professionally.

Once again, we have learned from experience that institutions that do not address these questions will eventually face these issues whether they want to or not. We were hired to conduct an online faculty training for a department in an institution that intended to offer online courses with or without institutional support. One faculty member decided to "play" with the student information tool embedded in the courseware and practice entering students into a course she had created as a part of the training. Although she had been given information about the correct way of doing so, she chose to create a softer, easier way, which crashed the server that housed the courseware. It took three days for the one instructional technologist hired by the institution to clean up the damage. And it took less than a week for the institution to engage in discussion to create policies for entering student information into courses, including who does so and how to do it. The result was the removal of the student information tool from the courseware. Information is now generated by registration and passed on to the instructional technologist who enters it into the course.

Technology Should Be Chosen by an Inclusive Committee

As we travel and consult with institutions, we are often asked by administrators, "How can we sell faculty on the idea of teaching online? This is the greatest obstacle we face." Inclusion in the decision-making process around the adoption and use of technology can greatly assist faculty in buying into the development and delivery of online courses and programs. They will feel more comfortable with the process if their voices are heard and if the focus remains on teaching and learning rather than maximizing profits. Furthermore, faculty, when involved in the process, can help to identify their training and support needs. If faculty are included in the planning process and there is a realistic assessment of student learning needs, that can help to avoid myriad problems and lead to the development of a responsible and responsive online program.

Faculty resistance also stems from fears that they will be overloaded in online course development and teaching responsibilities, especially in an area that may not contribute to promotion and tenure decisions. Developing clear policies in this area that recognize this work as scholarship and providing stipends or release time can help. Faculty fears and resistance can also be minimized if there is good training that focuses on pedagogy and if there is support for the delivery of courses. When faculty realize that it is the process of good teaching—a process they know about—that leads to success in the online classroom, and not the technology itself, then their anxiety level decreases.

A Look into the Near Future

As we look at the lessons from the cyberspace classroom that we have learned thus far—some of them painful, others positive—we are led to wonder what the future holds for online education. What can institutions and their faculties expect to see over the next few years as online learning becomes an even greater part of the academy? Although there are no certain answers to these questions, we suspect that we will see changes in the following areas: technology and software; accreditation, course, and program quality; course and program development; professional development; the ways in which faculty and students interact; and increased research into online education.

Let us now explore each of these, and in so doing, begin to fit together the pieces of the mosaic that is the future of online education and higher education as a whole.

Technology and Software

As computer hardware becomes increasingly affordable, and as access and quality in remote areas improve, it is likely that some of the tools that are currently difficult to use in an online classroom setting, such as chat, audio, and video, will become more accessible and therefore more usable in an online class. The responsiveness of courseware companies to the needs of their faculty and student constituents—in part as a result of the highly competitive marketplace in which they operate—should continue to lead to changes that make course software more user-friendly and more customizable, based on technology that is transparent to the course delivery process.

By calling for the certification of course authoring software, the Congressional Web-Based Education Commission (Carnavale, 2000c) is making one attempt to further development of software that is responsive to the marketplace. The commission is exploring the idea of creating a set of standards to measure software. The result would be a clearinghouse for approved software, allowing school districts and universities to make informed decisions and saving them both time and money. Although the commission is not interested in dictating educational policy in the area of online distance education, it is responding to those who are calling for federal guidelines to support technology standards.

In addition, it is hoped that a comprehensive set of technical standards will make it easier for institutions to transfer courses from one software platform to another, creating what has been termed the next generation of shareable courseware (Carr, 2000b). Current platforms are proprietary, sometimes making the transfer of content time-consuming and expensive. Because of the expense involved with the initial creation of online courses, universities want to ensure that the content in those courses is protected rather than lost should a move to a new platform become necessary or desired.

The bottom line is, as online distance education grows we are likely to see additional courseware players entering the market, causing increasing competition between software producers. Simultaneously, as universities become more informed consumers of technology products, increasing demand for responsiveness and quality standards is likely.

Accreditation, Course, and Program Quality

The issue of online program accreditation follows closely on the heels of the demand for quality standards in software development. Currently, online courses and programs are evaluated for accreditation based on standards developed for face-to-face courses and programs. Seen as unfamiliar and uncharted territory, decisions on the accreditation of distance learning programs are still pending (McMurtrie, 1999).

There is little agreement at present as to what constitutes a quality online course or program. Furthermore, the accrediting of Jones International University by North Central Association of Schools and Colleges raised significant concerns on the part of faculty and traditional institutions about how the accreditation of completely online programs might be accomplished. Questions included these: "Can accreditors truly evaluate a university based solely on distance learning—with classrooms, libraries, and faculty members located somewhere in cyberspace—in the same way that they evaluate a traditional institution? Can we really call those institutions 'colleges' or 'universities' if they lack both a critical core of full-time faculty members and a system of governance by which the faculty is responsible for developing curricula and academic policy? Can accreditors actually determine that new, on-line institutions meet the same basic criteria for quality—or at least equivalent criteria—that traditional accredited institutions must meet?" (Perley and Tanguay, 1999, p. B4). Just the fact that questions such as these are being asked indicates that a set of standards pertaining to online courses needs to be developed.

The benchmarking studies currently being done are an attempt to create agreement on quality in online programs. In addition, the attempts to develop a set of quality standards for courseware, discussed in the previous section, should help to create some uniformity among courses and programs as time goes on. We hope that these attempts at quality control will not produce standards so narrow that they stifle the creativity and experimentation with technique and course delivery that typify current course development. Additionally, we hope that standards will be created with an eye toward academic freedom. There is wide variation occurring in current course development, yielding a need for discussions of quality in online program development. The ideal outcome of those discussions, however, would be a range within which faculty, institutions, and the developers of course authoring software can comfortably work.

Course and Program Development

It is likely that as we move into the near future of online learning we will see more use of courses developed by private entities, textbook publishers, or faculty hired specifically to develop courses to be delivered by another instructor. The high cost of course development both in terms of faculty and staff time are leading institutions to seek cost-effective alternatives that will allow them to enter the online market.

Another trend that is beginning to emerge is partnerships between private entities and universities for the purpose of developing and delivering online degree programs. This is most pronounced in the area of business, where partnerships such as the one between University Access and the University of North Carolina or Pensare and Duke University have been entered into for the purpose of delivering executive MBAs. Individual institutions or groups of institutions are also beginning to form and spin off for-profit arms devoted to the development and delivery of online courses and programs. One such collaboration, called Fathom, has been made between Columbia University, the British Library, the Cambridge University Press, the London School of Economics and Political Science, the New York Public Library, and the Smithsonian Institution's National Museum of Natural History (Carr and Kiernan, 2000). Fathom will not be offering degrees or programs, but it will offer courses created by the member institutions.

Yet another form of combined resources to offer distance learning programs has been the development of consortia of academic institutions. The most widely known is the Western Governors' University and the failed California Virtual University, now reborn as the California Virtual Campus, representing the state's community colleges. The Massachusetts Distance Learning Consortium is unusual in that it combines two- and four-year institutions to deliver approximately twenty-five distance learning courses using television and the Internet. The Massachusetts consortium effectively blurs the lines between two- and four-year institutions by allowing students to mix and match course offerings (Carr, 1999). All of the consortia mentioned allow institutions to share technology and courseware and reduce the cost of course development by spreading it through all of the member institutions.

Finally, in the area of course and program development, the gap between higher education and the corporate sector is narrowing as corporations develop their own degree programs to encourage their employees to study where they work and to focus on the development of the knowledge workers who are in so much demand. Some corporations are also purchasing courses from and entering into alliances with course development companies such as Pensare, University Access, and Ninth House in order to move employee training online.

None of these developments indicate that course development will move out of the hands of university faculty, but they do indicate that a wider variety of options will become available to institutions for course creation and use. Some institutions are likely to use third-party courses as a way to get started and get faculty oriented to the online environment, perhaps moving to courses developed by their own faculty as they become more comfortable with what is needed to teach successfully online.

Professional Development

What does it really mean to be a "guide on the side" or a "learning facilitator" rather than an instructor? How does an instructor successfully make the transition required to teach an online course so that students become empowered learners and take charge of the learning process? Is it possible to develop every instructor into a good online instructor? How can institutions tell the difference between someone who will do well online and someone who will not, be they faculty or student?

The questions posed are designed to help stimulate thinking about what might be needed in a good training and development program for faculty. However, they also point out that we need to think carefully about who should be encouraged to teach online. Earlier in this book we made the point that not all faculty are suited to the online environment, just as not all students should consider taking online courses. We even put forth the fairly controversial idea that faculty who are highly entertaining face-to-face may not make the best online instructors. Not all faculty, even after participating in online teacher training, will do well in that environment. And although some authors predict that the face-to-face, traditional classroom will go the way of the Model T (Barone and Luker, 2000), we believe it is more likely that most colleges and universities will deliver at least a portion of their course offerings online (Katz, 1999). Consequently, there will still be room for those who choose to teach in the classroom along with those who choose to teach online.

Greater attention should be paid to what faculty need to be able to teach online successfully. Rather than focusing on the technology itself, training and faculty development should focus on increasing interactivity in online classes, building a learning community among the learners, delivering course content in new and creative ways, incorporating collaboration into the learning process, empowering learners, and evaluating learners and learning outcomes in ways that make sense in the online arena. As faculty become veteran facilitators online and as the online learning environment itself evolves, training and development needs will change. Consequently, faculty development to prepare faculty to teach successfully online should be fluid and responsive to the changes that are sure to come.

How Faculty and Students Interact

One of the changes already occurring that has been noted by many who write about online learning is the ways in which faculty and students interact (Barone and Luker, 2000; Duderstadt, 1999; Katz, 1999; Palloff and Pratt, 1999). Today's student is less likely to be an eighteen- to twenty-one-year-old seeking a one-time educational experience. Instead, today's student is likely to be an adult returning to school to obtain knowledge and skills needed to compete and advance in the workplace. The adult student is more likely to be a lifelong learner embarking on the beginning of what may be a learning process that results in the pursuit of multiple degrees, courses, or certifications. Although previously schooled to engage with instructors in traditional ways—expecting the instructor to be the expert with knowledge and wisdom to impart—lifelong learners are looking to enter a partnership that results in the achievement of their learning objectives (Bates, 2000).

The partnership students seek is with an academic institution that understands their needs and is capable of meeting them. Thus, there is a shift occurring in the academic world; academic institutions are recognizing that, like other types of organizations, they must be responsive to those they serve. The result is a shift from the traditional faculty-centered institution to a learner focus. Consequently, the relationship between faculty and student has to change as well.

Add technology and online teaching into the mix, and other changes begin to occur. Because the most effective way to achieve learning outcomes in the online classroom is by using active learning techniques, students are encouraged to become empowered learners. The more fully engaged, active learner is likely to bring new demands to the learning situation and will not be able to return to "business as usual" in subsequent learning situations, be they face-to-face or online. We noted earlier that the changed relationship between faculty and student in the online classroom is spilling over into the face-to-face classroom as faculty discover that active learning techniques work well there. Similarly, faculty who have historically made good use of active learning techniques face-to-face are finding that their transition to online learning is eased through the use of those techniques.

Bates (2000) notes, "Modern learning theory sees learning as an individual quest for meaning and relevance. Once learning moves beyond the recall of facts, principles, or correct procedures and into the area of creativity, problem solving, analysis, or evaluation (the very skills needed in the workplace in a knowledge-based economy, not to mention in life in general), learners need the opportunity to communicate with one another as well as with their teachers. This of course includes the opportunity to question, challenge, and discuss issues" (pp. 13–14).

Rather than feeling threatened by this shift in relationship, faculty should feel challenged by it. Faculty, too, are lifelong learners. The changing relationship between faculty and their students serves to expand the network through which faculty can learn. We always believe, when we enter a new online course, that we have as much to learn from our students as they do from us. We find this to be an exciting element of our online work and one that we welcome.

Research into Online Education

When we wrote *Building Learning Communities in Cyberspace* over two years ago, we found a paucity of research into online learning. However, we noted that interest in the area was growing and that the research would follow. That prediction has become increasingly true as online learning has established a stronghold in higher education. Individual faculty are writing and publishing articles about their experiences online. Studies are being conducted that compare face-to-face and online delivery of the same class for outcome effectiveness. The Institute for Higher Education Policy published a report (Phipps and Merisotis, 1999) reviewing contemporary research on the effectiveness of distance learning. Benchmarking studies are currently under way to determine the characteristics of effective online courses and the critical elements of the courseware that supports their development.

Because this is a new and growing area in academia, research efforts are likely to increase and continue. Those of us teaching online welcome the opportunity to contribute to this body of literature. The educational experiences that are the result of teaching online are so unique and different from those that we have had in the traditional classroom that we want to share them with our colleagues so that they might understand the power of this medium in delivering education in today's knowledge society.

James Duderstadt (1999) notes, "Today's technology is rapidly breaking the constraints of space and time. It has become clear that most people, in most areas, can learn—and learn well—using asynchronous learning (that is 'anytime, anyplace, anywhere' education). . . . Lifetime education is becoming a reality, making learning available for anyone who wants to learn, at the time and place of their choice, without great personal effort or cost. . . . Rather than an 'age of knowledge,' could we instead aspire to a 'culture of learning,' in which people are continually surrounded by, immersed in, and absorbed in learning experiences? . . . This may become not only the great challenge but the compelling vision facing higher education as it enters the next millennium" (pp. 24–25). Research that documents the effectiveness of our efforts in creating the culture of learning to which Duderstadt refers is important. Sharing our experiences and lessons learned, whether positive or negative, as we explore the territory of online learning is equally important.

We closed our previous book by commenting on our own experience of online teaching. We stated, "Not only are we helping to shape the creation of empowered, lifelong learners, our participation as equal members of a group of learners supports us in our quest for lifelong learning. For us, this is the power of online distance learning" (Palloff and Pratt, 1999, p. 168). Today, this not only remains true for us but increases with every online class we teach. We never cease to learn. We also never cease to wonder about and seek out what might be next. We have only begun to explore the cyberspace classroom and its important and powerful role in the future of education.

Tips for Creating Successful Courses and Programs

- Always strive to make online courses as interactive as possible.
- Use multiple means to deliver content and evaluate student progress.
- Give faculty a voice in the selection of course authoring software and in policy making around course ownership, governance, compensation, course loads and class size, and intellectual property.
- Provide training for both faculty and students in the new roles required to create online learning communities and complete courses successfully.
- Provide adequate administrative and technical support to faculty who are developing and delivering courses and to students who are enrolled in courses.
- Include issues such as course development, purchase of hardware and software, faculty compensation for course development and delivery, and training in the institution's strategic plan, and budget for a strong infrastructure to support online courses and programs.

A COMPARISON OF SYLLABI FOR ONLINE AND FACE-TO-FACE DELIVERY

Course Title: *Basic Addictions Studies*
Instructor: *Rena M. Palloff, Ph.D., LCSW*

I. Goals and objectives of this course:

At the conclusion of this course, the student should:

A. Know the background of society's use of drugs and its historical re-
    sponses to abuse and addiction
B. Know the evolution of the disease concept of chemical dependency,
    its definition, stages, and progression
C. Know a variety of theories which address the etiology of chemical de-
    pendency and can indicate a preferred approach and professional re-
    spect for other approaches
D. Identify the role denial plays in the assessment, intervention, and treat-
    ment process and can develop appropriate strategies to address this
E. Know the probable effects of chemical dependency on the family sys-
    tem, and can appropriately engage the family in the identification, in-
    tervention, and treatment process

    F. Know the basic approaches to the identification, intervention, and treatment of chemical dependency

    G. Know the importance of the 12 Step programs in the recovery process for both the chemically dependent and their families

    H. Be able to identify the salient issues involved in chemical dependency treatment as they relate to gender, culture, lifespan, and lifestyle

II. Methods by which these goals will be attained:

    A. Classroom presentations by instructor

    B. Group discussions

    C. Case studies provided by the instructor

    D. Films

    E. Required readings

III. Required Readings:

    A. Rotgers, Keller, and Morgenstern (1996), *Treating Substance Abuse*

    B. Palloff (1998), *Alcohol and Other Substance Dependence*

    C. Course Reader

IV. Evaluation:

Methods used to measure your goal attainment are:

    A. Case Studies

    B. Classroom Participation

    C. Brief report (3–5 pages typed) of attendance at any 3 of the following 12-Step meetings: *(Note: Choose 1 from each of the first 2 groups and then any third meeting)*

      • Alcoholics, Narcotics, Marijuana or Cocaine Anonymous

      • Alanon, Naranon, or Codependents Anonymous, or Adult Children of Alcoholics

      • Secular Organization for Sobriety, Rational Recovery, Women for Sobriety

    D. Brief (5–7 pages typed) research paper on any aspect of chemical dependency

V. Attendance requirements are the student's responsibility. However, it must be emphasized that much of the course material can only be learned through regular attendance. Therefore, all absences must be cleared in advance through the instructor. More than 2 absences in a quarter will affect your grade.

VI. Makeup work should be completed promptly by making arrangements with the instructor to avoid an incomplete grade. Assignments that are more than 2 weeks late will be not be accepted.

Syllabus: Basic Addictions Studies

(Note: Reading assignments are for the following class)
Wednesday, June 28, 2000

Introduction
    Student introductions
    Course overview
    "Quick and dirty" psychopharmacology

Assignments:
    Rotgers, Keller, and Morgenstern, Intro and Chapters 1 & 2
    Palloff, Lesson 1

Wednesday, July 5, 2000

Definitions of Alcoholism and Addiction
    Jellinek phases and stages
    Whole person concept
    Genetic factors
    Social/cultural factors
    Disease:
    Basic elements of disease model
    Evolution
    Continuum of use

Film: Bill Moyers, "The Hijacked Brain"

Assignments:
    Palloff, Lessons 2 & 3
    Reader, #1–4

Saturday, July 8, 2000

Assessment
    Screening instruments
    DSM-IV criteria
    Interviewing techniques

Working with concerned persons
Rights and releases
Continuum of care
Patient placement criteria

Concepts of Intervention
Creating a crisis
Concern, impact, and limitations
Patient placement criteria
Developmental model of recovery

Film: "Intervention"

Assignments:
Palloff, Lesson 4
Reader, #11–15
Practice Case Study (completed in class)
Complete Case Study 1 (homework)—Kathryn

Wednesday, July 12, 2000

Historical Models of Addiction and Treatment
Moral
Psychoanalytic
Behavioral
Current Addiction Treatment Efforts

Film: "Moyers on Treatment"

Assignments:
Palloff, Lesson 5
Reader, #5–9
Rotgers, Keller, and Morgenstern, Chapters 5 and 6
Case Study 1 due
Complete Case Study 2—Ron

Wednesday, July 19, 2000

Effects of Chemical Dependency on the Family
Adjustment of the family to the presence of addiction

The "life cycle" of the chemically dependent family
Family roles
Effective approaches to family treatment

Assignments:
  Palloff, Lesson 6
  Rotgers, Keller, and Morgenstern, Chapters 3 and 4
  Case Study 2 due
  Complete Case Study 3—Joe

Wednesday, July 26, 2000

Codependency/Adult Children of Alcoholics

Film: Moyers, "The Next Generation"

Assignments:
  Palloff, Lesson 6
  Rotgers, Keller, and Morgenstern, Chapters 7 and 8
  Case Study 3 due
  Complete Case Study 4—Raymond

Wednesday, August 9, 2000

Relapse
  Process
  Prevention

  Assignments:
  Reader, #17–20
  Case Study 4 due
  Complete Case Study 5—Cassie (to be distributed in class)

*** 12 Step Paper Due ***

Wednesday, August 16, 2000

Gender, Culture, Lifespan, and Lifestyle Issues in Chemical Dependency
  Adolescents
  Women

Elderly
Dual diagnosis
Working with cultural differences

Assignments:
Rotgers, Keller, and Morgenstern, Chapters 9 and 10
Reader, #21
Read Case Study material on Jane and Don (end of Lessons 4 and 6)
Case Study 5 due

Wednesday, August, 23, 2000

Becoming a chemical dependency counselor
Legal/ethical issues
Principles and practices of case management
Treatment techniques

Assignments:
Rotgers, Keller, and Morgenstern, Chapter 11
Palloff, Lesson 7
Reader, #16

Wednesday, August 30, 2000

Prevention
Future Trends in Treatment
The Biochemical Approach
                    *** Research Paper Due ***

◆ ◆ ◆

Course Title: **Basic Addictions Studies—Online Course**
Instructor: **Rena M. Palloff, Ph.D., LCSW**
   I. Goals and objectives of this course:

   At the conclusion of this course, the student should:

   A. Know the background of society's use of drugs and its historical
      responses to abuse and addiction.

B. Know the evolution of the disease concept of chemical dependency, its definition, stages, and progression.

C. Know a variety of theories which address the etiology of chemical dependency and can indicate a preferred approach and professional respect for other approaches.

D. Identify the role denial plays in the assessment, intervention, and treatment process and can develop appropriate strategies to address this.

E. Know the probable effects of chemical dependency on the family system, and can appropriately engage the family in the identification, intervention, and treatment process.

F. Know the basic approaches to the identification, intervention, and treatment of chemical dependency.

G. Know the importance of the 12 Step programs in the recovery process for both the chemically dependent and their families.

H. Be able to identify the salient issues involved in chemical dependency treatment as they relate to gender, culture, lifespan, and lifestyle.

II. Methods by which these goals will be attained:

A. Group discussions in the online classroom

B. Case studies provided by the instructor

C. Participation in an online team exercise in case management

D. Required readings

III. Required Readings:

A. Rotgers, Keller, and Morgenstern (1996), *Treating Substance Abuse*

B. Palloff (1998), *Alcohol and Other Substance Dependence*

C. Course Reader

IV. Evaluation

Methods used to measure your goal attainment are:

A. Case Studies—found in Palloff. Check the schedule of classes to see which case studies are due. Case study responses are to be posted to the course site.

B. Online Participation—in order to receive credit for participation, you *must* log on and make a contribution to the discussion *at least* twice a week.

C. Brief report (3–5 pages typed) posted to the course site of attendance at any 3 of the following 12-Step meetings:

(Note: Choose 1 from each of the first 2 groups and then any third meeting)

- Alcoholics, Narcotics, Marijuana or Cocaine Anonymous
- Alanon, Naranon, or Codependents Anonymous, or Adult Children of Alcoholics
- Secular Organization for Sobriety, Rational Recovery, Women for Sobriety

    D. Brief (3–5 pages typed) reflection paper on what you have learned about chemical dependency and how online learning contributed to or detracted from that experience.

  V. Participation requirements are the student's responsibility. However, it must be emphasized that much of the course material can only be learned through regular participation. Therefore, if you are having any difficulty, you must communicate with the instructor immediately. University policy is that more than 2 absences in a quarter will affect your grade. Lack of participation in weekly online discussion is considered an absence.

  VI. Make-up work should be completed promptly by making arrangements with the instructor to avoid an incomplete grade. Assignments that are posted more than 1 week late will be not be accepted.

  VII. Guidelines for Online Participation

Should you have questions or comments on any of these guidelines, let's discuss them! Also, please add any guidelines that you feel are appropriate.

"Attendance" and presence are required for this class. You are expected to log on at a minimum of twice per week (at any time during the week) and are expected to post a substantive contribution to the discussion at that time. Simply saying "hello" or "I agree" is not considered a substantive contribution. You must support your position or begin a new topic or add somehow to the discussion when logging on. You are also expected to attend two face-to-face meetings to begin and end the class. *The first meeting will be an online training and is very important to your success in this class!* The first meeting will be held on Thursday, June 29 at 7:15PM in the Computer Lab. The final meeting will be Thursday, August 31 at 7:15PM—room to be announced.

Discussions for the week begin on Sundays. I will post some questions for consideration to begin the discussion each week.

Your assignments will be posted online. You will be asked to comment on and provide feedback to one another on your work.

Instructions for the team simulation will be posted online the week prior to the start of the exercise.

Although I strongly suggest that all issues, questions, and problems be dealt with online, you can feel free to call or e-mail me regarding these issues at any time.

- Use good "netiquette" such as:
    Check the discussion frequently and respond appropriately and on subject.
    Focus on one subject per message and use pertinent subject titles.
    Capitalize words only to highlight a point or for titles—Capitalizing otherwise is generally viewed as SHOUTING!
    Be professional and careful with your online interaction.
    Cite all quotes, references, and sources.
    When posting a long message, it is generally considered courteous to warn readers at the beginning of the message that it is a lengthy post.
    It is considered extremely rude to forward someone else's messages without their permission.
    It is fine to use humor, but use it carefully. The absence of face-to-face cues can cause humor to be misinterpreted as criticism or flaming (angry, antagonistic criticism).
    Feel free to use emoticons such as:) or;) to let others know that you're being humorous.

Syllabus Basic Addictions Studies—Online Course

(Note: Reading assignments are for the following class)
Thursday, June 29, 2000

Introduction
    Student introductions—Complete a student homepage
    Computer training
    Course overview and discussion of guidelines
    Beginning discussion of "Quick and dirty" Psychopharmacology to be continued online

    Assignments:
    Rotgers, Keller, and Morgenstern, Intro and Chapters 1& 2
    Palloff, Lesson 1

Week of July 2

Definitions of Alcoholism and Addiction
    Jellinek phases and stages
    Whole person concept
    Genetic factors

Social/cultural factors
Disease:
Basic elements of disease model
Evolution
Continuum of use

Assignments:
Reader, #1, 2, and 4
Palloff, Lessons 2 and 3

Week of July 9

Assessment
Screening instruments
DSM-IV criteria
Interviewing techniques
Working with concerned persons
Rights and releases
Continuum of care
Patient placement criteria

Assignments:
Reader, #3
Rotgers, Keller, and Morgenstern, Chapters 3 and 4
Complete Case Study 1—Kathryn

Week of July 16

Concepts of Intervention
Creating a crisis
Concern, impact, and limitations
Patient placement criteria
Developmental model of recovery

Assignments:
Palloff, Lesson 4
Reader, # 10–15
Case Study 1 due
Complete Case Study 2—Ron

Week of July 23

Historical Models of Addiction and Treatment
   Moral
   Psychoanalytic
   Behavioral

Current Addiction Treatment Efforts

Assignments:
   Rotgers, Keller, and Morgenstern, Chapters 5 and 6
   Palloff, Lesson 5
   Reader, #5–9
   Case Study 2 due
   Complete Case Study 3—Joe

Week of July 30

Effects of Chemical Dependency on the Family
   Adjustment of the family to the presence of addiction
   The "life cycle" of the chemically dependent family
   Family roles
   Effective approaches to family treatment

Assignments:
   Rotgers, Keller, and Morgenstern, Chapters 7 and 8
   Case Study 3 due
   Complete Case Study 4—Raymond
                    *** 12 Step Paper Due ***

Week of August 6

Codependency/Adult Children of Alcoholics

Assignments:
   Palloff, Lesson 6
   Rotgers, Keller, and Morgenstern, Chapters 9 and 10
   Case Study 4 due
   Complete Case Study 5—Cassie (to be posted online)

Week of August 13

Relapse
    Process
    Prevention

Assignments:
    Reader, #21
    Case Study 5 due

Week of August 20

Becoming a Chemical Dependency Counselor—Treatment Team Simulation
    Legal/ethical issues
    Principles and practices of case management
    Treatment techniques

    Assignments:
    Reader, #17–20
    Read Case Study material on Jane and Don (end of Lessons 4 and 6)
    Begin online case management team process

Week of August 27

Gender, Culture, Lifespan, and Lifestyle Issues in Chemical Dependency
    Adolescents
    Women
    Elderly
    Dual diagnosis
    Working with cultural differences

Assignments:
    Rotgers, Keller, and Morgenstern, Chapter 11
    Palloff, Lesson 7
    Reader, #16

Wednesday, September 3

Final wrap-up—debrief online experience
Prevention
Future Trends in Treatment
The Biochemical Approach
                    *** Final Paper Due ***

RESOURCE B

SYSTEMS THEORIES COURSE
IN COURSEINFO AND eCOLLEGE

Exhibit B.1. Course Homepage: Blackboard

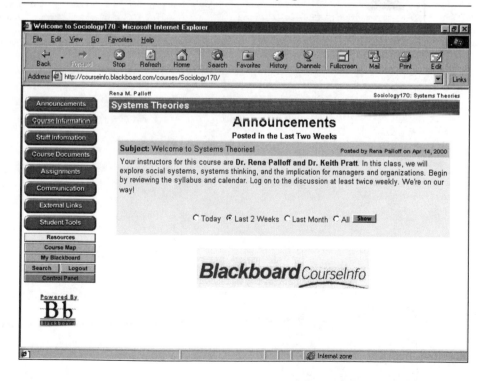

Exhibit B.2. Discussion Forums: Blackboard

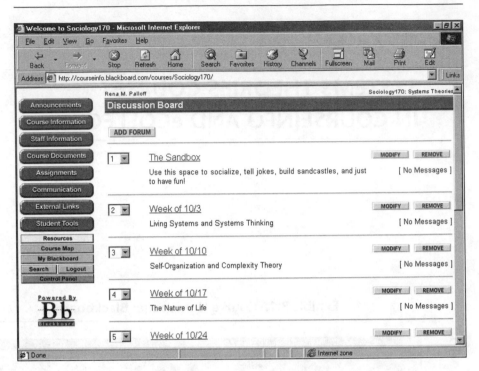

Exhibit B.3. Course Assignments: Blackboard

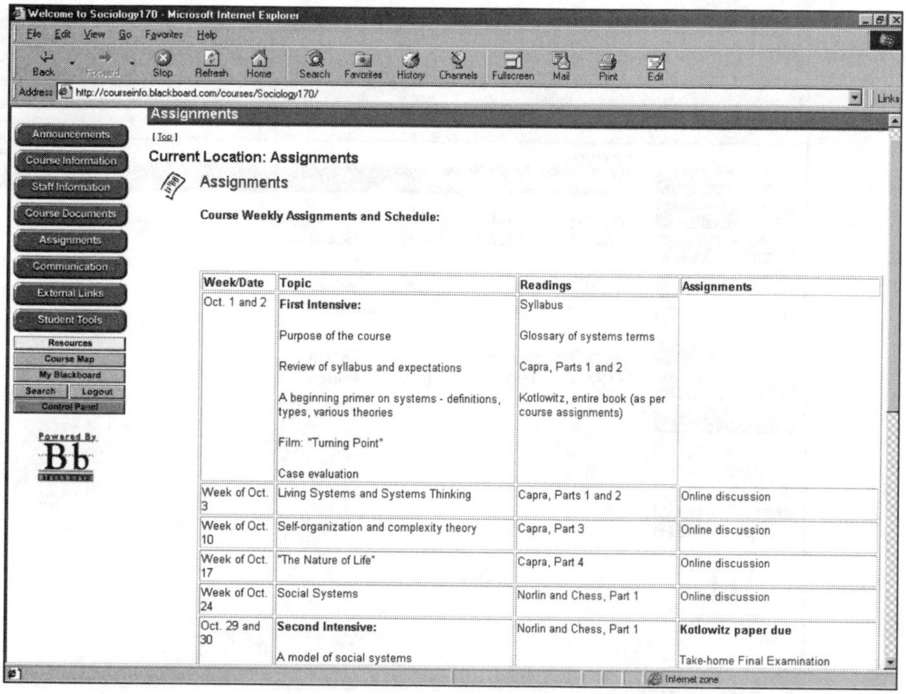

Welcome to Sociology170 - Microsoft Internet Explorer

File Edit View Go Favorites Help

Back Forward Stop Refresh Home Search Favorites History Channels Fullscreen Mail Print Edit

Address http://courseinfo.blackboard.com/courses/Sociology170/   Links

Assignments

Announcements
Course Information
Staff Information
Course Documents
Assignments
Communication
External Links
Student Tools
Resources
Course Map
My Blackboard
Search Logout
Control Panel

Powered By
Bb

[Top]

Current Location: Assignments

Assignments

Course Weekly Assignments and Schedule:

Week/Date	Topic	Readings	Assignments
Oct. 1 and 2	**First Intensive:** Purpose of the course Review of syllabus and expectations A beginning primer on systems - definitions, types, various theories Film: "Turning Point" Case evaluation	Syllabus Glossary of systems terms Capra, Parts 1 and 2 Kotlowitz, entire book (as per course assignments)	
Week of Oct. 3	Living Systems and Systems Thinking	Capra, Parts 1 and 2	Online discussion
Week of Oct. 10	Self-organization and complexity theory	Capra, Part 3	Online discussion
Week of Oct. 17	"The Nature of Life"	Capra, Part 4	Online discussion
Week of Oct. 24	Social Systems	Norlin and Chess, Part 1	Online discussion
Oct. 29 and 30	**Second Intensive:** A model of social systems	Norlin and Chess, Part 1	**Kotlowitz paper due** Take-home Final Examination

Internet zone

Exhibit B.4.   Student Communication Tools: Blackboard

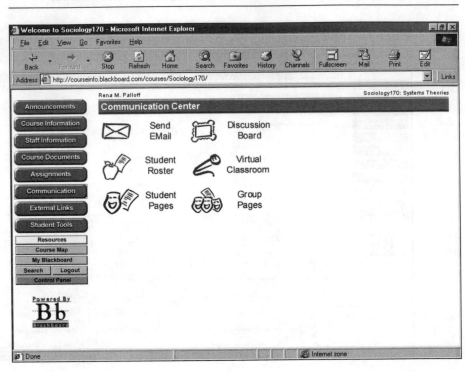

Exhibit B.5.   Course Syllabus: Blackboard

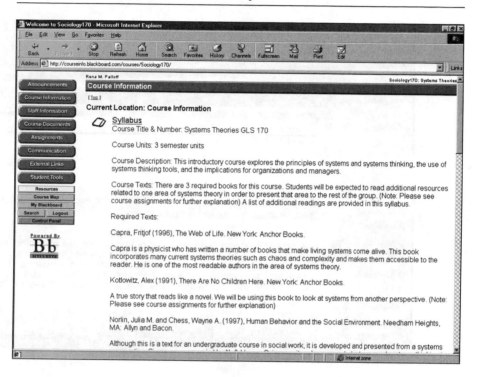

Exhibit B.6. Course Homepage: eCollege

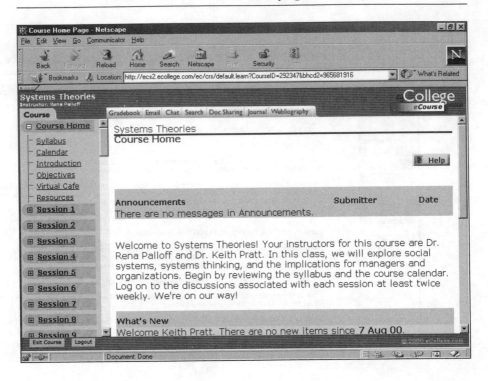

Exhibit B.7.   Course Assignments: eCollege

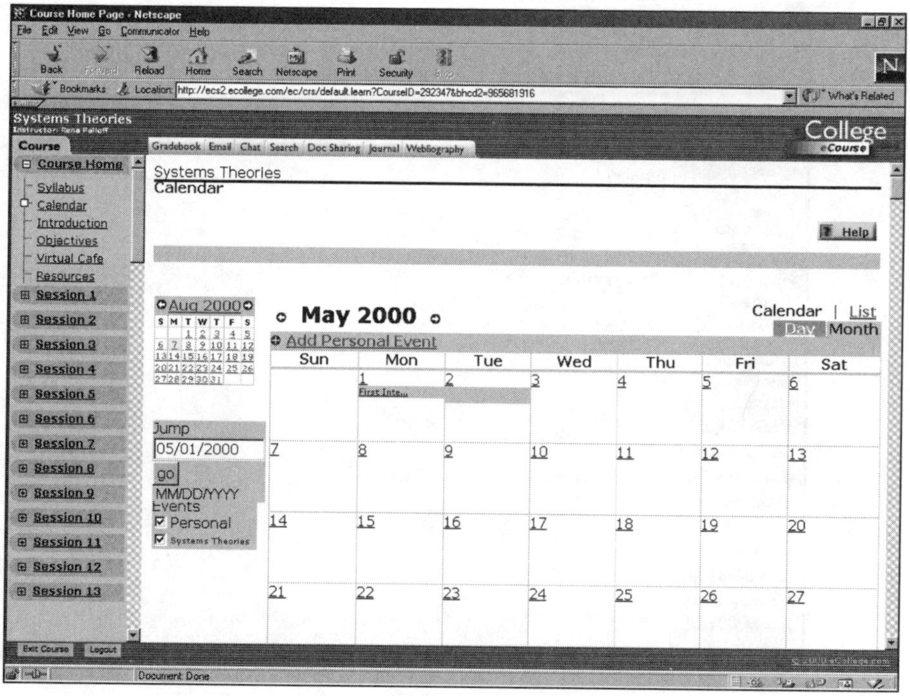

Exhibit B.8. Discussions: eCollege

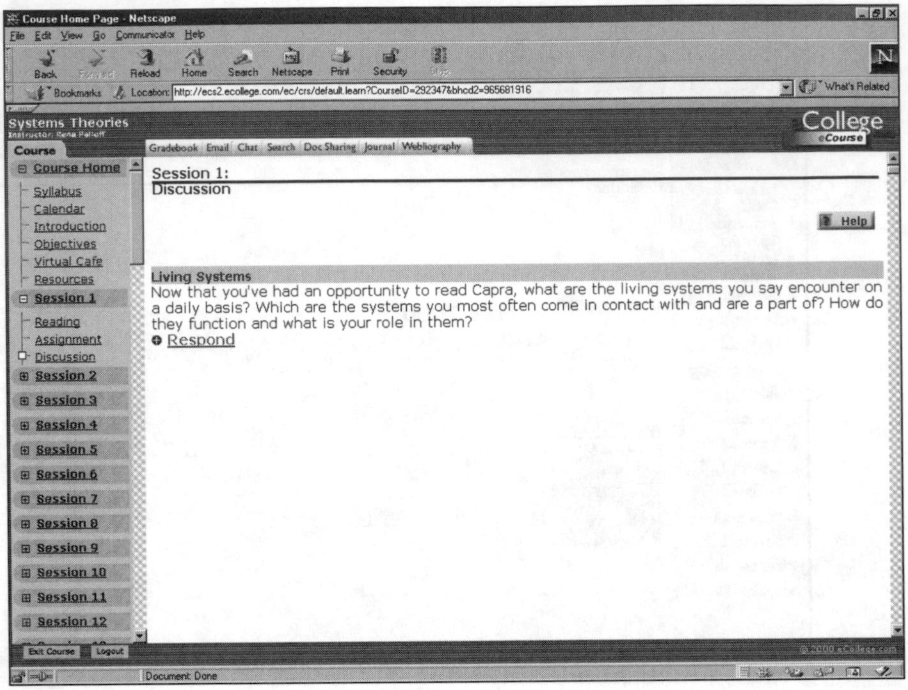

Exhibit B.9.   Student Communication Tools: eCollege

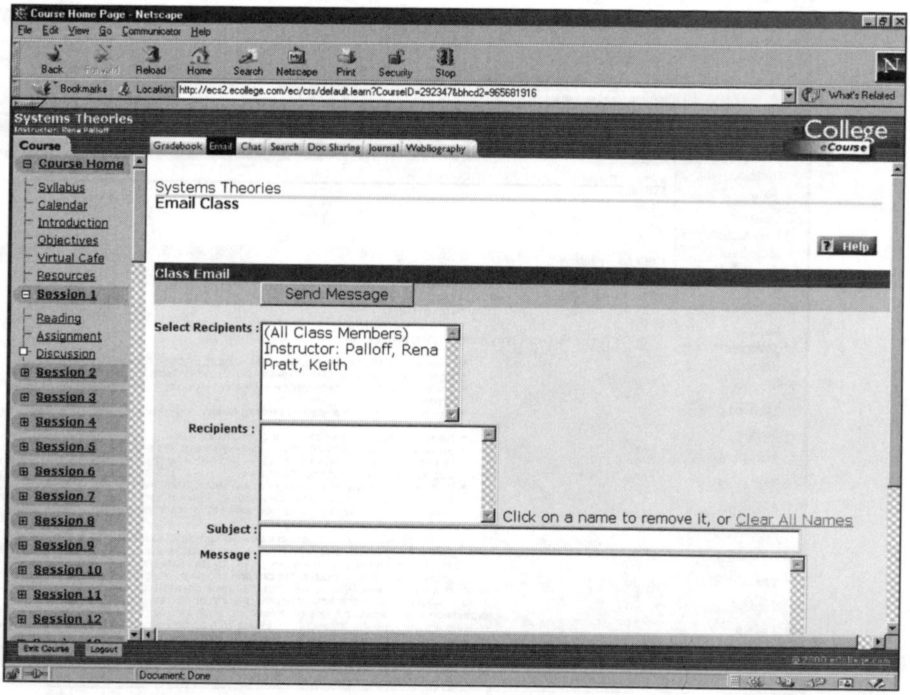

Exhibit B.10.   Course Syllabus: eCollege

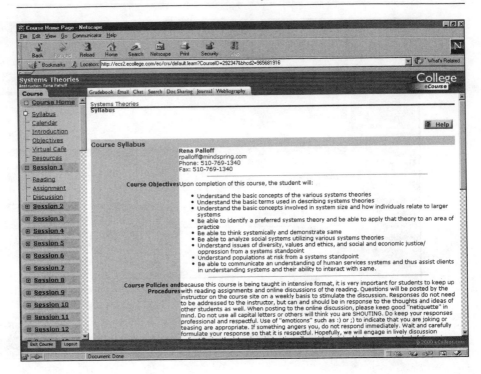

Exhibit B.11.   Course Homepage: Convene

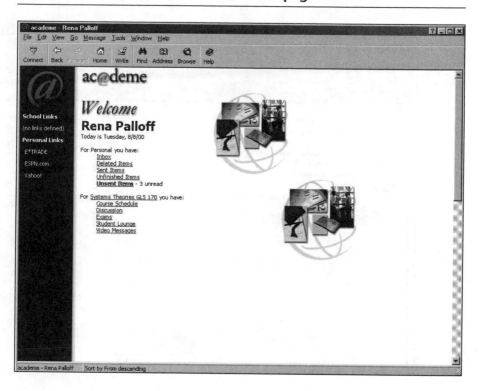

Exhibit B.12. Course Assignments: Convene

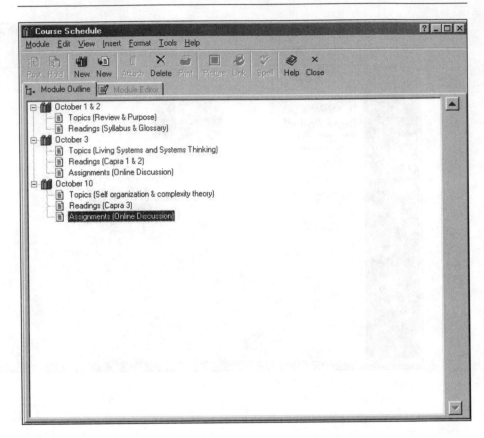

Exhibit B.13. Discussions: Convene

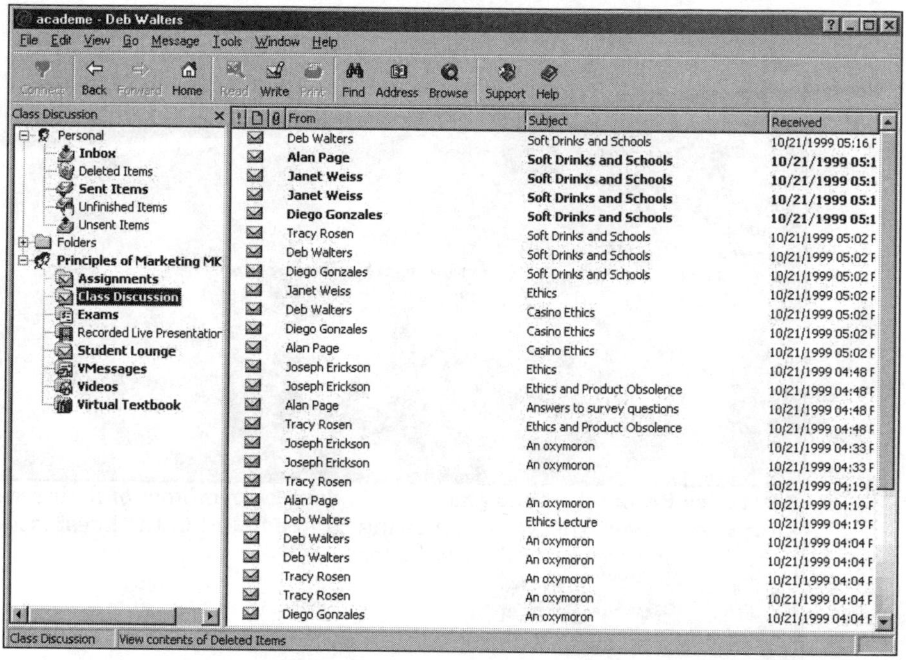

	From	Subject	Received
✉	Deb Walters	Soft Drinks and Schools	10/21/1999 05:16 F
✉	**Alan Page**	**Soft Drinks and Schools**	**10/21/1999 05:1**
✉	**Janet Weiss**	**Soft Drinks and Schools**	**10/21/1999 05:1**
✉	**Janet Weiss**	**Soft Drinks and Schools**	**10/21/1999 05:1**
✉	**Diego Gonzales**	**Soft Drinks and Schools**	**10/21/1999 05:1**
✉	Tracy Rosen	Soft Drinks and Schools	10/21/1999 05:02 F
✉	Deb Walters	Soft Drinks and Schools	10/21/1999 05:02 F
✉	Diego Gonzales	Soft Drinks and Schools	10/21/1999 05:02 F
✉	Janet Weiss	Ethics	10/21/1999 05:02 F
✉	Deb Walters	Casino Ethics	10/21/1999 05:02 F
✉	Diego Gonzales	Casino Ethics	10/21/1999 05:02 F
✉	Alan Page	Casino Ethics	10/21/1999 05:02 F
✉	Joseph Erickson	Ethics	10/21/1999 04:48 F
✉	Joseph Erickson	Ethics and Product Obsolence	10/21/1999 04:48 F
✉	Alan Page	Answers to survey questions	10/21/1999 04:48 F
✉	Tracy Rosen	Ethics and Product Obsolence	10/21/1999 04:48 F
✉	Joseph Erickson	An oxymoron	10/21/1999 04:33 F
✉	Joseph Erickson	An oxymoron	10/21/1999 04:33 F
✉	Tracy Rosen		10/21/1999 04:19 F
✉	Alan Page	An oxymoron	10/21/1999 04:19 F
✉	Deb Walters	Ethics Lecture	10/21/1999 04:19 F
✉	Deb Walters	An oxymoron	10/21/1999 04:04 F
✉	Deb Walters	An oxymoron	10/21/1999 04:04 F
✉	Tracy Rosen	An oxymoron	10/21/1999 04:04 F
✉	Tracy Rosen	An oxymoron	10/21/1999 04:04 F
✉	Diego Gonzales	An oxymoron	10/21/1999 04:04 F

Window title: academe - Deb Walters

Menu: File Edit View Go Message Tools Window Help

Toolbar: Connect Back Forward Home Read Write Print Find Address Browse Support Help

Left panel (Class Discussion):
- Personal
  - Inbox
  - Deleted Items
  - Sent Items
  - Unfinished Items
  - Unsent Items
- Folders
- Principles of Marketing MK
  - Assignments
  - Class Discussion
  - Exams
  - Recorded Live Presentation
  - Student Lounge
  - VMessages
  - Videos
  - Virtual Textbook

Status bar: Class Discussion   View contents of Deleted Items

Exhibit B.14.   Student Communication Tools: Convene

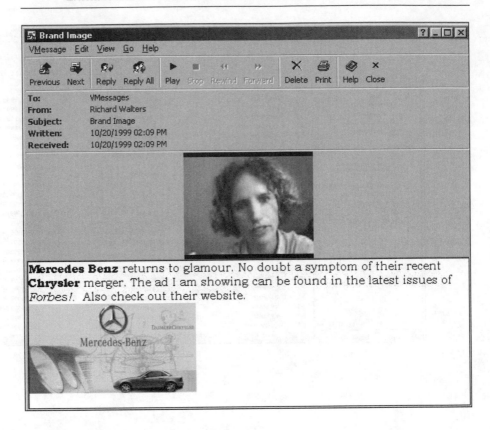

Exhibit B.15.   Course Syllabus: Convene

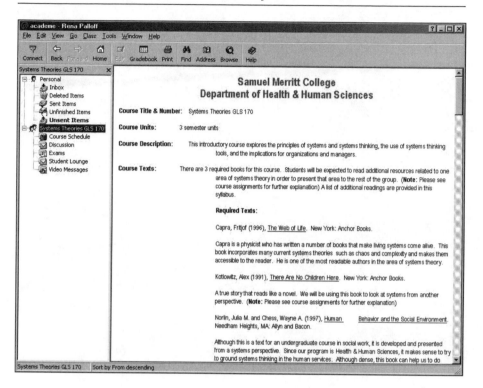

Samuel Merritt College
Department of Health & Human Sciences

Course Title & Number: Systems Theories GLS 170

Course Units: 3 semester units

Course Description: This introductory course explores the principles of systems and systems thinking, the use of systems thinking tools, and the implications for organizations and managers.

Course Texts: There are 3 required books for this course. Students will be expected to read additional resources related to one area of systems theory in order to present that area to the rest of the group. **(Note:** Please see course assignments for further explanation) A list of additional readings are provided in this syllabus.

Required Texts:

Capra, Fritjof (1996), The Web of Life. New York: Anchor Books.

Capra is a physicist who has written a number of books that make living systems come alive. This book incorporates many current systems theories such as chaos and complexity and makes them accessible to the reader. He is one of the most readable authors in the area of systems theory.

Kotlowitz, Alex (1991), There Are No Children Here. New York: Anchor Books.

A true story that reads like a novel. We will be using this book to look at systems from another perspective. **(Note:** Please see course assignments for further explanation)

Norlin, Julia M. and Chess, Wayne A. (1997), Human   Behavior and the Social Environment. Needham Heights, MA: Allyn and Bacon.

Although this is a text for an undergraduate course in social work, it is developed and presented from a systems perspective. Since our program is Health & Human Sciences, it makes sense to try to ground systems thinking in the human services. Although dense, this book can help us to do

ADDITIONAL ONLINE RESOURCES

The following is a collection of websites, Internet journals, and courseware for use in and assistance with computer-mediated distance learning. It should be noted that, at the time this book went to press, all URLs listed were current. With the rapidly changing nature of the Internet, however, some may have changed.

Course Authoring Software

Although many course authoring packages exist, the following are used most frequently. Each company also makes teaching and learning resources available on their websites.

WebCT: www.webct.com

Blackboard: www.blackboard.com

eCollege: www.ecollege.com

Convene: www.convene.com

Embanet: www.embanet.com

Jones Knowledge: www.e-education.com

Third-Party Course Development

Business courses:

Quisic: www.quisic.com

Ninth House: www.ninthhouse.com

Pensare: www.pensare.com

Examples of Online Courses

World Lecture Hall: www.utexas/world/lecture

University of Maryland, University College: www.umuc.edu/virtualteaching

Sites Comparing the Features and Function of Software

"Evaluation and Selection of Web Course Management Tools," Sunil Hazari, Ed.D.: http://sunil.umd.edu/Webct/

"University of Manitoba Feature Comparison of Web Course in a Box™, WebCT™, BlackBoard™, TopClass™": http://www.umanitoba.ca/ip/tools/courseware/model.html

"SCOET/CCIT/OLT Feature Comparison": http://www.ctt.bc.ca/landonline/

Technology Planning

The following sites include a number of links to technology plans:

http://www.mcli.dist.maricopa.edu/ocotillo/technoplan/

http://www.celtedge.celt.org/

The following are examples of technology policies and plans:

http://www.mde.state.mi.us

http://rohan.sdsu.edu/dept/senate/sendoc/distanceed.apr2000.html

Intellectual Property and Copyright

Numerous sites now exist on the Internet exploring the areas of intellectual property and copyright. These are but a few of the sites available:

Legal resources: www.copyrights-attorney.com

Copyright and distance education: http://library.cmsu.edu/paa/copyright/copy.htm

Intellectual property resources: http://www.ipmall.fplc.edu/

Papers and other resources: http://www.nea.org/he/techno.html

K–12 Resources

The Concord Consortium: www.concord.org

Virtual High School: http://vhs.concord.org

APEX Online Learning: www.apex.netu.com/

Archipelago: www.archipelago.com

State plans for K–12:

http://www.ed.gov

http://www.k12.ky.us/oet

Clearinghouse Sites on Distance Learning

- http://www.usdla.org/

The United States Distance Learning Association is a nonprofit organization formed in 1987 whose purpose is to promote the development and application of distance learning for education and training. The constituents served include pre-K through grade 12 education, higher education, home school education, continuing education, corporate training, military and government training, and telemedicine.

- http://www.uwex.edu/disted/home.html

   This comprehensive and widely recognized website brings together distance education information and resources from Wisconsin, national and international sources. Updated frequently.

- http://www.uwex.edu/disted/lobother.htm

   Many links to online resources for distance learning.

- http://ccism.pc.athabascau.ca/html/ccism/deresrce/institut.htm

   List of distance education organizations.

- http://webster.commnet.edu/HP/pages/darling/distance.htm

   Many distance learning resources.

- http://dir.yahoo.com/Education/Distance_Learning/

   Yahoo's directory for distance learning

REFERENCES

American Association of University Professors. "Distance Education and Intellectual Property." *Academe,* May-June 1999, pp. 41–45.

Arvan, L. and others. "The SCALE Efficiency Projects (The Sloan Center for Asynchronous Learning Environments)." *JALN,* Sept. 1998, *2*(2). [http://www.aln.org/alnweb/journal/vol2_issue2/arvan2.htm].

Barone, C., and Luker, M. "The Role of Advanced Networks in the Education of the Future." In M. Luker (ed.), *Preparing Your Campus for a Networked Future.* San Francisco: Jossey-Bass, 2000.

Barsch, J., "Barsch Learning Style Inventory," 1980. [http://hcc.hawaii.edu/intranet.vCom/guidebook/teachtip/lernstyl.htm].

Bates, A. W., *Managing Technological Change.* San Francisco: Jossey-Bass, 2000.

Blackboard, Inc. "Educational Benefits of Online Learning" (white paper), n.d. [www.blackboard.com].

Blustain, H., Goldstein, P., and Lozier, G. "Assessing the New Competitive Landscape." In R. Katz and Associates (eds.), *Dancing with the Devil.* San Francisco: Jossey-Bass, 1999.

Boettcher, J. "What Does Knowledge Look Like and How Can We Help It Grow?" *Syllabus,* Sept. 1999, pp. 64–66.

Boettcher, J., and Conrad, R. *Faculty Guide for Moving Teaching and Learning to the Web.* Mission Viejo, Calif.: League for Innovation in the Community College, 1999.

Boschmann, E. "Moving Toward a More Inclusive Reward Structure." *Horizon,* Oct. 1998. [http://horizon.unc.edu/TS/development/1998–10.asp].

Brookfield, S. *Becoming a Critically Reflective Teacher.* San Francisco: Jossey-Bass, 1995.

Brooks, J., and Brooks, M. *In Search of Understanding: The Case for Constructivist Classrooms.* Alexandria, Va.: Association for Supervision and Curriculum Development, 1993.

Carnavale, D. "Survey Finds 72% Rise in Number of Distance-Education Programs."
  Chronicle of Higher Education, Jan. 7, 2000a.
  [http://chronicle.com/free/v46/i18/18a05701.htm].
Carnavale, D. "Shopping for an Online Course? Kick the Tires and Check the Mileage."
  Chronicle of Higher Education, Feb. 2, 2000b.
  [http://chronicle.com/free/2000/02/2000020201u.htm].
Carnavale, D. "Survey Produces a List of 'Benchmarks' for Quality Distance Programs."
  Chronicle of Higher Education, Mar. 22, 2000c.
  [http://chronicle.com/free/2000/03/2000032201u.htm].
Carnavale, D. "San Diego State's Senate Creates a Detailed Policy for Distance Courses."
  Chronicle of Higher Education, Apr. 26, 2000d.
  [http://chronicle.com/free/2000/04/2000042601u.htm].
Carr, S. "Distance-Learning Group Blends Offerings of 2- and 4-Year Colleges." *Chronicle
  of Higher Education,* Oct. 1, 1999. [http://chronicle.com/cgi2-bin/].
Carr, S. "As Distance Education Comes of Age, the Challenge Is Keeping the Students."
  Chronicle of Higher Education, Feb. 11, 2000a.
  [http://chronicle.com/free/v46/i23/23a00101.htm].
Carr, S. "Wisconsin Project Seeks to Create a Common Standard for Online Courses."
  Chronicle of Higher Education. Feb. 17, 2000b.
  [http://chronicle.com/free/2000/02/200001701u.htm].
Carr, S., and Kiernan, V. "For-Profit Web Venture Seeks to Replicate the University
  Experience Online." *Chronicle of Higher Education,* Apr. 14, 2000, pp. A59–A60.
Cartwright, G. P. "Planning for Academic Computing: Important Trends and Issues." *Change,*
  July-Aug. 1996. [http://contract.kent.edu/change/articles/julaug96.html].
Casey, C. "Accessibility and the Educational Web Site." *Syllabus,* Sept. 1999, pp. 26–30.
Chambers, G. "Toward Shared Control of Distance Education." *Chronicle of Higher Education,*
  Nov. 19, 1999, pp. B8–B9.
Chisholm, W., Vanderheiden, G., and Jacobs, I. "Web Content Accessibility Guidelines."
  W3Cliability, 1999. [http://www.w3.org/TR/WAI-WEBCONTENT/].
Christiansen, E., and Dirckinck-Holmfeld, L. "Making Distance Learning Collaborative."
  1995. [http://www-cscl95.indiana.edu/cscl95/christia.html].
Clark, R. "Reconsidering Research on Learning from Media." *Review of Educational Research,*
  1993, *5*(3), 445–460.
Denning, P. "How We Will Learn." In P. Denning and R. Metcalfe (eds.), *Beyond Calculation.*
  New York: Springer-Verlag, 1997.
Dickinson, G., Agnew, D., and Gorman, R. "Are Teacher Training and Compensation Keep-
  ing Up with Institutional Demands for Distance Learning?" *Cause/Effect Journal,* 1999,
  22(3). [http://www.educause.edu/ir/library/html/cem9939.html].
Duderstadt, J. "Can Colleges and Universities Survive in the Information Age?" In R. Katz
  and Associates (eds.), *Dancing with the Devil.* San Francisco: Jossey-Bass, 1999.
Farrington, G. "The New Technologies and the Future of Residential Undergraduate
  Education." In R. Katz and Associates (eds.), *Dancing with the Devil.* San Francisco:
  Jossey-Bass, 1999.
Feenberg, A. "No Frills in the Virtual Classroom." *Academe,* Sept.-Oct. 1999, pp. 26–31.
Finnegan, D. "Transforming Faculty Roles." In M. Peterson, D. Dill, L. A. Mets, and Associates
  (eds.), *Planning and Management for a Changing Environment.* San Francisco: Jossey-Bass, 1997.
Foshee, D. "Instructional Technologies—Part One: Leveraging the Technology Menu—
  A Practical Primer for New Learning Environments." In *Teaching at a Distance: A Handbook*

for Instructors. Mission Viejo, Calif.: League for Innovation in the Community College and Archipelago, 1999.

Grimes, A. "A Matter of Degree." *Wall Street Journal*, July 17, 2000, p. R29.

Hampe, B. "What Video Does Well in Education—and What it Doesn't." *Syllabus*, Aug. 1999, pp. 12–14.

Hanson, D. and others. *Distance Education: A Review of the Literature*. (2nd ed.). Washington, D.C.: Association for Educational Telecommunications and Technology Research Institute for Studies in Education, 1997.

Harasim, L., Hiltz, S. R., Teles, L., and Turoff, M. *Learning Networks*. Cambridge, Mass.: MIT Press, 1996.

Hawke, C. S. *Computer and Internet Use on Campus: A Legal Guide to Issues of Intellectual Property, Free Speech, and Privacy*. San Francisco: Jossey-Bass, 2000.

Hazari, S. "Evaluation and Selection of Web Course Management Tools." 1998. [http://sunil.umd.edu/Webct/].

Jonassen, D. and others. "Constructivism and Computer-Mediated Communication in Distance Education." *American Journal of Distance Education*. 1995, *9*(2), 7–26.

Katz, R. "Competitive Strategies for Higher Education in the Information Age." In R. Katz and Associates (eds.), *Dancing with the Devil*. San Francisco: Jossey-Bass, 1999.

Kearsley, G. "A Guide to Online Education, 1997." [http://gwis.circ.gwu.edu/~etl/online.html].

Knowles, M. *The Adult Learner: A Neglected Species*. Houston, Tex.: Gulf, 1992.

Kolb, D. *Learning Style Inventory*. Boston: McBerr, 1984.

Litzinger, M., and Osif, B. "Accommodating Diverse Learning Styles: Designing Instruction for Electronic Information Sources." In L. Shirato (ed.), *What Is Good Instruction Now? Library Instruction for the 90s*. Ann Arbor, Mich.: Pierian Press, 1993.

Lynch, P., and Horton, S. *Web Style Guide*. New Haven: Yale University Press, 1999.

Lytle, S., Lytle, V., Lenhart, K., and Skrotsky, L. "Large-Scale Deployment of Technology-Enhanced Courses." *Syllabus*, Nov.-Dec. 1999, pp. 57–59.

Maloney, W. "Brick-and-Mortar Campuses Go Online." *Academe*, Sept.-Oct. 1999, pp. 18–25.

Martin, W. A. "Being There Is What Matters." *Academe*, Sept.-Oct. 1999, pp. 32–36.

McClure, B. *Putting a New Spin on Groups*. Hillsdale, N.J.: Erlbaum, 1998.

McGrath, J., and Hollingshead, A. *Groups Interacting with Technology*. Thousand Oaks, Calif.: Sage, 1994.

McMurtrie, B. "Decision Is Delayed on Agency's Authority to Accredit Distance-Education Programs." *Chronicle of Higher Education*, Dec. 7, 1999. [http://chronicle.com/].

Menges, J. "Feeling Between the Lines." *CMC Magazine*, Oct. 1996. [http://www.december.com/cmc/mag/].

Mennecke, B. E., Hoffer, J. A., and Wynne, B. E. "The Implication of Group Development and History for Group Support Systems Theory and Practice." *Small Group Research*, 1992, *23*, 524–572.

Merisotis, J. "The 'What's the Difference?' Debate." *Academe*, Sept.-Oct. 1999, pp. 47–51.

Merisotis, J. "Quality on the Line." Washington, D.C.: National Education Association and Blackboard, March 2000.

National Center for Education Statistics. *Distance Education at Postsecondary Education Institutions: 1997–98*. Washington, D.C.: U.S. Department of Education, Dec. 1999.

Nipper, S. "Third Generation Distance Learning and Computer Conferencing." *Mindweave*, 1989. [http://www-icdl.open.ac.uk/mindweave/chap5.html].

Olcott, D. "Instructional Technologies—Part Two: Strategies for Instructor Success—Selecting and Using Distance Education Technologies." In *Teaching at a Distance: A Handbook for Instructors*. League for Innovation in the Community College and Archipelago, 1999.

Palloff, R., and Pratt, K. *Building Learning Communities in Cyberspace: Effective Strategies for the Online Classroom*. San Francisco: Jossey-Bass, 1999.

Palmer, P. *The Courage to Teach*. San Francisco: Jossey-Bass, 1998.

Perley, J., and Tanguay, M. "Accrediting On-Line Institutions Diminishes Higher Education." *Chronicle of Higher Education*, Oct. 29, 1999, pp. B4–6.

Phipps, R., and Merisotis, J. *What's the Difference?* Washington, D.C.: Institute for Higher Education Policy, Apr. 1999.

Pratt, K. *The Electronic Personality*. Unpublished doctoral dissertation, Human and Organizational Systems Program, Santa Barbara, Calif.: Fielding Institute, 1996.

Rheingold, H. *The Virtual Community*. Reading, Mass.: Addison-Wesley, 1993.

Rockwell, S. K., Schauer, J., Fritz, S., and Marx, D. "Incentives and Obstacles Influencing Higher Education Faculty and Administrators to Teach Via Distance." *Online Journal of Distance Learning Administration*, 2(4), Winter 1999. [http://westga.edu/~distance/rockwell24.html].

Russell, T. *The No Significant Difference Phenomenon*. Chapel Hill: Office of Instructional Telecommunications, North Carolina State University, 1999.

Saunders, G., and Weible, R. "Electronic Courses: Old Wine in New Bottles?" *Internet Research*, 1999, 9(5), 339–347.

Schopler, J., Abell, M., and Galinsky, M. "Technology-Based Groups: A Review and Conceptual Framework for Practice." *Social Work*, May 1998, 4(3), 254–269.

Schutte, J. "Virtual Teaching in Higher Education." 1996. [http://www.csun.edu/sociology/virexp.htm].

Sherry, L. "Issues in Distance Learning." *International Journal of Educational Telecommunications*, 1996, 1(4), 337–365.

Strasburg, J. "Pushing for Net Access." *San Francisco Chronicle*, Mar. 26, 2000, pp. B1–B3.

Tomei, L. "The Technology Facade." *Syllabus*, Sept. 1999, pp. 32–34.

Truman-Davis, B., Futch, L., Thompson, K., and Yonekura, F. "Support for Online Teaching and Learning." *Educause Quarterly*, 2000, 2, 44–51.

Tuckman, B., and Jensen, M. "Stages of Small Group Development Revisited." *Group and Organizational Studies*, 1977, 2(4), 419–427.

Turkle, S. *Life on the Screen: Identity in the Age of the Internet*. New York: Simon & Schuster, 1995.

Wiggins, G. *Educative Assessment*. San Francisco: Jossey-Bass, 1998.

White, N. "Rena's Case Study." Posting to Online Facilitation listserv, Jan. 8, 2000.

Whitesel, C. "Reframing Our Classrooms, Reframing Ourselves: Perspectives from a Virtual Paladin." *Microsoft in Higher Education*, Apr. 1998. [http://www.microsoft.com/education/hed/vision.htm.]

Young, J. "University of Washington Tries a Soft Sell to Woo Professors to Technology." *Chronicle of Higher Education*, May 28, 1999a. [http://chronicle.com/free/99/05/99052401v.htm].

Young, J. "Author Warns Students—and Colleges—to Avoid On-Line Education." *Chronicle of Higher Education*, Nov. 3, 1999b. [http://chronicle.com/].

Index